Making
War,
Thinking
History

Making War, Thinking History

Munich, Vietnam, and Presidential Uses of Force from Korea to Kosovo

Jeffrey Record

Naval Institute Press
Annapolis, Maryland

Naval Institute Press
291 Wood Road
Annapolis, Maryland 21402

Library of Congress Cataloging-in-Publication Data
Record, Jeffrey.
    Making war, thinking history : Munich, Vietnam, and presidential uses of force from Korea to Kosovo / Jeffrey Record.
    p. cm.
    Includes bibliographical references and index.
    ISBN 1-55750-009-6 (acid-free paper)
    1. Presidents—United States—History—20th century. 2. United States—Foreign relations—1945–1989—Decision making. 3. United States—Foreign relations—1989—Decision making. 4. United States—Military policy. 5. Executive power—United States—History—20th century. 6. War (International law)—History—20th century. 7. Intervention (International law)—History—20th century. 8. Aggression (International law)—History—20th century. I. Title.
    E176.1.R298 2002
    973.92—dc21
                                        2001044764
Printed in the United States of America on acid-free paper ⊗
09 08 07 06 05 04 03 02   9 8 7 6 5 4 3 2
First printing

Contents

Making
War,
Thinking
History

Introduction

North Korea's invasion of South Korea on June 25, 1950, caught President Harry Truman vacationing in his hometown of Independence, Missouri. He ordered an immediate departure for Washington.

On the plane ride back to the White House, the former artillery officer, haberdasher, senator, and vice president employed his considerable knowledge of history to interpret the meaning of the North Korean attack. "I had time to think aboard the plane," he recounted in his memoirs. "In my generation, this was not the first occasion when the strong had attacked the weak. I recalled some earlier instances: Manchuria, Ethiopia, Austria. I remembered each time that the democracies failed to act it had just encouraged the aggressors to keep going ahead." Now, Truman reasoned, "Communism was acting in Korea just as Hitler, Mussolini, and the Japanese had acted ten, fifteen, twenty years earlier. I felt certain that if South Korea was allowed to fall Communist leaders would be emboldened to override nations closer to our shores." Ultimately, "it would mean a third world war, just as similar incidents had brought on the second world war."[1]

Long before he became president, Truman recalled, he had realized "that almost all current events in the affairs of governments and nations have their parallels in the past," and had concluded that "no decision affecting the people should be made impulsively, but on the basis of historical background and careful consideration of the facts as they exist at

1

the time. History taught me," continued this president well read in history, "that the leader of any country . . . must know the history of not only his own country but of all the other great countries, *and that he must make the effort to apply this knowledge to the decisions that have to be made.*"[2]

Thus, Truman applied the history of the 1930s—more specifically, what he perceived to be the lessons of the 1930s—when deciding whether or not to defend South Korea. His decision to fight was virtually dictated by the parallel he saw between Nazi and communist aggression, and it had enormous consequences for American foreign policy. It militarized the U.S. Cold War strategy of containment and extended it from Europe to Asia, setting the stage for the ill-advised U.S. intervention in Vietnam fifteen years later.

American presidents' uses of force are influenced by myriad factors, including personality, professional military advice, perceived stakes, anticipated enemy responses, and domestic political considerations. They are also influenced by ideas, including historical analogies. In some cases—i.e., in wars of necessity—the choice of force is mandatory. Enemy attacks on U.S. territory, U.S. military forces overseas, and on treaty allies automatically mean war. America's membership in NATO rests on a pre-hostilities judgment that the territorial integrity of the other members of the alliance is a fighting matter. Much more numerous—and controversial—than wars of necessity, however, are wars of choice. Indeed, none of America's wars since 1945 have been wars of necessity. The United States was not committed to defend South Korea in 1950, Kuwait in 1990, or Kosovo in 1999; nor was it legally bound to defend South Vietnam in 1965, although U.S. intervention there was certainly permissible under the vaguely worded 1955 SEATO Treaty. Domestic political controversy usually surrounds wars of choice precisely because military intervention is optional. The greatest controversy arises in cases of optional use of force on behalf of values as opposed to national interests, although most U.S. military interventions rest on a blend of the two.[3]

Both wars of necessity and wars of choice involve a great deal of choice about how to fight. For example, although the Japanese attack on Pearl Harbor (followed by Nazi Germany's gratuitous declaration of war) made World War II a war of necessity for the United States, President Franklin Roosevelt, anticipating U.S. entry, had already decided to pursue a "Germany first" strategy. The Johnson administration's decision to send U.S. ground combat troops into Vietnam in 1965 left open the question of how best to defeat the Vietnamese Communists. Gen. William Westmoreland's selection of an attrition strategy was challenged at the time within the U.S. military and to this day remains controversial.

Not least among the influences on presidents' use of force is what presidents believe history teaches about using force. Indeed, just as individuals make personal decisions based on daily experience, presidents cannot help but reason by historical analogy to some degree during a crisis involving possible use of force. Their reasoning may be sound or faulty, but reason by historical analogy they do. Historian Ernest R. May's groundbreaking *"Lessons" of the Past: The Use and Misuse of History in American Foreign Policy*, published in 1973, still stands as the seminal book in the field of examining foreign policy reasoning by historical analogy. Almost twenty years later, Yuen Foong Khong published his impressive study of the analogies at work behind U.S. entry into the Vietnam War, *Analogies at War: Korea, Munich, Dien Bien Phu, and the American Decisions of 1965*. For these and other scholars in the field, the starting point is Robert Jervis's observation, in his seminal *Perception and Misperception in International Politics* (1976), that "previous international events provide the statesman with a range of imaginable situations and allow him to detect patterns and causal links that can help him understand his world."[4] Specifically, according to Christopher Hemmer, analogies "are road maps that help policy makers maximize the national interest by guiding them through unfamiliar terrain by giving them information about the international ramifications of particular policies."[5] Analogies can help clarify the circumstances confronting decision makers, shed light on the stakes involved, and point to courses of action. For example, the punitive Versailles treaty of 1919 and its consequences for peace in Europe taught Allied leaders during World War II how not to treat defeated Nazi Germany and Imperial Japan.

This book examines presidential use-of-force decisions from the Korean War through the Kosovo crisis and reveals presidents extensively engaged in reasoning by historical analogy. Presidents have both *employed* analogies to inform their decision making and *deployed* them to mobilize public support for decisions made or about to be made. Presidents who believe that a particular historical analogy applies to the situation at hand display a propensity to use it to reinforce their case for action or inaction, and subsequently tend to deploy it to marshal popular and congressional support for the preferred course of action.

Presidential choices of foreign policy analogies are greatly influenced by generational experiences, especially war.[6] World War II and the events leading up to it exerted an enormous influence on the worldview of most Cold War presidents, including the last one, George Bush, who was also the last World War II veteran to occupy the White House. In contrast, Bill Clinton, the first post–Cold War president (and the first president born after World War II), represents the generation of the lost war in Southeast Asia, not the "good war" of 1941–45.

It should thus come as no surprise that the Munich and Vietnam analogies have weighed heavily on presidents faced with overseas crises. "Munich" refers, of course, to the infamous conference of September 1938 at which Great Britain and France handed Czechoslovakia's Sudetenland over to Hitler without a fight. But Munich has become shorthand for the democracies' appeasement of Hitler, Mussolini, and the Japanese throughout the 1930s, which is still believed to have foreordained World War II. The Vietnam analogy, of course, refers to America's ruinous military intervention in the Vietnam War.

The two analogies are quite different, although both can—and have— inform the same presidential decision. Munich is about *whether* to use force and about what can happen when force is *not* used. Munich teaches nothing about *how* force should be used. Unlike Vietnam, the Munich agreement entailed no loss of life and directly affected no American. *How* force should be used is a major theme of many of those who have sought to draw policy-relevant lessons from the Vietnam War. Others, however, believe that Vietnam teaches that force should never have been used in the first place, thus rendering moot discussions about the amount of force necessary and how it should have been employed. Here arises the greatest distinction between the two analogies insofar as they influence use-of-force decision making: while there is a broad consensus on the chief lesson of Munich, no such agreement exists on the lessons of Vietnam. Both individual and organizational policy makers have drawn lessons from Vietnam and in some cases have openly declared them to be guideposts for future uses of U.S. military power. But a great divide still separates the lessons drawn by those who believe the war was not winnable at any acceptable price and those who believe the war was winnable but that victory was self-denied.

Robert Timberg's best-seller *The Nightingale's Song* postulates the Vietnam generation as split at its core between those young men of military service age who went off to war and those who did not. For most of those who went, the issue was not whether or not U.S. forces should have been fighting there, but rather why the war was fought the way it was. For many of those who stayed home, the issue was why it was fought at all. The great divide between "whether" and "how" persists. There were also war "hawks"—now prominent among today's political elite—who succeeded in avoiding military service in Vietnam.

On the subject of force, the Vietnam War remains important precisely because it sparked a debate within the national political and military leadership over the uses of U.S. military power that continues unabated. A milestone in that debate was Secretary of Defense Caspar Weinberger's National Press Club speech of November 1984 in which he sought to establish rather narrow criteria for using force, prompting a counterspeech by Secretary of State George Shultz a month later. The debate has been heightened by the post–Cold War collapse of consensus on the organizing principle of American foreign policy and by controversial presidential uses of force in Somalia and the former Yugoslavia.

Generational change continues to exert an influence as the national political and military reins of power pass ever more quickly from those for whom the dominant foreign policy referent experience was Munich and World War II to those for whom it is Vietnam. The debate has been enriched by heightened congressional assertiveness in foreign policy and the professional military's increased influence on use-of-force decisions.

Munich and Vietnam are tightly woven into the fabric of the debate, and although Munich is more distant in time, it still informs policy makers. Indeed, both analogies were at work during the Persian Gulf crisis of 1990–91 and the Kosovo crisis of 1999. Saddam Hussein and Slobodan Milosevic were viewed as regional Hitlers whose aggression had to be checked before it got out of hand, and force was employed against both aggressors, but with the utmost determination to avoid protracted hostilities and politically unacceptable American losses. Munich urged intervention, but Vietnam counseled caution; together, they produced a search for painless victory. As commentator Daniel Schorr noted of NATO's war against Serbia: "If memories of Munich helped influence NATO's decision to go to war against Yugoslavia, memories of Vietnam influenced the decision to keep war high up in the air, above the quagmire, as long as possible." Indeed, "Munich and Vietnam are code words for 'appeasement' and 'quagmire,'" and "no expressions are more laden with the struggles of the past and hazards for future policy."[7]

The persistent influence of the Munich and Vietnam analogies in the formulation and implementation of American foreign policy stems in part from their apparent reinforcement by subsequent events. The very success of U.S. force against Iraq and Serbia seemingly validates the proposition that the only way to deal with aggressive dictators is to use force against them early and conclusively in order to prevent more costly aggression later on. "If you don't stop Hitler in Czechoslovakia, he'll go on for Poland and the rest of Europe," becomes, "If you let stand Saddam's aggression against Kuwait, the next thing he'll do is grab Saudi Arabia." And, "If you don't check Milosevic's bid to establish a greater Serbia out of the ruins of the former Yugoslavia, you are inviting the destabilization of all of southeastern Europe and perhaps a regional war." In short, the reasoning goes, small threats become ever-larger threats unless they are nipped in the bud. In contrast, the failed use of force in Lebanon and Somalia apparently confirms the propositions, depending on which of two basic contradictory lessons one chooses to draw, that the United States should stay out of foreign civil wars that do not directly threaten vital U.S. security interests, and, alternatively, that the United States should prosecute to victory any war it fights, regardless of the soundness of the original decision to fight.

This book pursues three purposes: First, to identify and assess the policy lessons the national political and military leadership have drawn from Munich and Vietnam. This task is much easier for Munich than for Vietnam; there is, to repeat, agreement on the great lesson of Munich, but continuing disagreement over the many lessons of Vietnam. Second, to trace the influence of those lessons in selected instances of presidential consideration or actual use of force since 1945. The cases examined in the chapters that follow all involve wars of choice. They include Truman's decision to fight in Korea in 1950; Eisenhower's decision not to intervene in French Indochina in 1954; Kennedy and Johnson's approach to military intervention in Vietnam; Nixon's decision to continue fighting in Vietnam for an "honorable" peace; Reagan's intervention in Lebanon and Grenada and noninterventions in Central America and Afghanistan; Bush's invasion of Panama and overthrow of Iraq's conquest of Kuwait, as well as his decision not to intervene in Bosnia; and Clinton's invasion of Haiti, escalation in Somalia, and double interventions in the former Yugoslavia. Third, to assess the usefulness of the Munich and Vietnam analogies as a means of informing past decisions to use or not to use force, and more generally the value of reasoning by historical analogy.

It is my hope to provide the reader not only with insight into past U.S. uses of force but also with an appreciation of the limitations of reasoning by historical analogy in a foreign policy crisis. If Munich and Vietnam were experiences no policy maker wishes to repeat, the same may be said for repetition of faulty historical reasoning. Unfortunately, there is no empirical means to determine the influence of a particular historical analogy on a past decision to use force relative even to other analogies at play, to say nothing of nonhistorical influences. But public and private testimony of presidents and their senior foreign policy and military advisers makes it clear that such reasoning is commonplace in use-of-force decision making. Munich played a key role in determining Lyndon Johnson's decision to intervene in the Vietnam War, and proved to be a faulty analogy in that case. But no one knows whether, absent Munich, Johnson would nonetheless have made the same decision. Other analogies were at work, including the analogy of the Korean War, during which the United States militarily reversed a communist invasion in yet another Cold War–divided country.

Chapter 1, "Munich and Vietnam: Lessons Drawn," identifies and discusses the lessons U.S. foreign policy makers—presidents first and foremost—and senior military leaders have drawn from Munich and Vietnam. The chapter starts with a factual review of the Munich conference and the Vietnam War conditioned by recognition that, unlike Munich, the Vietnam War remains a historiographical battleground on which even major issues of fact are vehemently disputed. The chapter then examines the public and private testimony, oral and written, of key decision makers expressing their views on Munich and Vietnam and their policy implications. The literature in both cases is extensive, and in the case of Vietnam the fact of competing—and in some cases irreconcilable—lessons drawn by different policy makers does not and should not obscure the significance of the relative consensus on the war's lessons within the professional military, the instrument of U.S. force. That consensus is embodied in the so-called Weinberger-Powell Doctrine, which continues to exert a major influence on use-of-force decisions. I do not hesitate to express my own views on what happened to the United States in Vietnam and why; I have devoted considerable study to that conflict, published extensively on it, and teach the Vietnam War elective course at the U.S. Air Force's Air War College.

The next several chapters examine the influence of the Munich and Vietnam War analogies with respect to specific presidential uses—and nonuses—of force. Historical analogies can encourage or discourage use of force. This examination covers three consecutive but different periods of American foreign policy since 1945. The first period runs from the end of World War II to the Johnson administration's decision to commit U.S. ground combat forces to the Vietnam War. Except for the first few years after World War II this period was characterized by strong consensus on the organizing principle of U.S. foreign policy, exceptional congressional deference to the White House on foreign policy and defense matters, and the dominance of a political generation for whom Munich and World War II were the most influential foreign policy referent experiences. During this period, David W. Levy observed, the president's "power to define the national interest, to lay out the defensive perimeters of the United States, to declare when and how the country's safety was threatened was virtually unassailable. His pronouncements on matters of the security of the United States were almost like royal decrees."[8]

The second period begins in 1965 and extends to the end of the Cold War. During this period, the Vietnam War and its outcome severely cracked the foreign policy consensus, especially within the Democratic Party, and Congress responded to the war by reasserting its constitutional prerogatives in foreign policy.

The last period stretches from the Cold War's demise to the present. This period has been characterized by the lack of foreign policy consensus, a weakened presidency, and the coming to power at last of a political generation for whom the Vietnam War itself—not Munich and World War II—is the dominant foreign policy referent experience.

In each use-of-force decision examined by this book, two basic questions are addressed: how influential was the analogy in question with respect to the use-of-force decision, and to what degree was the analogy useful as a tool of informing that decision? Because there is no way to determine empirically every factor behind past decisions and their relative contributions in producing those decisions, the influence of reasoning by historical analogy must be inferred from policy makers' statements and actions. For example, Truman's views on Munich and its lessons are known, and it is hard to believe that he would have decided on war in Korea had not the very term *appeasement* become synonymous in his own mind with foreign policy disaster. Because there is no way of empirically proving the utility of a historical analogy in a given crisis setting, judgment here, too, must necessarily be subjective. For example, it requires no special insight to conclude that the Munich analogy badly misinformed policy makers on Vietnam, and that the French experience in the First Indochina War should have been examined far more seriously than it was. *Subjective* does not mean uninformed by reason and fact.

Nor can the role of domestic political considerations be divorced from the study of historical analogies. Most examinations of the sources of U.S. foreign policy, including use-of-force decisions, pay insufficient attention to domestic politics, which since the Vietnam War and even more so since the end of the Cold War have intruded on foreign policy decision making as never before since the apogee of isolationism in the 1930s. Of particular significance during the Cold War was the Democratic Party's defensiveness on the issue of communist expansion overseas. Appeasement of Hitler produced a Second World War that expanded the Soviet empire in Europe and set the stage for communism's victory in China. In so doing, it made the Democratic Party for the remainder of the Cold War vulnerable to Republican charges—which were especially shrill during the late 1940s and 1950s—of being "soft on communism." In turn, the Vietnam War provoked a domestic political reaction that continues to influence the way the United States goes about using force.

Previous studies of official reasoning by historical analogy have not paid sufficient attention to what particular foreign policy lessons mean and why. For example, the tenets of the Weinberger-Powell Doctrine are not fully appreciated as the Pentagon's judgment of the lessons of the Vietnam War; nor is America's prosecution of the Gulf War comprehensible except as a deliberate and measured attempt to put those lessons into practice. In addition, most of the earlier studies focus on actual uses of force, ignoring equally important decisions *not* to use force. Military inaction can be just as good a gauge of analogical influence as military action. Truman's nonintervention in China's civil war, Eisenhower's nonintervention in the French-Indochina War, and Bush's nonintervention in Bosnia all testify to the power of non–foreign policy analogical influences on foreign policy decision making. Analogical pressures to intervene were offset or overwhelmed by other considerations. Finally, most earlier studies were denied the benefit of the Cold War's demise, which engendered the release of important new information and perspectives on such events as the North Korean attack on South Korea and the Cuban missile crisis. Stalin's role in the outbreak of the Korean War is much better documented today than it was even a decade ago, as is behind-the-scenes Soviet decision making on Cuba during the period from the aborted Bay of Pigs invasion through the thirteen-day U.S.-Soviet crisis of October 1962. Nor has any study to date covered the entire period from the outbreak of the Korean War to the termination of the Kosovo War. The influence of both the Munich and the Vietnam War analogies on the Bush and Clinton administrations' approach to Yugoslavia's violent disintegration is particularly deserving of further study.

In the pages that follow I hope to make some contribution to overcoming these deficiencies.

Munich and Vietnam:

Lessons Drawn

Munich was the most spectacular act of territorial appeasement in a chain of acts that began with Germany's uncontested military reoccupation of the Rhineland in 1936. As such, the very name "Munich" became, and remains to this day, synonymous with the larger phenomenon of the democracies' territorial appeasement in the 1930s of Nazi Germany in Europe, Fascist Italy in Africa, and Imperial Japan in China and Southeast Asia. The enduring symbol of Munich is Prime Minister Neville Chamberlain of Britain, having just deplaned at Heston Airport following his third trip to see Hitler, waving a copy of the agreement in his hand and pronouncing "peace in our time." War followed less than a year later.

The Munich Conference of September 1938, attended by Hitler, Mussolini, Chamberlain, and Premier Edouard Daladier of France, was held to discuss Hitler's demand for the incorporation into the Third Reich of those areas of Czechoslovakia—the Sudetenland—harboring ethnic German population majorities. The Sudetenland fronted the Czech-German border and contained powerful fortifications essential to Czechoslovakia's defense against German attack. At the time of the conference, to which Czech representatives were invited only as observers (they had to stay in their hotel rooms under Gestapo guard until the fate of their country was decided), Czechoslovakia enjoyed a defensive alliance with France.[1]

Hitler's demand for the Sudetenland was but the latest in a series of German moves that suggested his determination to expand the Third Reich to encompass, at a minimum, all German territory "lost" after World War I. During the first years of his dictatorship Hitler had denounced the Treaty of Versailles settlement imposed on Germany in 1919, initiated Germany's treaty-prohibited rearmament, and revoked Germany's membership in the League of Nations. In 1936, Hitler ordered the military reoccupation of the treaty-demilitarized Rhineland, and France did nothing, even though reoccupation dealt a disabling blow to the credibility of French military guarantees to other potential victims of Nazi aggression. The credibility of those guarantees rested on France's willingness to invade Germany through the undefended Rhineland. Once the Rhineland was invested with German troops, however, the price of invasion skyrocketed. In March 1938, Hitler engineered the union of Germany and Austria, a move also prohibited by the Versailles treaty.

At the Munich Conference Hitler claimed that the Sudetenland was his last territorial demand in Europe, implying that Nazi Germany's imperial ambitions did not extend to non-German territories or states, and walked away with the Sudetenland in his pocket. Six months later, German forces occupied the rest of Czechoslovakia, and some six months after that, Germany plunged Europe into World War II by invading Poland (to which Great Britain and France had belatedly given security guarantees). Germany went on to attack Denmark, Norway, Belgium, Luxembourg, the Netherlands, France, Great Britain, Yugoslavia, Albania, Greece, North Africa, and Russia, and then declared war on the United States.

What happened at Munich? France and Great Britain, as Hitler saw all too clearly, were gripped by a general fear of repeating the nightmare of World War I and a more specific fear of Germany's growing military might, whose strengths Nazi propagandists had deliberately inflated. The French and British governments were blind to the true scope of Hitler's ambitions in Europe, and in addition both, but more so the British, had to deal with widespread pacifism at home.[2] Accordingly, London and Paris appeased Hitler by giving him the Sudetenland. A crippled Czechoslovakia surely was a small price to pay for avoidance of another European war. Indeed, in a radio address to the British people, Chamberlain dismissed the entire Sudetenland issue as "a quarrel in a far away country between people of whom we know nothing."[3] Chamberlain changed his mind about Hitler only when the Germans grabbed the rest of Czecho-slovakia. As Henry Kissinger observed, "Hitler's transgression was to incorporate *non*-German populations into the Reich, thereby violating the principle of self-determination on behalf of which all his previous unilateral exactions had been tolerated."[4] But the horse had already left the barn. The Munich deal had sacrificed Czechoslovakia's formidable border fortifications, advertised French and especially British spineless-ness, whetted Hitler's appetite for territory, and convinced Stalin that he had to cut his own deal with Hitler, which he did less than a year later.

The democracies disastrously miscalculated at Munich on several fronts. First, they overrated Germany's military power. In 1938, the Czech army, assisted by Britain and France and by Czech fortifications in the armor-unfriendly terrain of western Czechoslovakia, probably could have defeated a German invasion.[5] That is the conclusion of journalist and historian William L. Shirer, who was exceptionally well informed about Germany and who covered the Munich Conference: "Germany was in no position to go to war on October 1, 1938 [the day after the Munich agreement was signed], against Czechoslovakia *and* France and Great Britain, not to mention Russia. Had she done so, she would have been quickly and easily defeated, and that would have been the end of Hitler and the Third Reich."[6] This was also the view of key German military leaders, including Wilhelm Keitel, Alfred Jodl, and Eric von Manstein, who so testified before the postwar Nuremberg Tribunal.[7] They were acutely aware of the Third Reich's relative military weakness at the time of Munich. Indeed, senior officers, including Army Chief of Staff Walther von Brauchitsch and Chief of the General Staff Franz Halder, strongly opposed risking war over the Sudetenland, and, as was revealed after the war, were contemplating Hitler's removal in the event that the democra-cies refused to back down to him in Munich.[8] Defeatism nonetheless pre-vailed in Paris and, especially, London. Chamberlain had convinced him-self that Britain and France were in no military position to prevent a quick German takeover of Czechoslovakia, and therefore that any threat-ened use of force would ring hollow in Berlin. Chamberlain believed that if force were threatened and Hitler called the democracies' bluff, another world war would ensue.[9]

Second, the French and British governments believed, or wanted to believe, that Hitler's ambitions were indeed limited to Germanic Europe. In this they were terribly mistaken. They also believed that Hitler's ambi-tions within the German nation were in large measure legitimate because they reflected a desire to overturn the unwise peace terms the democracies had imposed on a defeated Germany in 1919. Yet in the Sudetenland the democracies insisted on neither an uncorrupted plebiscite nor guarantees that non-Germanic minorities would be protected.

Third, although a mobilized France could have placed powerful forces on the side of Czechoslovakia's defense, the combination of a German-reoccupied Rhineland, a purely defensive military doctrine and force posture (symbolized by the Maginot line), and a political unwillingness, at the time, to fight Germany absent the British in a wartime alliance effectively removed France as a deterrent to German attack on any European state other than Great Britain and France itself.[10] France essentially ceded the most important decision a sovereign state can make to a British prime minister who at the time of Munich believed that Hitler could be trusted.

But for their defensive doctrine, the French could have threatened to invade the Rhineland. During the Munich crisis, the bulk of the German army and air force (including almost all of its mechanized units) was concentrated opposite the Czech border; the price of that concentration was a token defense of the Rhineland. In October 1938, the French army was better equipped and much larger than its German counterpart and could have launched a fifty-six-division invasion of a Rhineland held by only eight German divisions.[11] Thus, although the French were not in a position to offer a direct defense of Czechoslovakia (the two countries had no common border), they could have moved into Germany itself, posing a mortal threat to Germany's industrial heartland in the Ruhr. This is exactly what the nervous German generals feared. Indeed, in August, an emissary from the German army's General Staff was dispatched to Britain to brief Winston Churchill (then out of government) and others on Hitler's determination to invade Czechoslovakia and on the necessity of a firm British threat to deter him from doing so. Chamberlain knew of this extraordinary event but dismissed it.[12]

Clearly, the Munich agreement encouraged Hitler to believe that he could steal even more territory with little risk of war, just as his occupation of the Rhineland and incorporation of Austria into the Third Reich had encouraged him to believe he could get away with the Sudetenland. He believed he could move next against Poland with the same impunity with which he had gobbled up the rest of Czechoslovakia six months after Munich, even though Britain and France had subsequently extended guarantees to Poland. "Our enemies are worms," Hitler told his assembled generals on the eve of Germany's invasion of Poland. "I saw them at Munich."[13] Indeed, though France and Britain ultimately honored their defense commitment to Poland, both pressured Warsaw to appease Hitler's demands for Polish territory. Even after Hitler struck, there remained hope in London that he could be talked into a military withdrawal from Poland as a precursor to new negotiations.[14]

Appeasement also made the terms of war with Germany, when war finally came, much less favorable to the democracies. Hitler had in effect inflicted a strategic calamity on Great Britain and France, especially the latter, without firing a shot. "We are in the presence of a disaster of the first magnitude," declared Winston Churchill before the House of Commons.[15] William L. Shirer's diary entry on the day the Munich agreement was signed concludes that "France has sacrificed her whole Continental position" and characterizes Munich as Chamberlain's "diplomatic annihilation."[16]

The military price of stopping Hitler was to grow almost exponentially. Less than a year after Munich, a Nazi Germany now aligned with the Soviet Union occupied Poland and turned its gaze westward. (French forces sat quietly behind the Maginot line as Hitler picked off his latest victim.) By the end of 1940 Hitler had crushed France and marginalized British power in Europe. Britain could not hope to overturn Nazi control of Europe absent U.S. and Soviet entry into the war against Hitler, a condition fulfilled in 1941 only by Hitler's own folly: his invasion of Russia in June 1941 and utterly gratuitous declaration of war on the United States in December.

After the war, the influential British military commentator B. H. Liddell Hart observed that Munich was a great triumph "not only over [Hitler's] foreign opponents but also over his generals," and said that it encouraged Hitler's self-confidence in "a continued run of easy success." Munich also "changed the strategic balance in Europe." Afterward, no "acceleration of [French and British] armaments programs could be expected for a long time to offset the removal of Czechoslovakia's thirty-five well-armed divisions and the accompanying release of the German divisions they could have held in the balance."[17] Also subtracted from the scales was Czechoslovakia's armaments industry, the largest and best in Eastern Europe; it was quickly harnessed to the German war machine. It is little wonder that Germany's military leadership viewed the willingness of London and Paris to hand over such a strategic prize to Berlin with astonishment.

The elimination of Czechoslovakia as an eastern ally left only much weaker Poland as a substitute. But Britain and France were in no position to offer Poland meaningful military assistance; their post-Munich guarantee to Warsaw was a desperate effort to deter a German invasion of Poland. But their very behavior at Munich stripped the guarantee of any credibility. Worse still, by driving Stalin into Hitler's arms—via the infamous Nazi-Soviet Nonaggression Pact of August 1939—the Munich appeasers ensured that Germany's later attack on France could be conducted with a strategically secure rear in the east.

The scope of the democracies' defeat at Munich was not confined to the strategic realm. Munich was also a sellout of another democracy that looked for protection to Britain and, above all, France, which had a defense treaty with Prague. Churchill put it bluntly in his Commons speech: "All is over. Silent, mournful, abandoned, broken, Czechoslovakia recedes into the darkness. She has suffered in every respect by her association with the Western democracies and with the League of Nations, of which she has always been an obedient servant."[18] Munich was a moral travesty as well as an invitation to another world war.

Chamberlain was, to be sure, constrained at Munich by numerous factors other than his own misjudgment of Hitler. In the fall of 1938, Great Britain was just beginning to rearm; British intelligence greatly overestimated the German military threat; support for a war over Czechoslovakia was questionable among the British Dominions; Japan seemed poised to pounce on British assets in the Far East in the event of war in Europe; and public opinion at home appeared solidly pro-appeasement if not pro-German.[19] Additionally, much of Britain's ruling class continued to view Communist Russia as a greater threat to Europe's peace and stability than Nazi Germany, which was virulently anticommunist and formed a barrier against potential westward Soviet aggression. A decision to go to war over the Sudetenland in 1938 was highly unlikely under *any* British prime minister.[20]

But the obvious perils of counterfactual speculation do not budge the facts of Munich's strategic consequences for Britain and France. Nor do they absolve Chamberlain of wretched judgment. He sullied Britain's honor by participating in the dismemberment of a strategically important fellow democracy by a bloodthirsty tyrant. By late 1938, moreover, Hitler was manifestly untrustworthy; yet, after his first meeting with *Der Führer,* Chamberlain continued to believe that "in spite of the hardness and ruthlessness I thought I saw in his face . . . here was a man who could be relied upon when he had given his word."[21]

The great lesson the democracies, including the United States, drew from Munich was simple and clear: appeasement of aggression only invites more aggression, and it is therefore imperative that early and effective force be used to stop it. As Walter Lippmann, who believed Munich was "the equivalent of a major military disaster," put it in 1938: "Insofar as the fascist states believe that we will use only measures that are 'short of the application of force,' they will be undeterred by our wishes. I see no way of putting any stop to their aggrandizement except by convincing them that at some point they will meet overwhelmingly superior force."[22] Implicit in Munich's lesson is the principle that once a defense commitment is made, it must be honored at any cost; failure to do so will encourage further aggression by undermining the credibility of all commitments. Hence Vietnam. Also implicit in this lesson is the notion that the twentieth-century phenomenon of totalitarianism, be it fascism or communism, understands only the language of force.

Given the consequences of appeasement, Christopher Hemmer observed, "Munich tell[s] policy makers interested in protecting the interests of their state to oppose any form of aggression, no matter how slight, because appeasement only encourages future challenges and strengthens the aggressor."[23] Nazi Germany could have been stopped in 1938, or even in 1936, had the democracies been determined to act and had they appreciated the true scope of Hitler's ambitions. An important related lesson of the 1930s is that totalitarian states are inherently and endlessly aggressive, or, as Richard Lebow put it: "Aggression was the fuel totalitarian dictatorships burned to maintain legitimacy; they could not survive at home without seeking to expand abroad. Their appetites abroad were insatiable."[24] The presumption of insatiable aggressiveness irrespective of time and circumstances mandates war.

The association of aggression with large and powerful totalitarian states is certainly supported by the behavior of Nazi Germany, Fascist Italy, and Soviet Russia in the 1930s and later. But the implicit transference of insatiable aggressiveness to all states, large and small, seeking territorial acquisitions by force tends to downplay, or even altogether ignore, the great disparities in power among states as well as the historical circumstances peculiar to territories in disputes among states. Ho Chi Minh was a totalitarian, but his territorial ambitions were both limited and historically supportable. In any event, his North Vietnam, even when backed militarily by the Soviet Union and China, was not capable of sustaining a program of aggression beyond the borders of Indochina. In neither ambition nor capacity are most aggressors insatiable, which means that most cases of unchecked aggression do not inevitably mushroom, like cancer, into ever-larger conquests. Slobodan Milosevic launched four wars of aggression in the former Yugoslavia, but none of them reflected an imperial agenda in the rest of Europe.

✳ ✳ ✳

The Vietnam War conveys quite different messages to those who look to it for lessons. For starters, if Munich encourages using force, Vietnam encourages both an aversion to force and, paradoxically, an injunction to use it decisively if force cannot be avoided.

What happened to the United States in Vietnam? There is still no consensus among participants or historians on the reasons for America's defeat in Indochina, or even on the nature of the Vietnam War. The war continues to be passionately refought, and because the basic facts remain in dispute, some have argued that the war provides no meaningful lessons regarding future uses of force. The Vietnam War "does not provide us with a point of departure for common discourse about how to face that challenge," argued David Fromkin and James Chace ten years after Saigon's fall. "The Munich Pact was a disaster, but at least the Western world recognized it as such and learned that it would be a mistake to commit the same error again. The lesson of Munich can be misapplied— but the point is that it can also be *applied*. The lesson of Vietnam, if there is one, cannot be applied because we still do not agree about what happened."[25]

But the absence of consensus has not prevented presidents and other policy makers from drawing lessons. Nor has it prevented them from attempting to apply those lessons to policy formulation, including military action. The lack of consensus on what Vietnam can teach policy makers, however, makes it much more difficult to translate the Vietnam War experience into a reliable common guide for future decisions. There *is* absolute consensus on the imperative of avoiding a repetition of that war, and post-Vietnam presidents have so far avoided foreign policy mistakes of the kind that led to an eight-year war in which fifty-eight thousand Americans were killed. Post–Vietnam War presidents have been more careful than the Kennedy and Johnson administrations in picking overseas fights; indeed, they have picked relatively easy wins: Grenada, Panama, Iraq, and Serbia. They have also been more willing to cut U.S. losses in dead-end interventions—Lebanon and Somalia—than were Kennedy, Johnson, and Nixon in Vietnam. On balance, post-Vietnam presidents have displayed significantly greater risk aversion, and especially sensitivity to incurring casualties, than their predecessors. In this they have been reinforced by an even more timid Pentagon.

Indeed, during the 1970s and 1980s the professional military and many of its civilian supporters *did* draw a set of lessons from the war that commanded widespread agreement within the Pentagon. These lessons were translated into a doctrine that continues to exert a powerful influence on U.S. use-of-force decisions. Embodied in the tenets of what has become known as the Weinberger-Powell Doctrine, the lessons are hardly universally accepted. The point, however, is that they reflect the Pentagon's "take" on what went wrong in Vietnam.

Before examining these lessons, a survey of the state of the historical arguments over the Vietnam War is in order. What general propositions have been made over the past three decades about the war by various lesson drawers in the mainstream of the debate, and how does each fare in terms of the scope of its acceptance? I distinguish seven propositions, listed below in roughly ascending order of their contentiousness.

1. *American military intervention in the Vietnam War was a mistake.* This proposition seems, certainly in retrospect, to be self-evident. To be sure, some continue to argue that intervention demonstrated U.S. credibility as a guarantor and bought time for the rest of noncommunist Asia to progress economically and politically; others contend that the real mistake lay in the manner rather than the fact of intervention. Yet, whatever the U.S. motive and manner of action in Vietnam, intervention failed to save South Vietnam and inflicted enormous damage on both Vietnamese society and the American body politic. The anticipated consequences of U.S. defeat in Indochina—the loss of most or even all of the rest of Southeast Asia and the destruction of the credibility of U.S. defense commitments elsewhere—did not materialize. If intervention was not a mistake, then how is the persistence of the so-called Vietnam syndrome to be explained? The view that intervention bought time for the rest of Asia to strengthen its internal defenses against communism is not convincing either, especially given its association with the discredited architects of intervention.[26] The crushing of an attempted communist coup in Jakarta in October 1965 is cited as evidence for this view. But the

Indonesian generals who stopped the coup acted not because of the U.S. decision to defend South Vietnam but because they were fighting for their very lives. Certainly, no mainland Southeast Asian state beyond Indochina faced a communist insurgent or cross-border threat remotely approaching the magnitude of the Viet Cong and North Vietnamese army forces operating in South Vietnam.

Of course, no one can say for sure what the political map of Southeast Asia would look like today had the United States decided in 1965 to cut its losses rather than jump into the war. Vietnam almost certainly would have been reunified under communist auspices a decade earlier than it actually was, but the regional consequences of reunification in 1965 rather than 1975 remain inherently speculative. The United States might simply have fallen back to a politically and militarily much stronger position in Thailand, and in so doing reduced Cambodia's potential strategic importance to Hanoi. The end result—who knows?—might have been a Cambodia spared the horrors of the Khmer Rouge.

2. *American policy makers underestimated the military skill and political tenacity of the Vietnamese Communists.* This proposition also seems self-evident and is supported by the statements of key U.S. officials. For example, in 1965, Maxwell Taylor, the U.S. ambassador to South Vietnam and former chairman of the Joint Chiefs of Staff, marveled: "The ability of the Vietcong continuously to rebuild units and make good their losses is one of the mysteries of this guerrilla war. We still find no plausible explanation of the continued strength of the Vietcong."[27] A year later, Secretary of Defense Robert McNamara remarked to an acquaintance, "I never thought [the war] would go like this, I didn't think these people had the capacity to fight this way."[28] Secretary of State Dean Rusk later confessed: "Hanoi's persistence was incredible. I do not understand it even to this day."[29]

These declarations reflect a collective failure to recognize that the strength of the Communists' interest in the war greatly exceeded that of the United States. For Hanoi and the Viet Cong, the stakes were nothing less than national reunification, expulsion of hated foreign domination, and imposition of revolutionary social change. For these objectives the Communists had already been fighting for two decades when the first U.S. ground combat forces waded ashore in 1965. For the United States, in contrast, the stakes were limited and relatively abstract. U.S. intervention in the Vietnam War was hardly the last time policy makers failed to appreciate the strength of an adversary's interest in the struggle.

Official surprise at the Communists' fighting power also reflected, on the American side, a culture-based style of warfare that even today focuses on the measurable indexes of military power at the expense of such intangibles as the enemy's past performance, organizational quality, morale, discipline, courage, and willingness to die. U.S. military doctrine in 1965 treated war primarily as a firepower management challenge, and American culture exalted technocracy and the technocrat.

3. *Civilian authority imposed significant political restrictions on U.S. use of force in Indochina.* This is a proposition again in little dispute. Wars fought for limited political objectives entail political limits on the application of force. The argument, treated below, is not over the legitimacy of political supervision, but rather over the legitimacy of the specific restrictions President Johnson imposed on the U.S. war effort in Vietnam. "No major proposal required for war can be worked out in ignorance of political factors," observed Carl von Clausewitz, "and when people talk, as they often do, about the harmful political influence on the management of war, they are not really saying what they mean. Their quarrel should be with the policy itself, not with its influence."[30]

Johnson repeatedly boasted of his personal control over the selection of individual bombing targets in North Vietnam and over the rules of engagement. He also refused to permit U.S. ground forces to enter Laos and rejected repeated requests by the Joint Chiefs of Staff to authorize a reserve mobilization. Ever mindful of what had happened to the Truman administration in Korea, Johnson feared that an unlimited air war against North Vietnam would provoke direct Chinese intervention. Strictly limiting the application of military power also reduced the risk of losing control of the war to the professional military, whom the Texas populist regarded as warmongers.

In fairness to Johnson, he inherited a condition of bitter civil-military relations. Kennedy distrusted the Joint Chiefs of Staff, and McNamara's managerial revolution at the Pentagon had enraged the senior military leadership. Moreover, Johnson could hardly be blamed for the persistence of acute interservice rivalry and the institutional weakness of the Joint Chiefs, which made it next to impossible for them to provide civilian authority with timely and useful military advice.[31] The differences over war policy, especially between the air force and army, were as pervasive within the military as they were between the Chiefs and the civilians.

4. *The defeat of the American cause in Indochina—the preservation of an independent, noncommunist South Vietnam—was occasioned not by*

outright military rout but rather by the combination of a tenacious enemy and U.S. loss of political will to continue fighting. American military forces were not driven into the South China Sea by enemy action; they were instead unilaterally withdrawn from Vietnam by a Nixon administration under intense pressure to reduce U.S. casualties and end America's involvement in the war. South Vietnam did not fall to communist forces until 1975—more than two years after the last U.S. ground combat forces had left. The interim between the American troops' departure and the final communist victory unfortunately has permitted such commentators as former president Richard Nixon and retired general William Westmoreland to claim that the United States had actually won the war at the time the Paris Peace Agreement was signed in January 1973, only to see defeat snatched from the jaws of victory by the combination of poor South Vietnamese military performance and Congress's refusal to provide sufficient military assistance to allow South Vietnam to survive the communist onslaught of 1975.[32]

It is certainly understandable that both men would want to believe that the United States had actually won the war by 1973, or, to put it another way, that they bore no responsibility for what happened in 1975. But acceptance of that argument requires an enormous stretch of the imagination. Was not the war Americanized in the first place precisely because the South Vietnamese were being defeated on the battlefield? If 500,000 U.S. troops could not expel North Vietnamese regulars from South Vietnam, how was even the most lavishly equipped South Vietnamese army to survive a communist invasion without a U.S. ground combat presence? Did Nixon really believe that the "peace" of the Paris agreement was sustainable based on a settlement that mandated a U.S. departure from South Vietnam while letting the North Vietnamese army stick around in that country? (Certainly South Vietnam's president, Nguyen Van Thieu, was under no such illusion.)

It is helpful to remember that communist revolutionary war doctrine, especially the Vietnamese variant, emphasized the enemy's political will, not his forces, as the ultimate target of military operations, and the protraction of hostilities as the main means of breaking that will. "Protracted resistance," wrote Vo Nguyen Giap during the war, "is the essential strategy of a people . . . determined to defeat an enemy . . . having large and well-armed forces."[33] Thus, it really did not matter in the end that the Vietnamese Communists were never strong enough to inflict a Dunkirk on the United States. They did not have to.

5. *The war the United States entered in Vietnam was fundamentally a civil war among Vietnamese.* Official opinion insisted throughout the war that the conflict was a case of international communist aggression with the Vietnamese Communists serving as instruments of Moscow's and Beijing's imperial ambitions. Certainly, in the years following the Tet Offensive most of the original insurgency in the south dried up and North Vietnam became more and more militarily dependent on the Soviet Union for the increasingly conventional military operations it waged in the south.[34] (In 1978, Communist Vietnam became a formal military ally of the Soviet Union.) Yet, the war the United States chose to enter in 1965 was largely a politically and militarily self-sustaining insurgency based on legitimate political and social grievances and waged by southern-born and -raised Vietnamese who sought to overthrow their own government. The fact that the Communists were leading the insurgency does not strip the war of its primary identity as a fight between Vietnamese over political control of southern Vietnam and over the continued presence of Western influence there. In any case, the Vietnam War was hardly unique: civil wars often attract external intervention. America's own War for Independence, which was essentially a fight among Englishmen to determine who would rule British North America, attracted French troops, ships, and money, but French intervention did not make George Washington a flunky for the Bourbons. To be sure, in 1965 North and South Vietnam were territorially separate entities that had gained international diplomatic recognition. But does that mean that, had the Confederacy in 1862 attracted the diplomatic recognition of France and Great Britain, Union armies subsequently invading Virginia and Tennessee would have been transformed from agencies in an American civil war to instruments of international aggression?

6. *Vital U.S. interests were present in Vietnam in 1965.* Certainly the senior political and military leadership believed this to be true. Presidents Eisenhower, Kennedy, and Johnson all believed in the domino theory and saw the Communists' challenge in South Vietnam as a test of American resolve, specifically of the credibility of U.S. defense commitments worldwide. Spokesmen for all three administrations declared the outcome of the fight in Vietnam vital to U.S. interests. Some argued in private that even failed intervention was better than no intervention at all. In 1964, the president's national security adviser, McGeorge Bundy, argued that it was better to lose in South Vietnam after having committed 100,000 troops than to lose without making the commitment, and in the

following year he advised that the United States, even if it lost, could not afford the strategic consequences of not having been *seen* to have made the effort.[35] This same argument was revived in 1999 by Michael Lind in a controversial reinterpretation of the Vietnam War (discussed in chapter 4) that, among other things, claims that the Munich analogy was very relevant to what was happening in Southeast Asia in the 1960s.[36]

But the United States *did* lose the war, and where is the hard evidence of a connection between making the effort to win the war and East Asia's subsequent prosperity and partial democratization? Exactly what vital U.S. interest was compromised or overthrown by the fall of Saigon? Indeed, by what objective criteria, if any, is an interest deemed "vital"? Is it sufficient simply for a president to so pronounce an interest, as did Eisenhower, Kennedy, Johnson, and Nixon in Vietnam?

7. *The Vietnam War was winnable.* This most controversial of all propositions about the Vietnam War compels an analysis not only of why the United States lost but also of what would have constituted a victory. On the first issue there are two basic and fundamentally irreconcilable schools of thought, with several variants in between. The first school holds that the war the United States entered in Vietnam was essentially a revolutionary civil war and was probably not winnable at any acceptable military, political, and moral price.[37] Defeat was probable for one or more of the following reasons: (1) the United States faced a skilled and tenacious enemy who was prepared to fight longer and harder than the United States; (2) South Vietnam was a politically illegitimate and militarily incompetent client state; (3) the United States miscalculated the nature of the war, its strategic significance, and the enemy's fighting power; and (4) conventional military operations had a limited utility in the Indochinese setting. To this school of thought, "No more Vietnams" means no more entanglements in Third World civil wars not directly engaging vital U.S. security interests, although how these interests are defined is left open.

The second school of thought asserts that the Vietnam War was a case of state-on-state aggression and that a U.S. victory in Indochina was possible, even probable, but for the combination of crippling civilian intrusion on the conduct of military operations, a subversive domestic antiwar movement, and a hostile media.[38] For this school, "No more Vietnams" means fighting to win, or, as Richard Nixon put it, "'No more Vietnams' can mean we will not *try* again. It *should* mean we will not *fail* again."[39] Regardless of the reason for war, proponents of this view insist, once the decision for it has been made, force should be used decisively, if possible overwhelmingly. A small but highly influential variant of the "we defeated ourselves" school condemns U.S. military as well as civilian leadership. The former is criticized for disunity of command, choice of improper strategy, self-defeating personnel policies, reliance on lavish base camps, and lack of courage to confront civilian authority for failure to take their advice. Interestingly, much of this line of criticism has come from retired U.S. Army officers who served in Vietnam.[40]

There is no question that the professional performance of the U.S. military in Vietnam was deeply flawed, and it is to the credit of all the services, especially the army, that they did not shy away from hard postwar self-examination. The war generated fundamental reforms in training and doctrine, especially within the army, that paid off handsomely in the Gulf War. But no state loses a war without some help from the enemy. The conclusion that the United States was beaten in Vietnam by decisions made in Washington, Honolulu, and Saigon implicitly belittles decisions made in Hanoi and the remarkable fighting power of the Vietnamese Communists. The Sioux did, after all, have something to do with Custer's defeat at the Little Bighorn.

The issue of what a U.S. victory in Vietnam would have looked like is also bedeviling. U.S. war aims did not encompass North Vietnam's destruction or a change of regime in Hanoi. Nor did civilian or military authorities in Washington designate specific military objectives in Indochina as means of fulfilling the political objective of preserving an independent, noncommunist South Vietnam. Would victory have required the withdrawal of all North Vietnamese troops from the south? How would their return have been prevented? What about the indigenous communist insurgency in the south? How about defining victory as a declared percentage of population and territory under Saigon's control? Would a neutral Vietnam have been acceptable? For the Johnson administration, victory came to be defined simply as not losing for long enough to make the Communists tire and fold—a reckless and tragic conception based on an inability or unwillingness to grasp the magnitude of the Communists' stake in the war.

The strategic lessons that post–Vietnam War presidents and other defense and foreign policy makers have drawn from the war are many, and in some cases are as contradictory as the war itself. Certainly, it is easy to conclude that the best way to avoid another Vietnam is simply to stay out of Third World conflicts, especially civil wars. A variant of this prescription was the Nixon Doctrine, which reaffirmed U.S. defense commitments worldwide but declared in effect that the United States would never again Americanize a ground war on an ally's behalf. The United States would provide military assistance, including naval and air support, but allies would be expected to supply the manpower for their own defense. The United States had picked a poor client in the politically and militarily weak regime in Saigon and had to be more selective in the future. "The real question," observed Henry Kissinger in retrospect, "was not whether some dominoes might fall in Southeast Asia, which was likely, but whether there might not be better places in the region to draw the line."[41]

A different lesson, though compatible with greater discrimination in picking a fight, is the imperative of winning whatever war is at hand. Go in to win or don't go in at all. MacArthur's ringing declaration during the Korean War that "in war there is no substitute for victory" went unheeded in Vietnam, to the distress of those who found it difficult to accept political limits on the use of force.[42] To them, the only object of the war was to win, and absent that objective the United States should not have gone to war in the first place.

The most influential early professional military assessment of the lessons of the war was Harry G. Summers Jr.'s *On Strategy: A Critical Analysis of the Vietnam War,* published in 1982.[43] Using Carl von Clausewitz's masterpiece, *On War,* as the yardstick for judging U.S. political and military performance, Summers mercilessly condemned both. He censured the Johnson administration for failing to mobilize the national political will via dramatic exhortation and a formal declaration of war, and he indicted the military for having lost touch with the art of war, including the imperative not to confuse the administrative requirements involved in preparing for war with the operational requirements for waging war. Summers argued that the United States essentially waged a halfhearted war with no intention of winning; it lacked even a concept of victory, notwithstanding repeated proclamation of the presence of vital U.S. interests in Vietnam.

Although Summers's analysis was not well received by the senior army leadership, it electrified many younger officers and civilian defense analysts. Indeed, *On Strategy* laid the foundation for further discussion, which was not long in coming. Two years after Summers's book was published, Secretary of Defense Caspar W. Weinberger gave a speech, "The Uses of Military Power," that essentially summarized the basic lessons the professional military drew from the Vietnam War as they were seemingly reaffirmed by America's failed intervention in Lebanon in 1982–83.

The speech "illustrate[s] the growing consensus that has characterized the military's own views since its cathartic defeat in Southeast Asia," wrote Eric R. Alterman in 1986. "An examination of the intellectual evolution of the military elite since Vietnam and their reading of the 'lessons of Vietnam' clarifies the strategic, political, and intellectual underpinnings of Weinberger's doctrine for 'The Uses of Military Power.'"[44] The speech remains probably the single most influential contribution to the post–Vietnam War debate on the use of force. It was immediately tagged the "Weinberger Doctrine," and the doctrine's tenets continue to be popular within the Pentagon and on Capitol Hill, if not at the White House and State Department.

Weinberger was a secretary of defense who saw his role as being an uncritical advocate of the armed services' budgets and programs. He believed that civilians had no business telling the military how to conduct its business. In his memoirs, he argued that President Harry Truman was "seriously wrong . . . to limit General Douglas MacArthur's freedom of movement in Korea" and to reprimand the general "for going too far."[45] In his view, the lessons of Vietnam had been reaffirmed by the U.S. intervention in Lebanon, which he had opposed, and were waiting to be relearned yet again in a prospective U.S. military intervention in Central America. The U.S. assistance to the contras fighting to overthrow the Sandinista regime in Nicaragua and the U.S. advisory presence in neighboring insurgency-torn El Salvador portended a possible escalation into a Central American Vietnam. "The Uses of Military Power" was a warning against what Weinberger believed was a penchant of some policy makers, most notably his rival, Secretary of State George Shultz, for casual military intervention.[46]

The Weinberger doctrine amounts to six "tests" (his term) to be passed before the United States commits force—tests that by implication were not mastered in the Vietnam and Lebanon intervention decisions.

1. The United States should not commit forces to *combat* overseas unless the particular engagement or occasion is deemed vital to our national interest or that of our allies.
2. If we decide that it *is* necessary to put *combat* troops into a given situation, we should do so wholeheartedly and with the clear intention of winning.
3. If we *do* decide to commit forces to combat overseas, we should have clearly defined political and military objectives.

4. The relationship between our objectives and the forces we have com
mitted—their size and composition—must be continually reassessed
and adjusted if necessary.

5. Before the U.S. commits combat forces abroad, there must be some
reasonable assurance [that] we will have the support of the American
people and their elected representatives in Congress.

6. The commitment of U.S. forces to combat should be a last resort.[47]

Weinberger identified "gray area conflicts" as "the most likely challenge
to peace," yet warned that they "are precisely the most difficult challenges to which a democracy must respond." He further cautioned that if
"we are certain that force is required in a given situation, we run the risk
of inadequate national will to apply the resources needed." He then went
on to deplore post-Vietnam congressional intrusion in the making of foreign policy "and in the decision-making process for the employment of
military forces that had been thought appropriate and practical before."
The resulting "compromise" of "the centrality of decision-making authority in the executive branch" was not accompanied "by a correspond-
ing acceptance of responsibility by Congress."

Weinberger reserved his heaviest fire for those "theorists [who] argue
that military force can be brought to bear in any crisis," who "are eager to
advocate its use even in limited amounts simply because they believe
that if there are American forces of *any* size present they will somehow
solve the problem." He did not advocate a return to isolationism and the
dangers to core security interests isolationism had invited in the 1930s—
the Anglophile Weinberger worshipped Churchill and was a firm believer
in the great lesson of Munich as it applied to Soviet expansionism. But
neither could the United States embrace the "alternative [of] employing
our forces almost indiscriminately and as a regular and customary part of
our diplomatic efforts." To do so "would surely plunge us headlong into
the sort of domestic turmoil we experienced during the Vietnam War."

Weinberger was hardly the first major policy maker to draw such conclusions from Vietnam. Even before the war ended, Maxwell Taylor, a key
architect of U.S. intervention in Vietnam and an early enthusiast of grad-
ualist applications of force against Hanoi, conceded that piecemeal use
of force ended up "assuring a prolonged war which carried with it the
dangers of expansion." The "restrained use of our air power suggested to
the enemy a lack of decisiveness" and "encouraged the enemy to hang on
until his hopes were fulfilled in 1968 by a collapse of the American will to

persist in the bombing." Equally important, the "gradual erosion of public support for President Johnson should remind any future President of the many factors he must take into account before deciding to lead the American people into another intervention like Vietnam." Taylor cautioned that "before charging up the hill, he had better be sure that his troops will follow" by being "certain that the cause at stake is of clear, unchallengeable importance which can be explained in simple terms." Additionally, the president "should verify that there is a high probability of attaining his objective in a short time well within the probable limits of national patience."[48]

Both Taylor and Weinberger decried the use of force or threatened force as a means of political coercion. As a tool of coercive diplomacy, force had obviously failed against North Vietnam, and its failure was followed by a real war. Weinberger viewed the "intermixture of diplomacy and the military" as inherently dangerous because it meant "that we should not hesitate to put a battalion or so of American forces in various places in the world where we desired . . . stability, or changes of government, or support of governments or whatever else."[49] If the enemy then counterescalated, the United States would have to do the same. Weinberger essentially rejected force as a companion of diplomacy, and in his memoirs condemned the National Security Council staff for "spending most of their time thinking up ever more wild adventures for our troops."[50] Weinberger, in sum, saw force not as an arm of diplomacy, but rather as a substitute for it—something to be used only when diplomacy failed. This view in effect rejected the Clausewitzian dictum that war is a continuation of politics by other means and denied the continuum of agreement, negotiation, threat, coercive diplomacy, and war.[51]

The Weinberger Doctrine also assumes that failed coercive diplomacy leads inevitably to ever-widening war, which in turn implies loss of control over one's own foreign policy. Once the United States begins threatening and using even modest increments of force—a punitive air strike here, a naval demonstration there—it essentially hands the strategic initiative to the enemy, who makes the decision to counterescalate or deescalate. The only way to avoid the risk is to abjure threatened force in the first place. This in-for-a-dime-in-for-a-dollar determinism ignores both U.S. free will and the enormous qualitative differences in potential U.S. adversaries.

The Weinberger Doctrine was carried into the Bush administration by Gen. Colin Powell, who became chairman of the Joint Chiefs of Staff in

1989 and a key player during the Persian Gulf crisis of 1990–91. Indeed, his allegiance during the crisis to the tenets of the Weinberger Doctrine and his emphasis on the application of overwhelming force as a means of beating Iraq quickly and at minimum cost in U.S. casualties led commentators to start using the term "Weinberger-Powell Doctrine." Powell had, in fact, served as Weinberger's military aide and had helped the secretary of defense draft his famous speech. As a Vietnam veteran he passionately believed, as did many of his fellow officers who later planned and executed Operation Desert Storm, that U.S. military forces had been almost criminally misused in Vietnam by both the White House and the senior military leadership. "War should be the politics of last resort," Powell wrote in his best-selling memoirs. "And when we go to war, we should have a purpose that our people understand and support; we should mobilize the country's resources to fulfill that mission and then go in to win. In Vietnam, we entered a half-hearted war, with much of the nation opposed or indifferent, while a small fraction carried the burden."[52]

These words essentially restate the Weinberger Doctrine. Use of force should be highly restricted. It should be avoided in situations where political restrictions threaten to impede its effective use, where a clear and quick military win is not attainable, and where public and congressional opinion is indifferent or hostile to the purpose for which force is being used. For Powell, winning meant going in with overwhelming force, getting the job done quickly, and getting out cleanly—i.e., without posthostilities political obligations that might compel recommitment of U.S. forces in less than ideal circumstances.

Powell made avoidance of another Vietnam his life's mission. "Many of my generation, the career captains, majors, and lieutenant colonels seasoned in that war, vowed that when our turn came to call the shots, we would not quietly acquiesce in half-hearted warfare for half-baked reasons that the American people could not understand or support. If we could make good on that promise to ourselves, to the civilian leadership, and to the country, then the sacrifices of Vietnam would not have been in vain." Powell saw the greatest strike against the senior military leadership as its failure "to talk straight to its political superiors or to itself. The top leadership never went in to the Secretary of Defense or the President and said, 'This war is unwinnable the way we are fighting it.'"[53]

In 1992, after Bill Clinton was elected president but before his inauguration, Powell wrote an article for *Foreign Affairs* in which he elliptically warned his audience, presumably including the president-elect, against repeating the mistakes of Vietnam in the former Yugoslavia. He condemned gradualism and warned against "send[ing] military forces into a crisis with an unclear mission they cannot accomplish." He noted that "military force is not always the right answer," but urged that "when we do use it, we should not be equivocal: we should win and win decisively." He further cautioned that the intervention's objectives should be limited and achievable, and claimed that the Bush administration called off the Gulf War when U.S. objectives had been achieved and immediately evacuated Iraqi territory because the only alternative would have been "the inevitable follow-up" of "major occupation forces in Iraq for years to come and a complex American proconsulship in Baghdad."[54]

The Clinton administration inherited Powell as chairman of the Joint Chiefs of Staff, but there is no evidence that either the new president or his foreign policy principals had much use for the Weinberger-Powell Doctrine—or for Powell himself, who made his opposition to any U.S. military intervention in the crumbling Yugoslav state very clear. On the contrary, the administration displayed a propensity to use force in circumstances quite the opposite of those prescribed by the Weinberger-Powell Doctrine. U.S. military action was undertaken in Somalia, Haiti, Bosnia, and Serbia in the absence of either manifestly vital U.S. interests or reasonable assurance of public and congressional support. In the case of the war over Kosovo, there was a major mismatch between the immediate political objective sought and the military means employed.

But the Clinton administration was nonetheless compelled to pay lip service to the Weinberger-Powell Doctrine because of the doctrine's continuing popularity among the senior military leadership and especially on Capitol Hill, where Republican majorities were highly critical of the administration's uses of force. The administration's annual issues of *A National Security Strategy for a New Century* contain discussions of criteria for using force based on the weight of interest at stake. The December 1999 issue, for example, divides interests into "vital," "important," and "humanitarian and other." Where vital interests are at stake, it says, "our use of force will be decisive and, if necessary, unilateral." In situations involving important interests, "military forces should only be used if they advance U.S. interests, they are likely to accomplish their objectives, and the costs and risks of their employment are commensurate with the interests at stake, and other non-military means are incapable of achieving our objectives." For humanitarian and other interests, use of force will be highly selective and will focus "on the unique capabilities and

resources the military can bring to bear, rather than on its combat power."[55] The Clinton approach essentially graded U.S. interests in terms of
the means it was prepared to employ in their defense.

Clearly, the Clinton administration rejected the Weinberger-Powell
Doctrine's proscription of using force to defend less than vital interests.
But, as indicated in *A National Security Strategy for a New Century*, the
administration did declare that in every case in which use of force was
being considered, it would be necessary to ask a variety of questions that
in effect addressed most of the issues Secretary of Defense Weinberger
raised in 1984. "Have we explored or exhausted non-military means that
offer a reasonable chance of achieving our goals. Is there a clearly
defined, achievable mission? . . . What level of effort will be needed to
achieve our goals? What are the potential costs—human and financial—
of the operation?" The administration also recognized the imperative of
political support: "Sustaining our engagement abroad over the long term
will require the support of the American people and the Congress to bear
the costs of defending U.S. interests—including the risk of losing American lives."[56]

Implicit in the Weinberger-Powell Doctrine, in the various editions of
A National Security Strategy for a New Century, and, increasingly, in post–
Cold War actual uses of force is an assumption, rooted in the Vietnam War
and seemingly reaffirmed in Lebanon and Somalia, that the American
public and the Congress will not tolerate casualties sustained on behalf
of any use of force for other than manifestly vital interests. Pre–Vietnam
War presidents enjoyed what in retrospect seems a remarkable national
consensus on the organizing principle of American foreign policy and an
even more remarkable public and congressional deference to the White
House on matters of war and peace. Any decision to fight a communist
foe almost automatically commanded public and congressional support
even if the decision portended the loss of thousands of American lives. It
was unthinkable that such support could degenerate—in the middle of
an anticommunist war, no less—into domestic opposition sufficient to
compel a unilateral U.S. military withdrawal from the fight.

The Vietnam War changed all that. It provoked Congress to reassert its
prerogatives in foreign policy and made the American public both more
skeptical of the utility of force and more sensitive to the risk of casualties.
The Cold War's demise increased this skepticism and sensitivity. The
absence of a clear and present external danger to the United States has
not only destroyed what remained of the Cold War foreign policy consen-

sus but has also reduced public and congressional tolerance for incurring casualties in the kind of politically coercive military operations that have dominated the U.S. military's plate since the Persian Gulf War.

If anything, the Vietnam War produced a professional military excessively doubtful of the resilience and staying power of American democracy at war and less confident than the average citizen in the public's tolerance for casualties. "Vietnam had convinced U.S. soldiers that modern democracy's capacity to absorb the strains of war was severely limited," Andrew J. Bacevich observed. "In any conflict where success was not seen as forthcoming, popular impatience might lead all too easily into support withdrawn from the war with devastating consequences for the war's outcome and for those who fought it. . . . Therefore, an overriding imperative was to win quickly. . . . The corollary was equally important: situations where the prospect of an early decision appeared problematic were to be avoided at all costs."[57] The consequences of these Vietnam War lessons, especially of the apparent disparity in assumptions regarding casualty sensitivity between the senior political and military leadership, on the one hand, and the American people, on the other, are addressed in chapter 7.

"The legacy of Munich," wrote Norman Podhoretz in his controversial 1982 book, *Why We Were in Vietnam,* "had been a disposition, even a great readiness, to resist, by force if necessary, the expansion of totalitarianism; the legacy of Vietnam would obversely be a reluctance, even a refusal, to resist, especially if resistance required the use of force."[58] Podhoretz made this judgment, of course, before the West's conclusive victory over communist totalitarianism. Moreover, it is difficult to imagine how defeat in Vietnam could have had, for better or for worse, anything other than a chilling effect on U.S. willingness to use force. Finally, there is no question that Munich and the world war that followed promoted a fear that failure to use force against the expansion of communist totalitarianism would lead to yet a third world war. But for this conviction, however, it is improbable that the United States would have intervened in either Korea or Vietnam.

Truman in Korea

In his masterful *War and Politics,* the great American Cold War strategist Bernard Brodie reminded his readers that "the conviction that peace and security in the world were indivisible was strongly refortified by the events leading up to World War II. People who do not remember these events find it difficult to recapture the tremendously traumatic impact of the Munich Agreement on the thinking of the postwar world, especially in the United States."[1]

Indeed, Munich's influence has extended into the present post–Cold War era. President George Bush invoked the analogy during the Persian Gulf crisis of 1990–91, and even President Bill Clinton, the first president born after World War II, invoked it during the Kosovo crisis of 1999. But Munich's influence on U.S. foreign policy really began in the late 1940s as the Truman administration grappled with the implications of growing Soviet hostility. Within the space of just five years—from the end of World War II to the outbreak of the Korean War—the administration moved from the afterglow of wartime alliance with Moscow to the conclusion that Stalin's Russia, like Hitler's Germany, was an insatiably aggressive totalitarian state whose expansionism had to be contained, by force if necessary, as an alternative to a third world war. By the time North Korea invaded South Korea, many Americans had come to see the Soviet Union as no different from Nazi Germany in terms of the dual threat it posed to America's security and values. "American writers, political leaders, and opinion makers lost no time in applying to Stalin and the Communists the very same traits that had characterized the fallen Hitler and his Nazis," observed David W. Levy in *The Debate over Vietnam* (1995). "Stalin was no less totalitarian than the Fascists; he was no less ambitious to conquer the world; no less devious in his international dealings; no less brutal to his own enslaved population; no less the bitter foe of freedom, democracy, and religion."[2]

The policy of preventing the expansion of Soviet power and influence beyond those areas overrun by Soviet forces during World War II was thus a U.S. foreign policy response based on perceived strategic lessons of Munich. Although the actual application of this containment strategy varied widely during the Cold War,[3] its central tenet—that failure to resist Soviet expansionism simply invited more of it and inched the great powers closer to another world war—remained unchanged.

The shift toward containment began in 1946 with George Kennan's famous "long telegram" from Moscow to the State Department, which was published the following year in *Foreign Affairs* as "The Sources of Soviet Conduct." As conceived by Kennan in his telegram and other writings, the further expansion of Soviet power and influence in Europe was to be contained by restoring Europe's economy and political self-confidence. Kennan believed the Soviet threat was primarily political and psychological, not military, and that responses to it should be the same. Kennan also believed that the main task of containment was retaining control of the industrial plants of Western Europe and Japan and their potentially decisive war-making potential. The nonindustrialized areas of the world were, in his view, peripheral to U.S. security; thus, even communist victories in what became known as the Third World would not significantly affect the balance of power between the West and the Soviet Union.[4]

Kennan's conception of containment would have excluded U.S. military defense of either South Korea or South Vietnam. In his memoirs, Kennan recounted rejecting the Truman administration's interpretation of the North Korean attack "as merely the first move in some 'grand design' . . . on the part of Soviet leaders to extend their power to other parts of the world by the use of force." Kennan also believed that the Truman administration's decision to fight in Korea worked "to heighten the militarization of thinking about the cold war generally, and to press us into attitudes where any discriminate estimate of Soviet intentions was unwelcome and unacceptable."[5]

Kennan's view of Vietnam was consistent with his assessment of Korea. He testified before the Senate Foreign Relations Committee in 1966 that "Vietnam is not a region of major military, industrial importance. It is difficult to believe that any decisive development of the world situation would be determined in normal circumstances by what happens in that country." He added that "even a situation in which South Vietnam was controlled exclusively by the Viet Cong, while regrettable, and no doubt morally unwarranted, would not, in my opinion, present dangers great enough to justify our direct military intervention.[6]

But Kennan's concept of containment did not survive the outbreak of the Korean War. Indeed, by 1950 the Truman administration had become truly alarmed by the Soviet Union's behavior in Europe, most notably the attempted blockade of Berlin and the forcible installation of a communist regime in Prague in 1948—the second time in less than a decade that Czech democracy had been snuffed out by a totalitarian predator. Then came the communist victory in China and the unexpectedly early Soviet detonation of an atomic bomb. These events occurred against the backdrop of the Truman administration's continued refusal to rebuild demobilized U.S. military forces, notwithstanding its assertion of increasingly ambitious foreign policy objectives. The proclamation to Congress in 1947 of what became known as the Truman Doctrine—that henceforth "it must be the policy of the United States to support free peoples who are resisting attempted subjugation by armed minorities or by outside pressures"—was not accompanied by a request for an increase in defense spending;[7] nor was the historic assumption two years later of a formal NATO treaty commitment to defend Western Europe.

The Truman Doctrine was nonetheless a declaration of cold war against Soviet expansionism and the first of several presidential "doctrines"—it was followed by those of Eisenhower, Nixon, Carter, and Reagan—that pronounced, or by behavior otherwise conveyed, U.S. policy on using force to thwart the spread of communism. Truman painted the world in stark terms: "At the present moment in world history, nearly every nation must choose between alternative ways of life. . . . One way . . . is based upon the will of the majority, and is distinguished by free institutions, representative government, free elections, guarantees of individual liberty, freedom of speech and religion, and freedom from political oppression. The second way of life is based upon the will of the minority forcibly imposed upon the majority. It relies upon terror and oppression, a controlled press and radio, fixed elections, and the suppression of personal freedoms."[8]

Prompted by the threat of an insurgent communist victory in Greece and by Soviet pressure on Turkey to cede some control of the Dardanelles, Truman's declaration sought to secure passage by Congress of a $400 million assistance bill to aid the two beleaguered countries. Yet the doctrine was couched in universal terms, making no distinction between the strategic importance or internal political composition of states threatened or potentially threatened by communism. The so-called Free World included every noncommunist state, democracies and dictatorships alike. Nor did the doctrine restrict U.S. containment to countries threatened by traditional cross-border aggression; on the contrary, it included countries threatened by "attempted subjugation by armed minorities." In this regard, the Truman Doctrine reached beyond the great lesson of Munich, which dealt with the handover, under duress, to Nazi Germany of territory belonging to another sovereign state. Intervention against "armed minorities" invited entanglement in foreign civil wars, and in fact the provision of U.S. military assistance to the Greek government beginning in 1947 was precisely that.

Yet the Truman administration was not yet prepared to put military teeth into its sweeping doctrine. Despite the stark portrait of the Soviet threat Truman painted before the Congress (designed in part to scare the tightfisted legislators into providing assistance to Greece and Turkey), Truman remained preoccupied with the domestic economy and balancing budgets. The great gap during the late 1940s between the political objective of containment and the military means to support that objective was brutally exposed in the opening months of the Korean War. But a National Security Council study of the issue known as NSC-68 had already been completed before the North Korean attack and was sitting on Truman's desk.

NSC-68 is the seminal document of the Cold War because it became the foundation of U.S. policy for four decades, and because it took a much more alarmist view of the Soviet threat and called for a much more ambitious response to that threat than did Kennan's concept of containment.[9] NSC-68 treated the Soviet Union and communism as one and the same thing, a Moscow-directed movement aimed, like Hitler's Germany, at world domination: "The Kremlin is inescapably militant," it insisted, ". . . because it possesses and is possessed by a worldwide revolutionary movement, because it is the inheritor of Russian imperialism, and because it is a totalitarian dictatorship."[10] NSC-68 also perceived the communist threat as primarily a military one fostering armed revolution and cross-border aggression, requiring the permanent rearmament of the United States: "The Soviet Union is developing the military capacity to support its design for world domination . . . and possesses armed forces far in excess of those necessary to defend its national territory."[11] Most significant of all, however, was the document's conclusion that any further loss of territory to communism "would raise the possibility that no coalition adequate to confront the Kremlin with greater strength could be assembled."[12] The "assault on free institutions is worldwide now, and in the context of the present polarization of power a defeat of free institutions anywhere is a defeat everywhere."[13]

NSC-68 also addressed America's hesitancy to use force relative to that of the Soviet Union. Indeed, it said, "differences between our fundamental purpose and the Kremlin design . . . are reflected in our respective attitudes toward and use of military force." The Kremlin did not hesitate to use "its vast forces to intimidate its neighbors, and to support an aggressive foreign policy."[14] In contrast, the United States used force "only if the necessity for its use is clear and compelling and commends itself to the overwhelming majority of our people. The United States cannot therefore engage in war except as a reaction to aggression of so clear and compelling a nature as to bring the overwhelming majority of our people to accept the use of military force."[15]

It is thus small wonder that the Truman administration interpreted the North Korean attack through the lens of Munich. Truman suspected that the attack was a move by "the Russians . . . to get Korea by default, gambling that we would be afraid of starting a third world war and would offer no resistance."[16] In a 1951 radio address on the Korean War and U.S. policy in the Far East, Truman referred to the lesson of the 1930s. "It is easier to put out a fire in the beginning when it is small than after it has become a roaring blaze," he said. "And the best way to meet the threat of aggression is for the peace-loving nations to act together. . . . If they had followed the right policies in the 1930s—if the free countries had acted together to crush the aggression of the dictators, and if they had acted at the beginning when the aggression was small—there probably would have been no World War II. If history has taught us anything, it is that aggression anywhere in the world is a threat to peace everywhere in the world."[17] In his book *Diplomacy,* published in 1994, Henry Kissinger observed that "without exception, the key members of the Truman administration believed in a global communist design and treated [North] Korean aggression as the first move in a coordinated Sino-Soviet strategy which might well be the prelude to a general assault."[18] The Munich analogy "was irresistible," agreed historians Richard E. Neustadt and Ernest R. May. "Everyone saw events of the 1930s being replayed, and everyone agreed about the central lesson of those events: that aggression has to be resisted."[19] But was the analogy valid as a tool for informing the Truman administration about what to do in Korea? Specifically, was the communist regime in North Korea an agent of Soviet aggression, and how did Stalin's Russia really compare to Hitler's Germany?

It was not unreasonable for the Truman administration to interpret North Korea's attack as a Soviet-sponsored move in the larger Cold War. Soviet forces had occupied northern Korea in 1945 and had used the occupation to install the regime of Kim Il Sung, who during much of World War II had served as an officer in a multinational Soviet army unit. Unlike Mao Zedong and Ho Chi Minh, the two other communist leaders in Asia, Kim had thus been put in power by foreigners. Beginning in March 1949, Kim made repeated entreaties to Stalin for permission to attack South Korea.[20] The very fact that Kim felt the need to get Stalin's permission stripped the Pyongyang regime of any pretense of independence. Indeed, a recent examination of North Korea's relationship with Moscow and Beijing as it affected the decision for war concludes that throughout the early post–World War II years, "North Korea can justly be called a Soviet satellite."[21]

Kim Il Sung, whom Stalin had personally selected to be the leader of Korea, did not possess the military wherewithal for decisive action against the south until Stalin provided it in the form of T-34 tanks. The invasion plan itself was drawn up by Soviet military advisers, who until the invasion were present throughout the North Korean army down to the battalion level. Indeed, the evidence suggests that the North Koreans' failure to follow the plan contributed in part to its defeat.[22]

The attack, moreover, served Stalin's strategic agenda. Stalin had been reluctant to give Kim permission while he thought there was a possibility that the United States might respond with force. By the spring of 1950, however, events had conspired to change Stalin's mind, among them signs of hardening Western resolve to contain the Soviet Union militarily in Europe, the withdrawal from South Korea of the last remaining U.S. occupation forces, and the public exclusion of Korea from America's defense perimeter in East Asia by both U.S. Far East commander Gen. Douglas MacArthur and Secretary of State Dean Acheson.[23]

A successful North Korean invasion of South Korea could serve Stalin's interests by distracting the attention of the United States from Europe, adding yet another communist victory in the Cold War, and reminding Mao Zedong, whom Stalin did not trust, who was actually in charge of the communist world. (Stalin told Kim that the Soviet Union would not come to his aid if the Americans intervened, thus leaving Mao's China holding the military bag in Korea after MacArthur's rout of the North Korean army in late 1950.)[24] In addition to demonstrating his support of communism in Asia, William Lee observed in his book on the Korean War, Stalin wanted to "preempt Mao's assertion of traditional Chinese hegemony in Korea."[25] He saw the rise of the Chinese Communist Party (CCP) as a potential threat to Soviet dominance of the international communist movement. For Stalin, the success of the CCP was a double-edged sword. On the one hand, it enlarged the Soviet Union's buffer zone and helped spread communist influence in Asia. On the other hand, once the Chinese gained military strength, they had the potential to become a rival power in the East.[26] Stalin also had his eye on South Korea's warm-water ports. Additionally, by 1950 Stalin was on the defensive in Europe, having failed in his attempts to blockade Berlin, discipline Tito, and thwart the formation of a West German state.

Obviously, Stalin miscalculated in Korea, but his sponsorship of North Korea's attack was hardly reckless under the circumstances of an apparent U.S. strategic write-off of Korea. Permitting Kim Il Sung to invade South Korea may well have been Moscow's greatest single Cold War mistake because it triggered implementation of NSC-68's recommendations, but Stalin had no reason to believe that it would do so. Recklessness was, in fact, the greatest distinction between Hitler's Germany and Stalin's Russia. Both men were totalitarian dictators with global imperial agendas hostile to the United States and the West, and both ruled states possessing enormous actual and latent military power. Both also threatened to upset the balance of power in Europe, for which the United States began to shoulder primary responsibility in the late 1940s. Yet Hitler was reckless because he was convinced that he and he alone possessed the genius to accomplish his dream of a Nazi-controlled Europe, which meant that he had to subdue all of Europe during his lifetime. It is Kissinger's view that since, "on the basis of his family history, he had estimated that his life would be relatively short, he was never able to permit any of his successes to mature, and pushed forward according to a timetable established by his assessment of his physical powers. History offers no other major example of a major war being started on the basis of medical conjecture."[27] This impatience-induced recklessness drove Hitler into war simultaneously with the British Empire, the Soviet Union, and the United States, a war he could not win, and one that he alone among European leaders in the late 1930s wanted.

Stalin, in contrast, was, as George Kennan recognized, a patient and cautious man. He pushed until he encountered resistance, and then backed off to look for another opening. He was a prober, not an attacker, and unlike Hitler he never let ideology fatally impair his strategic judgment. Moreover, Stalin's ideology informed him that communism's ultimate triumph over capitalism was a historical inevitability and therefore did not depend on his personal will. What did depend on his personal will was the survival of the Soviet state, and he therefore avoided exposing the USSR to unnecessary danger. Hitler forced war on him in 1941, but Stalin can hardly be accused of provoking him. Hitler would have invaded Russia sooner or later regardless of Stalin's behavior.

Yet, these personal differences between Hitler and Stalin, important as they are in explaining the fates of the two men, do not undermine the essential correctness of the Truman administration's interpretation of the outbreak of the Korean War based on the Munich analogy. The North Korean attack was, in fact, a Soviet-sponsored probe aimed at gaining additional real estate for communism. The fact that the war was also a civil conflict between Koreans does not alter this judgment. North Korea in 1950 was not North Vietnam in 1965; Ho Chi Minh had not been installed by Soviet troops, and he never felt the need to ask a foreign state's permission to take over South Vietnam. The 1950 attack was a conventional cross-border invasion; in contrast, the war in South Vietnam in 1965 was largely a self-sustaining insurgency.

Clearly, Munich exerted a profound influence on Truman's decision to opt for war in Korea, and it was probably the single most important influence. But the decision was also inseparable from domestic political calculations and from another legacy of appeasement: the failure of the League of Nations. Presidents are not in the habit of making significant use-of-force decisions without weighing the potential domestic political consequences, and Americans in 1950 still had high hopes that the United Nations could succeed where the old league had failed. The United Nations was but five years old, and the North Korean attack was the first critical test of the collective security organization.

The primary domestic political consideration was the potential penalty of doing nothing in the face of yet another act of communist aggression. During the half decade separating the end of World War II and the beginning of the Korean War, congressional Republicans, including Senators William Knowland and Joseph McCarthy and Congressman Richard Nixon, attempted to paint the Democratic Party as "soft" on communism both at home and abroad. The partisan indictment included the Yalta agreement's "sellout" of Eastern Europe to Stalin, the "loss" of China to the Communists, and the Soviet theft of U.S. atomic secrets. By 1950, Truman and Secretary of State Dean Acheson were already on the political defensive against Republican red-baiters, who could have had a field day had the administration stood by and watched the Communists brazenly grab more real estate. Whether the prospect of a Republican backlash was alone sufficient to dictate resistance in Korea cannot be known, but domestic politics, certainly in combination with the interpretation of the North Korean attack through the prism of Munich, reinforced the case for intervention. One observer of congressional anticommunist behavior during the period concluded that "Truman and Acheson knew that the entire world would be watching their response [in Korea]. Failing to respond decisively to communist aggression in Asia would undoubtedly expose Truman to charges from Republicans that he had allowed two Asian nations to fall into communist hands within the span of nine months. Had Truman wavered or refused to assist South Korea in the critical days following the invasion, it would have effectively ended his presidency and spelled an end to Democratic control of Congress."[28] The Korean War was not the last American war in which a Democratic president felt threatened by the prospect of being politically assaulted from the Right for being insufficiently anticommunist. This albatross weighed even more heavily on Lyndon Johnson than it did on Harry Truman.

There was, too, the Truman administration's recognition that the North Korean attack did indeed constitute a critical test of the United Nations. The failure of the League of Nations during the 1930s to do anything about Japan's aggression against China and Mussolini's conquest of Ethiopia was a lesson not lost on either the United States or the United Nations. Truman sought and received UN authorization for an international military response to the North Korean attack, calling that response a "police action." In fact, in this instance the United Nations, because of the unexpected absence of the Soviet ambassador, worked as its enthusiasts had hoped it would: the Security Council voted to authorize UN member states to use force to repel North Korea's aggression. This success was not repeated during the rest of the Cold War.

Truman did not seek a congressional declaration of war because he apparently regarded the combination of the UN authorization and his own constitutional prerogatives as commander in chief of U.S. armed forces as sufficient. Truman consulted with congressional leaders, practically none of whom insisted on a formal declaration of war, before making his decision; according to Dean Acheson, the president did not want to give "the irreconcilable minority" on Capitol Hill the opportunity to debate and delay a war declaration resolution.[29]

The decision not to seek formal congressional authorization proved to be a mistake. The war quickly turned sour with China's intervention, which prolonged the fighting for almost three years. Truman's popularity plummeted, and the absence of a declaration of war freed his critics in Congress to attack Truman's war policy with less restraint than they otherwise would have been forced to use. They made the most of Truman's imposition of political restrictions on U.S. military operations, and especially his decision to fire Gen. Douglas MacArthur for publicly challenging those restrictions.

The necessity of resisting communist aggression in Korea, however, was accepted by most of Truman's critics, including isolationist Senator Robert Taft. The great lesson of Munich loomed large across party lines in 1950. Forcible resistance to communist expansion remained the heart of the political consensus on containment until 1965, when the first small fissures appeared over the issue of direct U.S. military intervention in Vietnam.

Yet the Munich analogy focused on halting aggression, not eliminating the aggressor. Like containment, the analogy was defensive. At the heart of the Truman-MacArthur controversy was the general's insistence on a wider war with China, which he saw as an opportunity to overturn the communist revolution there. Truman, supported by the Joint Chiefs of Staff, opposed escalation because it threatened to bog down scarce U.S. military resources in an open-ended war on the Asian mainland at a time when Europe was defenseless against a Soviet invasion. JCS chairman Omar Bradley called MacArthur's pleas for permission to blockade China, bomb its Manchurian industries, and "unleash" Chiang Kai-shek across the Formosa Strait "the wrong war, at the wrong place, at the wrong time, and with the wrong enemy."[30]

Yet, the Truman-MacArthur dispute, which was essentially a profound disagreement over U.S. war aims, would not have arisen had the United States stuck to its original objective of restoring South Korea's territorial integrity. The decision, following MacArthur's stunning victory at Inchon in September 1951, to cross the thirty-eighth parallel into North Korea and liberate that country as a precursor to the Korean nation's reunification under Western auspices, provoked China's intervention, which in turn provoked the crisis in U.S. civil-military relations. In retrospect, the decision to grab North Korea appears casual to the point of recklessness. Truman, swept up in the euphoria of Inchon and the apparent collapse of the North Korean army, seems to have taken at face value MacArthur's personal assurance that the Chinese would not, indeed could not, intervene effectively. China's attempts to warn the United States that it would not tolerate the loss of North Korea were ignored or dismissed; no senior-level American decision maker seemed capable of imagining how strategically threatening MacArthur's headlong rush to the Yalu might appear to Beijing.

Truman's decision to limit the war to Korean territory, and in the end to settle for essentially a restoration of the status quo ante bellum, was thus quite consistent with the instruction of the Munich analogy. Truman and the Democratic Party, however, paid a stiff domestic political price for an unpopular and seemingly indecisive war that was finally settled through negotiations with Chinese and North Korean Communists. As they did later, during the Vietnam War, critics on the Right condemned presidential interference in what they believed would otherwise have been decisive military operations. No such charge, however, could be convincingly leveled at a Republican war hero.

3

Eisenhower
in Indochina

The power of analogies to encourage the use of force can be offset, even overwhelmed, by other analogies and nonanalogical considerations discouraging the use of force. The literature on use-of-force official reasoning by historical analogy focuses on decisions to *use* force rather than on decisions to refuse force. Yet negative decisions can be just as consequential and analogically informed as positive decisions. The democracies' refusal to employ force against Hitler until 1939 rested in part on a dread of repeating the horrors of World War I, yet their appeasement of the German dictator (and of the Japanese in the Far East) made World War II virtually inevitable. During the first two decades of the Cold War, the United States, having learned the lesson of Munich, attempted to apply it in Asia, using force in Korea in 1950 and in Vietnam in 1965 to stop the spread of communism. Yet in one instance—in Indochina in 1954—it refrained from military intervention even though the price of inaction was the establishment of a new communist state, North Vietnam, that was ultimately to defeat a subsequent U.S. intervention and conquer South Vietnam.

The same arguments that would be made for intervention in 1965 were made in 1954 by, among others, Secretary of State John Foster Dulles and Vice President Richard Nixon. But President Dwight Eisenhower decided differently in 1954 than did President Lyndon Johnson eleven years later.

Harry Truman's successor in the White House also believed that the Munich analogy was applicable to the communist threat. During his 1952 campaign for the presidency, Eisenhower attacked the Truman administration for failing to apply the lesson of Munich to communist expansion in China and Korea. "World War II should have taught us all one lesson," he declared in *Time* magazine. "The lesson is this: To vacillate, to hesitate—to appease even by merely betraying unsteady purpose—is to feed the dictator's appetite for conquest and to invite war itself. That lesson—which should have firmly guided every great decision of our leadership through these later years—was ignored in the development of the Administration's policies for Asia."[1] As a Republican and a war hero, however, Eisenhower was insulated from the prospect of a significant domestic political backlash in his administration's responses to communist aggression. This insulation permitted Eisenhower in 1954 to resist considerable pressures within his own administration to intervene in the French-Indochinese War.

It is not clear that Eisenhower ever seriously considered intervention, although he went through very public motions of doing so. He established political conditions for U.S. intervention that could not possibly be satisfied under the circumstances, however, and it is difficult to believe that he ever thought that they could be. To be sure, he wrote to Winston Churchill that what was happening in Indochina engaged the lessons of the 1930s, but Eisenhower had excellent reasons for staying out of the war even though nonintervention ensured a communist victory.

The situation Eisenhower faced in Indochina in 1954 differed greatly from the one that Truman had faced in Korea four years earlier. The French-Indochinese War was a contest over continued colonial rule. As such, it was, in Eisenhower's own words, "our tradition of anti-colonialism" that proved the "strongest reason of all for the United States' refusal to respond by itself to French pleas" for intervention.[2] The war was not a case of Soviet-sponsored cross-border aggression, but rather a guerrilla conflict waged by communist-controlled forces—the Viet Minh—that commanded broad nationalist appeal. No Chinese communist forces were in the field (though Chinese military advisers were present and Beijing supplied modern artillery to its Vietnamese communist brethren). There was, too, the issue of whether U.S. intervention could have saved French rule in Indochina. Even had the French been prepared to grant their Indochinese subjects genuine independence (which they were not), it is not clear that the United States could have prevented at least a partial communist succession. The U.S. Army chief of staff, Matthew B. Ridgway, took it upon himself to find out and ordered a professional military assessment that concluded that nothing short of a massive buildup of U.S. ground forces in Indochina could do the job. Nor was there public and congressional sentiment for intervention. The American people were war-weary in 1954; they had been at war for seven of the last thirteen years, and many men had performed military service in both World War II and the Korean War. Congress—in the midst of the notorious army-McCarthy hearings—was preoccupied with alleged communist subversion at home; there was no sentiment there for U.S. intervention on the ground, and little even for air strikes to support the besieged French garrison at Dien Bien Phu.

That Eisenhower and his senior foreign policy lieutenants, notably Secretary of State John Foster Dulles, viewed communism through the Munich analogy is indisputable. In a letter to Winston Churchill urging Britain's support for a regional grouping of anticommunist states in Southeast Asia, Eisenhower reminded Churchill that "we failed to halt Hirohito, Mussolini and Hitler by not acting in unity and in time. That marked the beginning of many years of stark tragedy and desperate peril. May it not be that our nations have learned something from that lesson?"[3] It was Eisenhower who also first compared the potential victims of communist aggression in Asia to a row of dominoes, a row that would fall just as the European dominoes had fallen to Hitler. At a press conference just one month before the fall of Dien Bien Phu, Eisenhower was asked to comment on the strategic importance of Southeast Asia and what would happen if the Communists won in Indochina. "The 'falling domino' principle," he said. "You have a row of dominoes set up, you knock over the first one, and what will happen to the last one is the certainty that it will go over very quickly. So you could have a beginning of a disintegration that would have the most profound influences."[4] In his letter to Churchill he cited the dominoes by name. "It is difficult to see how Thailand, Burma and Indonesia could be kept out of Communist hands. The threat to Malaya, Australia and New Zealand would be direct. The offshore island chain would be broken. . . . [I]t is difficult to see how Japan could be prevented from reaching an accommodation with the Communist world."[5]

In a speech titled "The Threat of a Red Asia," Dulles warned that a communist victory in Indochina would propel the Communists to "resume the same pattern of aggression against other free peoples in the area." The "propagandists of Red China and Russia make it apparent," he said, "that the purpose is to dominate all of Southeast Asia." He then declared that "sometimes it is necessary to take risks to win peace just as it is necessary in war to take risks to win victory. The chances for peace are usually bettered by letting a potential aggressor know in advance where his aggression could lead him."[6]

Pressure for at least air intervention in Indochina was also strong within Eisenhower's administration. Dulles leaned toward intervention; Adm. Arthur Radford, the chairman of the Joint Chiefs of Staff, favored it; and on April 16, 1954, Vice President Richard Nixon gave a speech to the American Society of Newspaper Editors in which he suggested that the United States might have to send in troops. Nixon clearly favored intervention, and even as late as 1985, in his book *No More Vietnams,* he argued that America's "first critical mistake in Vietnam was not to have intervened in the battle of Dien Bien Phu." By not intervening, he continued, "the United States lost its last chance to stop the expansion of communism in Southeast Asia at little cost to itself."[7] Radford not only favored the use of massive U.S. air power to relieve the siege of Dien Bien Phu, but actually proposed the use of tactical nuclear weapons to visiting French general Paul Ely.[8] The rest of the Joint Chiefs were opposed.

Happily for the United States, sound judgment prevailed. The influence of the Munich analogy was trampled by overriding domestic and international political considerations and by the possibility of limiting the potential damage of a communist victory. The United States was not about to go to war to preserve French colonial rule anywhere in the world, and the French were unwilling, despite U.S. pressure, to grant the measure of independence to their subjects in Indochina that might have compromised the Communists' powerful appeal to Vietnamese nationalism. There was, moreover, strong opposition among the congressional leadership, with whom Eisenhower met several times, to any unilateral U.S. military intervention. Nor were the British prepared to participate, despite Eisenhower's letter to Churchill. Intervention was probably never really in the cards precisely because Eisenhower established French political reforms in Indochina, congressional support, and British participation as conditions for it. (The congressional leadership also insisted on British participation.)

The likely domestic political and strategic costs, however, were the most important factors working against intervention. The crisis occasioned by the Communists' siege of Dien Bien Phu arose less than a year after the Korean War ended, and the Eisenhower administration's popularity had been greatly enhanced by its success in achieving an armistice in what had become a bloody and highly unpopular war. To have then entered a second war on the Asian mainland, and one to preserve French colonial rule, at that, would have been an act of staggering political incompetence. As Herbert Parmet summed it up, the administration "was in no mood to forfeit credit for what was obviously becoming its most popular accomplishment by, less than a year later, sending fresh American troops to a new Asian battlefield."[9]

The issue of intervention's effectiveness also may have figured strongly in Eisenhower's calculations. Nixon later argued that the Dien Bien Phu "situation was tailor-made for the use of our air power," and that "if we had sent in fleets of heavy bombers to drop conventional explosives, we could have crippled the Viet Minh in a matter of days."[10] Nixon's retrospective judgment ignored America's own subsequent experience with air power in Indochina and begged the question of how saving Dien Bien Phu would have altered long-term prospects for France's position in Indochina, which by 1954 had become politically and militarily untenable. Ridgway clearly understood that it was not enough to lift the siege of Dien Bien Phu via air strikes; the Viet Minh could be decisively defeated only on the ground. The army position paper Ridgway had ordered on the subject stated that at least seven U.S. divisions and supporting naval and air forces would be required to accomplish that, and they could not be accommodated quickly because of Indochina's logistical primitiveness.[11] In his memoirs, Ridgway insisted that the Korean War had proved that air and naval power alone could not defeat a determined Asian enemy on the ground and went on to declare that "it was incredible to me that we had forgotten that bitter lesson—that we were on the verge of making that same tragic error."[12] Ridgway believed that the army report "played a considerable, perhaps a decisive, part in persuading our government not to embark on that tragic adventure,"[13] but Eisenhower's memoirs do not even mention it.

Operational feasibility considerations alone were probably strong enough to torpedo any decision to intervene. Combined with political considerations—the indefensibility of the French cause in Indochina and the absence of any enthusiasm in the United States for intervention—the question of feasibility made inaction almost inevitable. Ridgway, to his great credit, tackled the issue of military feasibility with a determination and thoroughness that had no parallel in the deliberations within the Johnson administration as it moved toward intervention in the spring of 1965. Neither Nixon nor Dulles seems to have pondered the questions of what it would take militarily to defeat the Viet Minh conclusively and whether beating the Viet Minh was worth the anticipated price. And if the answers to these questions were decisive in Eisenhower's decision not to intervene, he carefully concealed them behind his public insistence on congressional support, allied participation, and French political reforms in Indochina.

U.S. intervention in Indochina also would have prevented Eisenhower from implementing a new defense policy based on a conviction that insolvency was as great a threat to America's long-term national security as communism. This policy, known as the New Look, essentially rejected conventional military competition, especially in ground warfare, against the Soviet Union and China in favor of a strategy of massive nuclear retaliation.[14] Eisenhower saw in America's nuclear superiority a means of both deterring communist aggression and avoiding the potentially ruinous cost of trying to match Soviet and Chinese ground forces. Indeed, Eisenhower believed that the Soviet Union sought to bankrupt the American economy by forcing it into a soldier-for-soldier, tank-for-tank arms race, and that entering such a race would also threaten America's democratic institutions by turning the country into a garrison state.[15] (He returned to this theme in his famous Farewell Address, warning against the acquisition of unwarranted influence by the "military-industrial complex.") "I refused to turn the United States into an armed camp," Eisenhower recounted in his memoirs, and "I saw no sense in wasting manpower in costly small wars that could not achieve decisive results. . . . [T]his kind of military policy would play into the hands of a potential enemy whose superiority in available military manpower was obvious."[16] Jumping into another such war in Indochina would have made it impossible for Eisenhower to shift half the defense budget into nuclear weapons and long-range bombers.

Eisenhower and Dulles's conviction that the potential damage of a Viet Minh victory in Indochina could be limited also worked against intervention. In fact, at the Geneva Conference that settled the French-Indochinese War, the Vietnamese Communists were forced—although by their erstwhile Chinese and Soviet brethren rather than by the United States—to make political and territorial concessions incompatible with their commanding military position. Additionally, the United States leveraged the crisis into the creation of an alliance—the Southeast Asia Treaty Organization (SEATO)—aimed at stopping further communist aggression in Indochina and ultimately into the establishment of an anticommunist state in South Vietnam.

All the Vietnamese Communists got at Geneva was the northern half of Vietnam. For overriding strategic reasons of their own, Russia and even more so China pressured the Viet Minh to accept a simple military truce in place of a definitive political settlement and a temporary division of Vietnam much farther north (at the seventeenth parallel) than the Viet Minh could otherwise have successfully insisted on.[17] Reunification elections, which Ho Chi Minh undoubtedly would have won, were postponed until 1956, affording the United States the opportunity to create an anticommunist South Vietnam that in turn refused to participate in any such elections. Indeed, the Geneva-mandated French withdrawal from Indochina removed the albatross of colonialism from around the neck of anticommunism, which in turn permitted the establishment of SEATO, an organization dedicated to containing further communist advances in Indochina. Although SEATO did not mandate U.S. defense of South Vietnam, it provided a basis for voluntary intervention. Thus the apparently decisive Viet Minh military victory of 1954 turned out to be but a partial political success that postponed complete victory for three decades. The Geneva peace accord was, in retrospect, no small accomplishment. Because the Communists' victory was limited, because there was strong public and congressional opposition to unconditional intervention, and because the president himself was a Republican and a war hero, the decision of 1954 not to intervene cost the Eisenhower administration little politically.

The question of whether the Munich analogy was valid in Indochina in 1954 is moot because the argument that it was valid was overwhelmed by other considerations that discouraged intervention. But by the early 1960s a new administration was in power, and the factors that had worked against intervention in 1954 were being supplanted by factors working in favor of it. To be sure, the validity of a particular analogy is not a function of whether decision makers believe it to be valid or behave accordingly, but rather whether it is reflected in their words and deeds.

Eisenhower declined U.S. military intervention in Indochina for much the same reasons that Truman had declined it in China, even though the Republicans had pummeled Truman for "losing" China. The acceleration of China's civil war after the Japanese surrender in 1945 elicited an initial administration attempt to broker a negotiated settlement in the form of a coalition government that included Chiang Kai-shek's Nationalist Party and Mao Zedong's Chinese Communist Party. When that failed, the Truman administration continued modest military assistance to Chiang

Kai-shek while resisting Republican calls for massive aid. By mid-1947, both Truman and Secretary of State George C. Marshall had concluded that the Nationalist regime was a lost cause both militarily and politically. This judgment was explicated by Marshall's successor, Dean Acheson, in a letter to Truman that accompanied the delivery to the White House of the State Department's white paper on China in August 1949. Nationalist armies had been defeated not because of inadequate aid but because the Nationalist leaders "proved incapable of meeting the crisis that confronted them, [Nationalist] troops had lost the will to fight, and the Government had lost popular support. . . . The Nationalist armies did not have to be defeated; they disintegrated." The only alternative to nonintervention open to the United States "was full-scale intervention in behalf of a Government which had lost the confidence of its own troops and people. Such intervention would have required the expenditure of even greater sums than have been fruitlessly spent so far, the command of the Nationalist armies by American officers, and the probable participation of American armed forces—land, sea, and air—in the resulting war." In the final analysis, Acheson concluded, "the ominous result of the civil war in China was beyond the control of the government of the United States."[18]

The bottom line for the Truman administration from the outset, however, was the a priori judgment that the United States possessed no strategic interests in China worth a war. This nonintervention "decision" was greatly reinforced, analyst Tang Tsou suggested in 1963, by "the rapid demobilization of the [U.S.] armed forces, the unwillingness of the American people to send their boys to fight in China for a decadent government, and the reluctance to use force without both an unambiguous moral issue and an immediate threat to survival."[19] The United States virtually disarmed itself in the latter 1940s, and not even the harshest Republican critics of Truman's China policy favored direct U.S. military intervention on the ground. Even had the U.S. military not been in the process of postwar demobilization, there was grave doubt that any external military intervention could save a regime as venal and militarily incompetent as the Nationalist government had become by 1947. Other factors favoring nonintervention included concern that it would provoke a direct Soviet counterintervention and violate the established American strategic injunction against becoming involved in a ground war on the Asian mainland. Additionally, both the Truman administration and its China policy critics understood the war in China for what it fundamentally was: a civil war, albeit one involving indirect outside intervention on both sides. Finally, there was growing concern over sharpening U.S.-Soviet tensions in Europe, including what seemed to be a growing possibility of war. It would have been strategically reckless to risk being drawn into China's civil war at a time when Western Europe remained virtually defenseless against a Soviet invasion. It was for this very reason that Truman and the Joint Chiefs of Staff later rejected MacArthur's call to expand hostilities in Korea to mainland China.

To be sure, both the Munich analogy and its specific expression in the Truman Doctrine of 1947 argued for intervention. The Chinese Communists may not have been Soviet surrogates, but they were, by the end of 1946, the recipients of massive Soviet arms transfers. And although Stalin was wary and suspicious of Mao Zedong (as he was of anyone whose behavior he could not completely control), he stood to benefit strategically from a Communist China materially and ideologically dependent on the Soviet Union. Yet, as in the case of Eisenhower later in Indochina, nonanalogical factors, including strategic common sense, an appreciation of the limits of U.S. military power in China, and domestic political imperatives, prevailed. If Truman had seen a lost cause in China after World War II, Eisenhower saw one in Indochina in 1954. What separated the two presidents was Eisenhower's personal and political immunity to the charge of being "soft" on communism.

A final note: The Truman administration's decision not to intervene militarily on behalf of the Nationalist government—i.e., to cut its losses in China—obviously did not pass unnoticed by the communist leaderships in Korea and Indochina. Potential adversaries constantly monitor the behavior of one another, drawing lessons from instances of military action and inaction that then become analogical tools available to decision makers in future crises. Reputations are established on the issues of the willingness to use force and the ability to use it effectively. Yet, unpredictability can itself be a reputation, and the United States surprised more than one aggressor in the twentieth century by opting for a military response.

The U.S. acquiescence to a violent communist takeover in China, an American ally in World War II and the principal object of American diplomatic sympathy in East Asia since the beginning of President William McKinley's Open Door policy in 1899, argued in favor of similar American inaction in South Korea in 1950 and South Vietnam in 1965. Because neither of these small states could possibly loom as large and important as China, was it not reasonable for Pyongyang and Hanoi to assume, everything else being equal, that the United States would not fight to save anticommunist governments in Seoul and Saigon? Unfortunately for Kim Il Sung and Ho Chi Minh, everything else was not equal. The very fact of China's loss contributed significantly to the American decisions for military action in South Korea and South Vietnam, and in the case of Korea, ironically, U.S. action compelled China's counterintervention to save the North Korean regime from certain destruction.

Kennedy and
Johnson in Vietnam
and the Caribbean

Presidents Kennedy and Johnson were, if anything, even more captivated than Eisenhower by the Munich analogy and its domino theory corollary. As a student at Harvard, John F. Kennedy had written his senior honors thesis on "Appeasement at Munich: The Inevitable Result of Slowness of British Democracy to Change from a Disarmament Policy." (His father, Joseph P. Kennedy, though notoriously pro-appeasement during his service as U.S. ambassador to Great Britain from 1937 to 1940, had his son's thesis rewritten and published as the best-seller *Why England Slept*.)[1] In a famous speech delivered in 1956, then-Senator Kennedy declared: "Vietnam represents the cornerstone of the Free World in Southeast Asia, the keystone to the arch, the finger in the dike. Burma, Thailand, India, Japan, the Philippines and obviously Laos and Cambodia are among those whose security would be threatened if the red tide of communism overflowed into Vietnam."[2] President Kennedy even cited Munich as the mandate for his tough stance during the Cuban missile crisis of 1962. In his address to the nation on October 22, Kennedy warned that the "1930s taught us a clear lesson: aggressive conduct, if allowed to go unchecked, ultimately leads to war."[3] Indeed, Ernest May and Philip Zeilkow postulated in *The Kennedy Tapes* that, for Kennedy, Munich and appeasement "connoted not only past events and their supposed lessons but also his own need continually to prove that his views were not his father's."[4]

President Johnson also saw Munich lurking in Indochina. After he left the White House, he told Doris Kearns that "everything I knew about history told me that if I got out of Vietnam and let Ho Chi Minh run through the streets of Saigon, then I'd be doing exactly what Chamberlain did. . . . I'd be giving a fat reward to aggression."[5] In early 1964, he told his secretary of defense, Robert McNamara, that if the United States pulled out of Vietnam, "the dominoes would fall and a part of the world would go to the Communists."[6] He also cautioned "those who advocate retreat or appeasement" in Vietnam that "we modestly suggest that . . . on history's face the blotch of Munich is still visible."[7] Johnson, who in the 1960 Democratic nomination fight had attacked Kennedy for his father's support of the Munich agreement (sneering, "I wasn't any Chamberlain umbrella man"), believed that the post–World War II wave of communist aggression had replaced the 1930s fascist wave, and that the Communists had to be taught, as the fascists had been, that the democracies could and would fight.[8]

For Secretary of State Dean Rusk, who served both Kennedy and Johnson, Munich was what communist aggression in Southeast Asia was all about. No U.S. foreign policy maker believed more strongly than he that what was happening in Southeast Asia in the 1960s was a replay of what had happened in Europe in the 1930s. For Rusk, the principal issue at stake in Vietnam was the credibility of the United States as guarantor of the security of potential victims of communist aggression. Failure to stop the Communists there would invite another world war. Even in retirement he maintained that the "overriding problem before us in Southeast Asia . . . was how to prevent World War III."[9] Rusk dismissed those who questioned the relevance of the Munich analogy: "There are those who object to analogies—that Mao Tse-tung is not a Hitler, that Ho Chi Minh is not a Mussolini," he told an American Legion convention. "But one robber may be named John Doe, another robber may be named Richard Roe—there may be infinite differences between the two, but what they have in common, namely robbery, is what sends them to prison."[10]

The quintessential Munich-influenced policy maker of the 1960s, however, was the brilliant McGeorge Bundy, a strong proponent of U.S. intervention in Vietnam who served Kennedy and Johnson (until 1966) as national security adviser. Before he joined the Kennedy administration, he taught government at Harvard and was famous on campus for his standing-room-only lecture on the Munich crisis and its lessons. He believed the lessons of Munich were universal and once chided John

Kenneth Galbraith, who did not: "Ken, you always advise against the use of force—do you realize that?" Bundy as national security adviser linked Vietnam to Munich and argued relentlessly that the latter mandated an American military stand in the former.[11]

Munich, to be sure, was hardly the only historical analogy at work among Vietnam policy makers. In his survey of analogies that policy makers approaching military intervention in Vietnam referred to in public and private, Yuen Foong Khong discovered that the Korean War was the most frequently invoked, even more than the appeasement of the 1930s. Other analogies included the Greek, Malayan, and Filipino insurgencies; the French experience in Indochina; World War II; and the Cuban missile and Berlin crises.[12] Yet Khong's conclusion that the Korean War analogy was more influential than Munich ignores the fact that the U.S. decision to fight in Korea was virtually dictated by the Munich analogy.[13] Had there been no appeasement of fascism in the 1930s, there probably would have been no decision to stand in Korea, and therefore almost certainly no decision to commit to Vietnam. "Without U.S. involvement in Korea there would have been little reason for the United States to become involved militarily in Vietnam," historian Robert D. Schulzinger noted in his book on U.S.-Vietnam relations, *A Time for War.*[14]

In any event, the Korean analogy's influence was less on the decision to go to war in Vietnam than it was on how to fight that war, and Khong's analysis does focus extensively on this point. The analogy seemed to suggest that South Vietnam could be successfully defended, as South Korea was, and the conclusion that successful military intervention was feasible undoubtedly reinforced the decision to intervene. Implicit in most decisions to use force is the a priori judgment that it has a good chance of success. But the Korean analogy also suggested that great care had to be taken in using force so as to avoid provoking Chinese intervention, as MacArthur's pell-mell rush to the Yalu had done in 1950. President Lyndon Johnson lived in dread of doing anything that might trigger China's intervention, and this dread accounted in large measure for the restraints he imposed on U.S. air operations against North Vietnam.[15]

In addition to other analogies at play, there were also analogically based domestic political considerations behind the decisions that led to the U.S. intervention in Vietnam. Such considerations had argued strongly against intervention in 1954, but the picture had changed by the early 1960s. As Democrats, both Kennedy and Johnson were leaders of a political party that since the end of World War II had been savaged by Republican critics as "soft" on communism. Around the party's neck hung the Yalta "sellout" of Eastern Europe, the Soviet theft of U.S. atomic secrets, the "fall" of China, the perfidy of alleged traitors within the State Department, and the denial of a "decisive" victory in Korea to MacArthur. No post–McCarthy era Democratic president could afford to give up additional real estate to communism without a fight; to do so would invite a right-wing backlash.

The Democrats' vulnerability on this issue constitutes one of several arguments against the proposition that Kennedy, had he not been assassinated, would have cut American losses in Vietnam sometime in 1964. After the Cuban missile crisis, Kennedy told Senator Mike Mansfield, a Vietnam skeptic, "If I tried to pull out completely now from Vietnam, we would have another Red scare on our hands."[16] In July 1963 he is said to have told reporters at an off-the-record news conference: "We don't have a prayer of staying in Vietnam. . . . But I can't give up a piece of territory like that to the Communists and get the American people to reelect me."[17]

Lyndon Johnson too was apparently obsessed by the prospect of a domestic political reaction. As a fast-rising member of the Senate in the late 1940s and early 1950s, Johnson had a front-row seat when the Republican Congress assaulted the Truman administration for its alleged failures in the fight against communism at home and abroad. It was a politically ugly period. A Johnson administration perceived as not allocating sufficient resources to defeat communism in Vietnam would provide opponents of the ambitious Great Society agenda with the perfect argument against proceeding with the costly domestic social and economic reforms Johnson's program would entail. "Conservatives in Congress," Johnson told Doris Kearns, "would use [the war] as a weapon against the Great Society. You see, they'd never wanted to help the poor or the Negroes in the first place. But they were having a hard time figuring out how to make their opposition sound noble in a time of great prosperity. But the war. Oh, they'd use it to say that they were against my programs, not because they were against the poor . . . but because the war had to come first."[18] Even the emergence of a strident, leftist antiwar movement didn't faze Johnson, who once cautioned Undersecretary of State George Ball to "pay no attention to what those little shits on the campuses do. The great beast is the reactionary elements in this country."[19] In his memoirs, Johnson declared that "I knew our people well enough to realize that if we walked away from Vietnam and let Southeast Asia fall, there would follow a divisive and destructive debate in our country. This had happened when the Communists took power in China. . . . A divisive debate about 'who lost Vietnam' would be, in my judgment, even more destructive to our national life than the argument over China had been."[20]

Kennedy and Johnson also embraced a new defense policy that, in contrast to Eisenhower's New Look, actually encouraged intervention in Vietnam. The strategy that became known as Flexible Response called for the United States to be able to counter communist aggression at whatever level—nuclear, conventional, or insurgent—it was launched. Kennedy and Johnson sought to maintain U.S. nuclear superiority while at the same time rebuilding the country's conventional military power. Proponents of Flexible Response believed that nuclear weapons were not an effective deterrent to communist conventional aggression outside Europe and that the Communists were exploiting new possibilities for nonnuclear aggression, especially so-called wars of national liberation in the decolonizing Third World. "The struggle had been switched from Europe to Asia, Africa, and Latin America," observed John Lewis Gaddis, "from nuclear and conventional weaponry to irregular warfare, insurrection, and subversion."[21] Vietnam was seen as a test case for implementing Flexible Response, specifically as a test of America's ability to defeat a communist-sponsored war of national liberation. Kennedy's obsession with defeating such wars was manifest in his glorification of the U.S. Army's green-bereted Special Forces.

The argument that Kennedy would have avoided major U.S. combat intervention in Vietnam is not convincing.[22] To be sure, Kennedy was skeptical of South Vietnam's prospects for survival even with U.S. military assistance, but so too was Lyndon Johnson, whose senior foreign policy advisers were all Kennedy appointees who in 1965 pressed for ground combat intervention. Kennedy dramatically increased the number of U.S. military advisory personnel in South Vietnam and permitted them to cross the line into direct participation in combat operations. He was also, by his own admission, hostage to the domestic political consequences of a major communist victory overseas on his presidential watch. Moreover, his administration's complicity in the overthrow and assassination of President Ngo Dinh Diem saddled the United States with a heavy moral responsibility to stay the course in South Vietnam. And while Kennedy apparently believed that the war was ultimately South

Vietnam's to win or lose, he also believed that the strategic stakes involved in the struggle were paramount to successful American competition with the Soviet Union in the Cold War. He came into office believing that the United States was losing the Cold War and that its outcome would be decided in the Third World. He was subsequently humiliated by the Bay of Pigs fiasco and then insulted by Soviet premier Nikita Khrushchev at the Vienna Summit. He left Vienna believing, as he told *New York Times* columnist James Reston, that "now we have a problem in trying to make our power credible, and Vietnam looks like the place."[23]

Kennedy might have recognized military stalemate earlier in Vietnam than Johnson did, and might therefore have been more open to cutting U.S. losses there earlier than Johnson and certainly Nixon did. But would he have refused to deploy at least some U.S. ground combat forces in 1965 to stave off South Vietnam's imminent military collapse? The choices in 1965 were the same regardless of who occupied the White House.

The influence of the Munich analogy on the behavior of the Kennedy and Johnson administrations' foreign-policy makers with regard to Indochina is beyond dispute, though its influence relative to other factors that produced U.S. intervention in the Vietnam War cannot be accurately gauged. Moreover, the disastrous outcome of that intervention would seem conclusive proof of the analogy's misapplication in Southeast Asia in the 1960s. U.S. defeat in Indochina, however, does not, ipso facto, close the books on this issue; even the best reasoning by historical analogy is hardly a guarantee of successful use of force. A decision to fight offers no instruction on *how* to fight. Yet poor reasoning by historical analogy can distort perceptions of reality to the point at which misuse of force becomes probable, even unavoidable. The great Prussian theorist of war, Carl von Clausewitz, convincingly argued that the "first, the supreme, the most far-reaching act of judgment that the statesman and commander have to make is to establish . . . the kind of war on which they are embarking; neither mistaking it for, not trying to turn it into, something that is alien to its true nature. This is the first of all strategic questions and the most comprehensive."[24]

The case for the Munich analogy's suitability as a tool for policy makers with regard to events in Southeast Asia is difficult to make because it assumes that the threats posed by Nazi Germany in Europe in the 1930s and the Communists in Southeast Asia thirty years later are comparable. Worse still, it fails to recognize the compatibility of communism and nationalism. In essence, the United States mistook a powerful, communist-led, *nationalist* revolution in a historically xenophobic land for an extension of a centrally directed international communist movement. The communist leadership was dismissed as alien to Vietnamese nationalism, and the presence of genuine revolutionary grievances in South Vietnam was more or less ignored. The fact that the Communists exploited nationalism as a means of gaining power in Vietnam, as did Mao in China and Castro in Cuba, does not mean that they were not nationalists themselves or that liberation from alien rule was not a genuine issue. The Vietnamese communist revolution was nationalist long before it imposed communism on the Vietnamese people.[25]

A propensity to ignore, even deny, the legitimacy of nationalism in anticolonial and postcolonial revolutions in the Third World was a prominent feature of the official U.S. mentality in the pre–Vietnam War years. Communist aggression by definition had to be "foreign," and therefore illegitimate; otherwise, no convincing case could be made for military intervention to stop it. In 1950, Secretary of State Dean Acheson declared that Russia and China's diplomatic recognition of the Viet Minh as the Democratic Republic of Vietnam "should remove any illusions as to the 'nationalistic' nature of Ho Chi Minh's aims and reveal Ho in his true colors as the mortal enemy of native independence in Indochina."[26] Judgments like these prompted John Kenneth Galbraith to observe later that in "the conspiratorial vision of world communism that developed following World War II, one thing was axiomatic. Communism outside the Soviet Union could never successfully identify itself with nationalism. It was a foreign as well as a wicked thing which no country could have except as it might be imposed or infiltrated from abroad."[27] In 1951, Dean Rusk characterized Mao Zedong's communist regime as "a colonial Russian government—a Slavic Manchukuo on a large scale. It is not the government of China."[28] In fact, all of the world's most prominent communist leaders of the day—Stalin, Mao, Tito, and Ho Chi Minh—had successfully harnessed nationalism to their revolutions. Moreover, China was—and remains—Vietnam's hereditary enemy. The two-thousand-year history of Vietnam is largely a record of fierce Vietnamese resistance to Chinese aggression. The Vietnamese Communists were never agents of either Soviet or Chinese imperial ambitions, and throughout the Vietnam War they successfully played off Moscow and Beijing against one another. Ho Chi Minh's early service as a Comintern agent and his subsequent acceptance of Soviet and Chinese advice and assistance did not make him or his senior lieutenants simply extensions of foreign imperial agendas. He was no Vidkun Quisling or Walter Ulbricht. Like Tito, Ho Chi Minh had an independent power base within his own country as well as an independent national agenda. A communism that truly dissolved national antagonisms would have prevented, after the fall of South Vietnam, Communist China's invasion of Communist Vietnam as a means of punishing Communist Vietnam's invasion of Communist Cambodia.

Even at the time, senior U.S. government officials' dismissal of the nationalist content of communist-led revolutions in the Third World dismayed those who knew better. Paul Kattenberg, a Foreign Service expert on Vietnam, recounted being in a meeting with Rusk, McNamara, and other senior Vietnam policy makers: "I listened for about an hour and a half to this conversation. . . . There was not a single person there that knew what he was talking about. . . . They were all great men. It was appalling to watch. . . . They didn't know Vietnam. They didn't know the past. They had forgotten the history. They simply didn't understand the identification of nationalism and Communism, and the more this meeting went on, the more I sat there and thought, 'God, we are walking into a major disaster.'"[29]

Comparing Ho Chi Minh to Hitler, and North Vietnam in the 1960s to Nazi Germany in the 1930s, reveals few similarities and overwhelming differences. Both Ho and Hitler were, to be sure, totalitarian rulers who sought to expand the territorial scope of their rule. But Hitler's ambitions and power to act on them dwarfed Ho Chi Minh's, and Hitler was acting in a place of far greater strategic importance to the United States than Indochina could ever be. Hitler sought nothing less than the subjugation of all of Europe, and he had at his disposal Germany's (and later, continental Europe's) enormous actual and latent military power. Hitler was not interested in simply reunifying the German nation in Europe, which was the fatal assumption underlying Franco-British appeasement at the Munich Conference. He wanted control of Europe from the Atlantic to the Urals, which would have upset the global balance of power to the grave strategic disadvantage of the United States. In contrast, the Vietnamese Communists' ambitions were limited to the reunification of Vietnam and the establishment of friendly governments in the rest of Indochina. Hanoi's military resources, even given its access to Soviet and Chinese assistance, bore no comparison to those of Nazi Germany. In Europe in the 1930s and early 1940s, aggression was centrally directed from Berlin; in Indochina in the 1960s, communist aggression was locally directed from within.

To make the case that the United States was right to intervene in Vietnam in 1965 virtually mandates the reenlistment of the Munich analogy as applicable. This is exactly what conservative author Michael Lind did in his 1999 revisionist polemic, *Vietnam: The Necessary War.* In this work Lind conceded that Ho Chi Minh's North Vietnam does not bear apt comparison to Hitler's Germany. But he reduced Ho Chi Minh to a communist stooge of the Kremlin—a Vietnamese Ulbricht devoid of any political legitimacy. He further cast the war in Vietnam as a Soviet test of U.S. credibility in "a proxy war between the United States [and] the Soviet Union," reflecting the fact that "there *was* an international communist conspiracy."[30] "As the lesson of Munich predicted," Lind continued, "the forfeiture of Indochina by the United States between 1968 and 1975 encouraged Soviet leaders to engage in more assertive and reckless imperialism throughout the world, with a greatly reduced fear of confrontation with the United States."[31] The "Soviet elite viewed the victories of their clients in Indochina as the first in a series of successes, which included the rise to power of pro-Soviet regimes in Angola, Mozambique, Guinea-Bissau, Ethiopia, Nicaragua, and Afghanistan."[32] Lind's view has much in common with that of Richard Nixon, who wrote in 1985: "Our defeat in Vietnam sparked a rash of totalitarian conquests around the world as we retreated into a five-year, self-imposed exile."[33]

The Lind thesis revives the myth of the global communist monolith and fails to address the question of whether the United States might have been more selective in picking its Cold War proxies. Did Munich really dictate selection of a client as politically illegitimate and militarily incompetent as South Vietnam? Might not Thailand have been strategically firmer ground on which to make a stand in Southeast Asia? Worse yet, Lind would have his readers believe that the post-Vietnam expansion of Soviet influence in such Third World backwaters as Guinea-Bissau, Mozambique, and Afghanistan was as strategically consequential for the United States as Hitler's post-Munich invasion and conquest of Europe from Brest to the outskirts of Leningrad and Moscow. Indeed, though, is it not the case that the very recklessness of Soviet imperialism in the Third World—most notably in Afghanistan—contributed mightily to the Soviet Union's own dissolution in 1991? And if this is so, cannot a case be made that U.S. "forfeiture" of South Vietnam laid the foundation of America's victory in the Cold War? Was Lyndon Johnson a closet strategic clairvoyant?

Overestimation of communism's ability to replace nationalism was perhaps the greatest strategic misjudgment that both Washington *and* Moscow made during the first two decades of the Cold War. In the end, it was communism, not nationalism, that ended up on the trash heap of history. And one of the many tragedies of U.S. intervention in the Vietnam War was that the predominantly nationalist character of the Vietnamese Revolution was evident to anyone not blinded by the lenses of America's Cold War ideology—an ideology spawned in part by the perceived lesson of Munich. "That containment was misapplied in Vietnam . . . seems beyond debate," concluded George Herring, the dean of American historians of the Vietnam War, in *America's Longest War.* "By wrongly attributing the conflict to external sources, the United States drastically misjudged its internal dynamic. By intervening in what was essentially a local struggle, it placed itself at the mercy of local forces, a weak client, and a determined adversary. What might have remained a local conflict with primarily local implications was elevated into a major international conflict with enormous human costs that are still being paid."[34]

It is no coincidence that prominent proponents of the "realist" school of international politics—men like George Kennan, Walter Lippmann, and Hans Morgenthau—opposed intervention. They viewed the world in discriminating, balance-of-power terms, not through the prism of NSC-68. They opposed containment's militarization and blanket extension to East Asia, and recognized the powerful national tensions within the so-called communist bloc—itself a term that hardly encouraged threat discrimination. In 1965, Morgenthau lamented that the United States was prone to "seeing in every Communist Party and regime an extension of hostile Russian or Chinese power." He pointed out the China was the hereditary enemy of Vietnam, and that the "United States today encounters less hostility from Tito, who is a Communist, than from de Gaulle, who is not."[35]

Dean Rusk's comparison of international aggressors to common robbers illustrates the dangerous simplicity in applying Munich to Vietnam. Setting aside the issue of whether or not what was going on in Vietnam was an act of international aggression (again, did the Army of the Potomac commit such an act when it entered Virginia?), the comparison begs three issues: the importance of the goods the robber attempts to steal; who should be responsible for stopping the robber; and, indeed, whether the robber can be stopped at an acceptable price.

❋ ❋ ❋

If the Munich analogy encouraged Kennedy and Johnson to intervene in Vietnam, it also encouraged intervention in the Caribbean. Kennedy launched the ill-fated Bay of Pigs invasion of Cuba in April 1961 in an attempt to topple what was fast becoming the Soviet Union's only client state in the Western Hemisphere. Indeed, during the 1960 presidential elections candidate Kennedy had accused the Eisenhower-Nixon administration of being "soft" on Cuba, a rare instance of a Democrat turning a favorite Republican charge against a Republican. In 1962, Kennedy threatened world war over the Soviet Union's surreptitious attempt to install nuclear missiles in Cuba. In 1965, Lyndon Johnson invaded the Dominican Republic to forestall its becoming a Cuban-promoted communist "domino."

The Bay of Pigs was an attempt not to contain but rather to "roll back" the communization of Cuba, but it was motivated by a perception of Castro's Cuba as the progenitor of future communist aggression in the hemisphere. Reversing Castro's victory was thus tantamount to containing communist expansion in the Caribbean and Latin America. The invasion as it was planned, using fourteen hundred poorly trained Cuban exiles and based on the assumption that it would trigger a popular uprising against Castro, was from the start a harebrained scheme doomed to defeat.[36] It was launched against a Cuba that President Kennedy believed was being transformed into "a base for subverting the survival of other free nations throughout the hemisphere."[37] Indeed, Cuba's leaders, Kennedy claimed, were "puppets and agents of an international conspiracy" aimed at spreading communism throughout Latin America.[38] Cuba, itself a Soviet domino, was in turn seeking to do Moscow's bidding by toppling other hemispheric dominoes. The communization of an island state just ninety miles off the U.S. coastline was a major Soviet political and propaganda victory over the United States, and the Kennedy administration's acute hostility to Castro was hardly a secret.[39]

The invasion's failure did not change the Kennedy administration's view of the Cuban threat or its allegiance to the domino theory in both Latin America and Southeast Asia. In both areas, communist advances were viewed as products of a monolithic, centrally directed conspiracy, a definition of the threat that discounted the association of communism with genuine local nationalist yearnings. (Like Ho Chi Minh, Fidel Castro, if not his brother Raul, was a nationalist long before he became a Communist, and neither substituted communism for nationalism.)

Yet the fate of communism in Cuba was not the issue in the Kennedy administration's second and far graver crisis involving Cuba: the deployment of Soviet nuclear missiles and conventional combat forces on the island. A major objective of the deployment was to compromise the clear-cut U.S. superiority over the Soviet Union in intercontinental ballistic missiles. Soviet medium-range ballistic missiles deployed in Europe and Asia posed no direct threat to the United States, but when moved within range of American territory they automatically became "strategic." Khrushchev also sought to provide a deterrent to any U.S. invasion of Cuba. Operation Anadyr, as the plan to convert Cuba into a Soviet military bastion was code-named, called for the emplacement of medium-range ballistic missiles and the deployment to the island of four Soviet motorized regiments, two tank battalions, a MiG-21 fighter wing, forty-two Il-28 light bombers, two cruise missile regiments, air defense units, and fifty-one thousand military personnel.[40]

Khrushchev's gamble was a direct extension of Soviet military power into a region that the United States had long declared to be its sphere of interest via proclamation of the Monroe Doctrine and subsequent corollaries to it. As such, it was an aggressive act worthy of comparison to the Munich analogy, which indeed President Kennedy invoked in his famous televised speech to the nation on the night of October 22, 1962. After referring to the lesson of the 1930s, Kennedy went on to declare that "this urgent transformation of Cuba into an important strategic base—by the presence of these . . . clearly offensive weapons of mass destruction— constitutes an explicit threat to the peace and security of all Americans."[41] Privately, he complained to his Executive Committee (of the National Security Council), or ExComm, advisers that Khrushchev's actions constituted "a provocative change in the delicate status quo" that was unacceptable to the United States even at the risk of a third world war.[42] Appeasement was unthinkable. The Russians had attempted to alter the existing nuclear balance on the sly and cheap—just as the Germans had altered the continental military balance in 1936 when they reoccupied the Rhineland without a French or British military whimper. Putting medium-range nuclear missiles in Cuba transformed them into a strategic threat and reduced the warning time of a Soviet nuclear strike to mere minutes. To let Moscow get away with such an abrupt compromise of U.S. intercontinental nuclear supremacy, advised Dean Rusk, "would free [the Soviets'] hands for almost any kind of intervention that they might want to try in other parts of the world. If we are unable to face up to the situation in Cuba against this kind of threat, I think they would be critically encouraged to go ahead and eventually feel like they've got it made as far as intimidating the United States is concerned."[43]

The Munich analogy clearly encouraged—indeed, mandated—action to compel the removal of the Soviet missiles, but it provided no instructions for how to go about it. Although the Joint Chiefs and others urged direct military action, the president looked for a nonviolent way to resolve the crisis. Kennedy had devoured *The Guns of August*, Barbara Tuchman's gripping analysis of World War I, and feared stumbling into a world war as had Europe's great powers in 1914. Here entered yet another analogy that counseled against an invasion of Cuba, favoring instead the naval "quarantine" option that President Kennedy finally selected. During ExComm's tense deliberations over the thirteen days of the Cuban missile crisis, the Japanese attack on Pearl Harbor was employed and deployed at least a dozen times as an argument against a surprise attack on Cuba. Undersecretary of State George Ball said that such an attack, "a Pearl Harbor, just frightens the hell out of me" because you "go in there with a surprise attack [and] put out all the [Soviet] missiles. This isn't the end. This is the *beginning*."[44] For Ball, a "Pearl Harbor" against Cuba meant perhaps war with the Soviet Union. It also meant taking action "contrary to our traditions, by pursuing a course of action that would cut directly athwart everything we have stood for during our national history, and condemn us as hypocrites in the opinion of the world."[45] The president's brother and attorney general, Robert F. Kennedy, also opposed a military strike because "it would be a Pearl Harbor type of attack."[46] At one point while listening to those arguing for invasion, he passed a handwritten note to presidential speechwriter Theodore Sorenson: "I know how Tojo felt when he was planning Pearl Harbor."[47] Indeed, by the sixth day of the crisis President Kennedy himself was referring to the massive air strike/invasion option as "this particular Pearl Harbor recommendation."[48]

Cuba without Soviet military support—the Bay of Pigs Cuba—was a strategic nuisance, not a threat. In contrast, Cuba as an extension of Soviet military power—the missile crisis Cuba—was indeed a threat. Thus the Munich analogy was much more informative to the Kennedy administration in 1962 than it had been in 1961.

It was also more informative in 1962 than it was in 1965, when Lyndon Johnson ordered U.S. soldiers and marines into the Dominican Republic. The events prompting intervention were complicated and confused. Following the long nightmare of the Trujillo dictatorship on the island there emerged a democratically elected government headed by a progressive but weak leader, Juan Bosch. A military coup, however, deposed Bosch in September 1963. On April 24, 1965, younger military officers and Bosch supporters launched a counterrevolt to overthrow the ruling military junta and restore constitutional government and Bosch to power. The fighting consumed much of downtown Santo Domingo, endangering the lives of American citizens there. Four days later, Lyndon Johnson ordered U.S. forces—first marines and a day later U.S. Army soldiers—into the country, more than twenty-two thousand men in all.

Although initially justified as a means of protecting Americans, the size and duration of the intervention, as well as administration statements within days of the first marine landings, confirmed that Johnson had acted out of fear of a communist takeover of the Dominican Republic. There was no evidence that Bosch was a Communist, and the administration had considerable difficulty identifying known Communists among those who were fighting to restore constitutional government in the Dominican Republic. But Johnson apparently convinced himself that the turmoil presented opportunities for a Castro-like outcome.[49] In his memoirs he wrote that "just beyond the horizon lay Cuba and Castro. The Communist leader in Havana was always alert to any exploitable weakness among his neighbors. He was promoting subversion in many countries in the Western Hemisphere, and we knew he had his eye on the Dominican Republic." Johnson continued: "The last thing I wanted—and the last thing the American people wanted—was another Cuba on our doorstep."[50] Another communist domino in the Caribbean was unacceptable to any American president in the spring of 1965, especially a Democratic president who was at the same time setting the stage for massive U.S. intervention to prevent the fall of a far more distant domino in Southeast Asia. Whether the communist threat in the Dominican Republic was real or not, Johnson "believed domestic pressures compelled him to act as he did."[51] As Undersecretary of State George Ball observed in retrospect, "Johnson's reaction could be understood against a backdrop of Castro's subversion of Cuba which had become a nagging source of worry and mischief; it had produced the Bay of Pigs and the Missile Crisis in the Kennedy Administration. In addition [there was] a wider preoccupation. We were just on the verge of committing American combat forces to Vietnam and the President feared that a disaster close to home might lead more Americans to challenge our adventure ten thousand miles away."[52]

It is difficult to argue that the Munich analogy was relevant to dealing with a revolt in a small, impoverished country to restore constitutional order and return to power a legitimately elected leader who was clearly not a Communist. Johnson seems to have panicked at the remote prospect of a second Cuba in the Dominican Republic. With respect to Vietnam, Johnson both employed and deployed the Munich analogy; he really saw parallels between the situation in Southeast Asia in the 1960s and Europe in the 1930s. In the case of the Dominican intervention, however, Johnson seems to have been driven by a vivid imagination reinforced by fear of the perceived domestic political price he would pay if he failed to act.

5

Nixon and Kissinger
in Vietnam

The Nixon administration inherited the consequences of an intervention decision made by its predecessor and continued to wage war in Vietnam for four more years. The administration accepted its predecessor's "domino" and "credibility" arguments about the consequences of a U.S. defeat in Vietnam, regarding communism in the Third World as an extension of Soviet power. The Nixon administration was the first to draw explicit "No more Vietnams" foreign policy lessons from the war, generating a new policy that became known as the Nixon Doctrine.

Additionally, the Nixon administration was the first to base its foreign policy on exploiting the collapse of what previous administrations had considered an internationally monolithic communism. Nixon embraced Communist China in a tacit strategic alliance against the Soviet Union. He understood that the Sino-Soviet split was rooted primarily in national antagonisms and approached both countries on the basis of national interest. Nixon nevertheless remained a Cold Warrior who believed that a communist victory in Indochina, even though not directed from Moscow or Beijing, threatened U.S. interests in the Third World.

Both Nixon and his chief foreign policy lieutenant, National Security Adviser and later Secretary of State Henry Kissinger, were as determined as Johnson and Rusk had been to prevent a communist victory in South Vietnam. But their military leverage in Indochina, especially on the ground, declined steadily from 1969 to 1973 as domestic political opposition to the war mounted. The administration was compelled to undertake a series of unilateral U.S. troop withdrawals from South Vietnam that steadily diminished its bargaining leverage with Hanoi. Indeed, in May 1971 the administration dropped the long-standing U.S. insistence that a reciprocal North Vietnamese troop withdrawal from South Vietnam be part of any negotiated settlement of the war; in so doing, it abandoned the very reason for intervention in 1965.

Nixon and Kissinger believed that a "peace with honor" was essential to maintain America's credibility as a guarantor of its allies' security and that a "dishonorable" peace would encourage further expansion of Soviet power and influence in the Third World. The Nixon administration in effect extended U.S. intervention in the Vietnam War for four years on basically the same premise that the Johnson administration had begun it: defeat in Vietnam would start the dominoes falling and endanger America's credibility as an ally. For the Nixon administration, however, the dominoes were not just neighboring Southeast Asian states but also the future of the U.S. will to use force.[1] Certainly Nixon, an old red-baiter of Democrats he labeled "soft" on communism, wanted to be seen as having made the maximum effort possible before allowing yet more real estate to fall to communism.

Kissinger's memoirs are explicit on the reason why the administration he served rejected the option of cutting U.S. losses early on in Vietnam:

> Leaders are responsible not for running public opinion polls but for the consequences of their actions. They will be held to account for disasters even if the decision that produced the calamity enjoyed widespread public support when it was taken. In 1938 the Munich agreement made Chamberlain widely popular and cast Churchill in the role of alarmist troublemaker; eighteen months later Chamberlain was finished because the Munich agreement was discredited. With the Vietnam War the problem was more complex. Rightly or wrongly—I am still convinced rightly—we thought that capitulation or steps that amounted to it would usher in a period of disintegrating American credibility that could only accelerate the world's instability.[2]

Nixon's retrospective on the Vietnam War contends that the Communists' ultimate victory in Vietnam vindicated the domino theory: "The dominoes fell one by one; Laos, Cambodia, and Mozambique in 1975; Angola in 1976; Ethiopia in 1977; South Yemen in 1978; Nicaragua in 1979."[3] The dominoes fell, Nixon argued, precisely because America's defeat in Vietnam shattered U.S. credibility by sapping the national will to use force to stop communism's spread in the Third World. Defeat "left the United States so crippled psychologically that it was unable to defend its interests in the developing world," with domestic critics "brandish-[ing] 'another Vietnam' like a scepter, an all-purpose argument-stopper for any situation where it was being asserted that the United States should do something rather than nothing."[4]

But the dominoes listed by Nixon were hardly the strategic equivalent of the Rhineland, the Austrian Anschluss, the Sudetenland, Czechoslovakia, and Poland; and it would have been as strategically misguided to have committed U.S. military power to defend the nations on Nixon's list as it was to intervene in the Vietnam War itself. Indeed, Soviet overextension in the Third World during the 1970s and 1980s, although almost certainly encouraged by the U.S. defeat in Vietnam, contributed mightily to the strains that ultimately destroyed the Soviet Union. In Afghanistan, the Soviets even repeated America's disastrous misadventure in Vietnam. Ironically, it may have been America's post-Vietnam *failure* to contain Soviet expansion in the Third World that accelerated the Soviet Union's demise.

Yet Nixon was right in anticipating that the experience of the Vietnam War would significantly influence future U.S. uses of force in the Third World, especially in circumstances not involving clear threats to manifest strategic interests. During the decade following the Paris agreement the United States seemed fearful of using force under almost any circumstances, and even as that fear subsequently faded, continued to display an aversion to the risks of using force decisively. The "Vietnam syndrome" was—and remains—a powerful influence on American statecraft.

Nixon had always seen avoidance of an Asian Munich as the great stake in Vietnam. In 1964, he criticized those who derided the importance of Southeast Asia for wanting to "reach agreement with our adversaries—as Chamberlain reached an agreement with Hitler at Munich in 1938."[5] In 1965, he wrote a *Reader's Digest* article in which he said that if the United States abandoned South Vietnam, the Pacific Ocean would "become a Red Sea" and "Indonesia, Thailand, Cambodia, and Laos" would "inevitably fall under communist domination."[6] In 1967, he went so far as to declare in a speech that "if the credibility of the United States is destroyed in Vietnam, it will be destroyed in Europe as well."[7] In his memoirs he approvingly quoted Churchill's condemnation of Munich in 1938 and then went on to conclude that "what had been true of the betrayal of

Czechoslovakia to Hitler in 1938 was no less true of the betrayal of South Vietnam to the communists advocated by many in 1965."[8]

What had changed by 1969 was lack of confidence in a military solution. During the Tet Offensive of 1968, Nixon told his speechwriters, "I've come to the conclusion that there's no way to win the war. But we can't say that, of course. In fact, we have to seem to say the opposite, just to keep some degree of bargaining leverage."[9] In September 1969, Kissinger drafted a memorandum for Nixon in which the national security adviser concluded that the United States could not win the war under the existing military and political circumstances.[10] He doubted whether Vietnamization would ever work, a doubt that resurfaced in his memoirs: "I had my doubts about Vietnamization; nor did I think we had the time for victory—that opportunity, *if it ever existed,* had been lost by our predecessors."[11] Kissinger understood the Vietnam War to be predominantly a civil conflict, and used the terms "civil war" and "cruel civil war" to describe it in his memoirs. This implies that the decision to intervene in Vietnam in 1965 was a mistake, and in fact Kissinger, unlike Nixon, who insisted to his dying day that the conflict in Vietnam was not a civil war, did not argue otherwise. Indeed, Nixon himself acknowledged that if the Vietnam War "had been a civil war, we probably should not have intervened in the first place."[12]

The Nixon administration ended up using force against North Vietnam to maximize the time separating the departure of U.S. combat forces and the likely eventual communist takeover of South Vietnam. The 1972 air campaigns called Linebacker I and Linebacker II were intended to—and did—diminish Hanoi's military capacity and compel concessions on war settlement terms. By the early 1970s, the war had become predominantly a conventional military contest between the North Vietnamese army and American air power. Linebacker I smashed Hanoi's Easter Offensive and shut down Haiphong Harbor in the spring of 1972, and the following December, Linebacker II crippled North Vietnam's air defenses. By January 1973, when the Paris Peace Agreement on Ending the War and Restoring Peace in Vietnam was signed, North Vietnam was in no military or political position to take South Vietnam by force. More than two years of military recovery were required to reconstitute sufficient force for Hanoi's final offensive, but even then the communist leadership was stunned by the rapidity of South Vietnam's collapse.

The two-year hiatus permitted Nixon, Kissinger, and other administration war policy apologists to distance themselves from responsibility for the defeat and instead to blame both Congress, which prohibited further U.S. military action in Indochina and drastically reduced military assistance to South Vietnam, and even South Vietnam itself. Making matters worse, when the onslaught finally came in 1975, South Vietnam's president, Nguyen Van Thieu, fatally mishandled the country's military defense by ordering an abrupt evacuation of the Central Highlands under fire.

It is hard to believe that either Nixon or Kissinger in 1973 had much confidence in South Vietnam's survival given the combination of a peace agreement that did nothing to remove North Vietnamese forces from South Vietnam and growing public and congressional opposition to further U.S. military involvement in Indochina. To believe otherwise is to believe that South Vietnam had a better military chance against North Vietnam without the presence of 500,000 U.S. troops than it did with that presence. In a July 1970 conversation with news commentators, Nixon expressed confidence that "the South Vietnamese can defend themselves if there is a mutual withdrawal of outside [U.S. and North Vietnamese] forces [from South Vietnam]."[13] Yet his administration subsequently dropped its demand for a North Vietnamese withdrawal as a condition for U.S. withdrawal.

The claim that Linebacker II—the so-called Christmas bombing of targets in the Hanoi-Haiphong area—forced North Vietnam back to the bargaining table is true, but it is also irrelevant. The bombing was militarily devastating but strategically inconsequential. Hanoi returned to the table to sign an agreement—the terms of which had already been settled in October—that placed South Vietnam at an enormous military and political disadvantage. Indeed, the real target of the bombing was President Thieu, who rightly regarded the Paris agreement as an undated death warrant for his regime. As historian Stephen Ambrose noted, it was not Hanoi, "it was the Americans—in response to demands from President Thieu—who backed off the October agreements. . . . But Nixon could not have Kissinger straightforwardly tell the American people his administration was bombing Hanoi to convince Thieu to sign." Something "had to be done to convince Thieu that, whatever the formal wording of the cease-fire agreement, he could count on Nixon to come to the defense of South Vietnam if the [North Vietnamese army] broke the cease-fire."[14] Even with the bombing, Nixon had to use the explicit threat of a separate peace with Hanoi to compel Thieu's acceptance. As U.S. Air Force historian Earl H. Tilford Jr. concluded in his analysis of Linebacker

II, "Air power, marvelous in its flexibility, had succeeded in bombing a United States ally into accepting its own surrender."[15]

After the war, Nixon claimed that the Johnson administration's decision to Americanize the war was a great mistake. But there is no evidence that he objected to it at the time, and his complaint begs the question of what alternatives to Americanization were available in 1965 other than a communist takeover.[16] Richard Kimball, who has produced the best study on Nixon's Vietnam War policies to date, concluded that "what happened in Indochina between January 1973 and April 1975 was virtually preordained by the terms of the Paris Agreement and the circumstances of power that Nixon left behind in Southeast Asia and the United States."[17]

Nixon and Kissinger were right to worry about the impact of a defeat in Vietnam on America's will to use force effectively overseas. For better or for worse, the war did exert a chilling effect on that will that continues to this day; had the United States eschewed intervention in Vietnam, there would have been nothing like the national debate on the very issue of force use of the past three decades. Moreover, all the evidence suggests that, as Nixon had predicted, defeat in Vietnam did encourage the further expansion of Soviet power and influence in the Third World.

But at this point analogies with the 1930s in Europe quickly turn sour. Soviet gains in the Third World in the 1970s and early 1980s were gains along the Cold War's periphery. They did not affect the central balance of military power between the United States and the Soviet Union; on the contrary, those gains quickly turned out to be liabilities. In contrast, Hitler's successes in the Rhineland and Czechoslovakia undermined the European balance of power and sped the planet to another world war. To equate, as Lind did in *Vietnam: The Necessary War,* the Soviet invasion of Afghanistan, to say nothing of Soviet "triumphs" in places like Ethiopia and Guinea-Bissau, with Hitler's occupation of the Rhineland and Czechoslovakia is to dismiss the critical distinction that George Kennan made—and NSC-68 rejected—between the center and the periphery. The Soviet invasion of Afghanistan was a strategic dead end in very much the same way that intervention in the Vietnam War proved to be for the United States. Indeed, both interventions reflected not only an overvaluation of the Third World's strategic importance as a whole but also a failure to make key distinctions of importance within the Third World. For the United States, who runs Afghanistan, Ethiopia, and Guinea-Bissau is simply not as important a question as who runs Saudi Arabia, South

Africa, and Mexico. Strategically, "dominoes" come in different weights and sizes, and the fall of one here may not matter compared with the fall of one there.

Indeed, the very term *Third World* told Cold War policy makers only that the region was neither Western nor communist. The argument of Kennan and other "realists" for containment's *selective* application—based on the inherent strategic significance and availability of U.S. defense resources—was sound, but it always ran afoul of the dominant NSC-68 view that in the struggle against communism (as opposed to the more specific item of *Soviet* power and influence), a defeat anywhere was a defeat everywhere. For Truman, Eisenhower, Kennedy, Johnson, and Nixon, perceptions of change in the East-West balance of power were as important as, perhaps even more important than, the actual balance itself. They believed that such perceptions were influenced by small changes in local balances even in places of little or no intrinsic importance. These men, especially the Democrats, also had limited domestic political maneuverability in dealing with communist expansion abroad.

The major lesson President Nixon drew from the Vietnam War was that the United States should never assume the primary burden of an ally's defense. Americanization of the Vietnam War, he believed (at least retrospectively), was a mistake because it imposed an enormous military burden on the United States while simultaneously absolving South Vietnam from the main responsibility for its own defense.

What became known as the Nixon Doctrine first surfaced at a 1969 presidential news conference in Guam in response to a question about the future of U.S. counterinsurgency tactics in Asia. Nixon replied that the United States remained prepared to help countries threatened by communism, but that "where we draw the line is in becoming involved heavily with our own personnel, doing the job for [allies], rather than helping them do the job for themselves."[18] Nixon added that "certainly the objective of any American administration would be to avoid another war like Vietnam any place in the world." The United States could learn from past mistakes, he said, and "if we examine what happened in Vietnam—how we became so deeply involved—. . . we have a good chance of avoiding that kind of involvement in the future."[19]

By November these offhand remarks had been enshrined as a formal declaration of policy. In an address to the nation Nixon criticized the "policy of the previous administration" for "our assuming the primary responsibility for fighting the war" and for failing to "adequately stress the goal of strengthening the South Vietnamese so that they could defend themselves when we left."[20] The president described the Nixon Doctrine as "a policy which not only will help end the war, but which is an essential element of our program to prevent future Vietnams." Specifically, the United States would keep its commitments and continue to provide extended nuclear deterrence to allies. "But we shall look to the nation directly threatened to assume the primary responsibility of providing the manpower for its defense."[21] The doctrine was further elaborated in a 1971 presidential report to Congress. "The Nixon Doctrine will enable us to remain committed in ways that we can sustain," it declared. The Vietnam War would not be permitted to become a justification for a return to isolationism, and commitments had to be both politically and militarily sustainable. "There are lessons to be learned from our Vietnam experience—about unconventional warfare and the role of outside countries, the nature of commitments, the balance of responsibilities, the need for public understanding and support. But there is also a lesson *not* to be drawn: that the only antidote for undifferentiated involvement is indiscriminate retreat."[22]

The Nixon Doctrine essentially recognized the limits of American power and called for greater selectivity in picking fights. In this regard it seemed to lean away from NSC-68 and toward George Kennan's conception of containment. But the doctrine begged the very question that faced the Johnson administration in 1965: What should the United States do when an ally *is* bearing the primary responsibility for its defense—i.e., is supplying the manpower and taking the casualties—but nonetheless is facing imminent defeat by a communist foe? Jump in with both feet, or let the ally go down? This Hobson's choice does not arise with politically determined and militarily competent allies. Should not the United States be just as careful in picking allies, then, as in picking fights? Does a commitment, once made, remain an absolute obligation regardless of changing circumstances? Internally weak allies invite excessive dependence on the United States, which in turn encourages Americanization of effort. The Nixon Doctrine failed in Vietnam as it later failed in Iran not because its precepts were unsound, but because it was misapplied on behalf of ineffectual clients facing revolutionary unrest at home.

Choice of allies was central to the success or failure of American use of force during the Cold War. Western Europe and Japan were obvious choices because of their manifest strategic vitality to the United States and because they were threatened by a powerful Eurasian hegemon. Less obvious were nonindustrial Third World states. Some were quite important because of the resources they controlled (Saudi Arabia), others because they lay astride strategic lines of communication (Panama). South Vietnam fitted neither bill, and worse still, it was governed by a politically weak regime. South Vietnam's only claim to U.S. attention was the fact that it was an anticommunist state facing an immediate communist threat. As such, it met the requirements of NSC-68, though not of George Kennan's selective approach to containment. Yet "realists" Nixon and Kissinger stuck with that poor client, extending the war they had inherited for four additional years and in the end accepting a sham negotiated settlement.

What happened to the United States in Vietnam reaffirmed an established lesson of international politics: weak allies can be worse than no allies. The great strategic successes of Great Britain and the United States against Imperial Japan and Nazi Germany, and of the United States against the Soviet Union, derived in substantial measure from their richness in allies. In contrast, Germany in both world wars and the Soviet Union in the Cold War ended up with allies, such as Austria-Hungary, Fascist Italy, and Communist Cuba, that proved to be strategic liabilities.

6

Reagan in Lebanon, Grenada, Central America, and Afghanistan

Presidential uses of force between the Nixon and Reagan administrations were limited to two hostage rescue missions: one in the Gulf of Thailand (the *Mayaguez* incident) and the other in Iran (Operation Desert One). Neither raid was undertaken or promoted as a vehicle for a larger regional or global policy; nor were the Munich and Vietnam historical analogies relevant or officially seen to be so.

The foreign policies of the Gerald Ford and Jimmy Carter presidencies were circumscribed by Vietnam War–inspired congressional restrictions on potential uses of force and by strong public opposition to virtually any kind of U.S. military action in the Third World. The country was suffering from overseas intervention fatigue. A malady that became known as the Vietnam syndrome, an acute aversion to even indirect military intervention in foreign wars—especially in the Third World—gripped America's political and military leadership. Potential Vietnams were seen in virtually every potential U.S. military commitment outside Europe and northeastern Asia, and for the remainder of the Cold War, the original foreign policy consensus on the need to contain the spread of communism worldwide remained badly battered. The Soviet Union's post-Vietnam strategic overextension in sub-Saharan Africa, the Middle East, South Asia, and Southeast Asia encountered no direct U.S. military opposition. During the 1970s and much of the 1980s, Congress was in a profound anti-intervention mood.

Indeed, during the first three years of his administration Carter rejected anticommunism as the organizing principle of U.S. foreign policy, and also, by implication, the relevance of the Munich analogy to policy. Early in his first year in office he declared in the major foreign policy speech of his presidency that "we are now free of that inordinate fear of communism which once led us to embrace any dictator who joined us in that fear." The Vietnam War had "produced a profound moral crisis, sapping worldwide faith in our own [containment] policy" and making it impossible any longer to "separate the traditional issues of war and peace from the new global questions of justice, equity, and human rights."[1] Carter believed that the greatest international political fault line ran North–South (i.e., economic), not East–West (i.e., political), and that America's chief purpose in the world should be the promotion of human rights.[2] He also believed that the lesson of the Vietnam War was that the United States should not "become militarily involved in the internal affairs of another nation unless there is a direct and obvious threat to the security of the United States or its people."[3]

Unfortunately for Carter, his declaration that the time had come for the United States to relax its policy of containment was premature. The Soviet invasion of Afghanistan in December 1979 provoked an abrupt return to containment. Carter declared to the nation that a "Soviet-occupied Afghanistan threatens both Iran and Pakistan and is a stepping stone to possible control over much of the world's oil supplies," adding that "history teaches perhaps very few clear lessons. But surely one such lesson learned by the world at great cost is that aggression, unopposed, becomes a contagious disease."[4] Carter went even further in his January 1980 State of the Union Address, calling the Soviet invasion possibly "the most serious threat to peace since the Second World War" and deploring "the steady growth and increased projection of Soviet military power beyond its own borders." He then announced what would come to be known as the Carter Doctrine. "Let our position be absolutely clear: An attempt by any outside force to gain control of the Persian Gulf region will be regarded as an assault on the vital interests of the United States of America, and such an assault will be repelled by any means necessary, including military force."[5] The doctrine was attended by the initiation of the first U.S. military buildup since the end of the Vietnam War, a buildup that was expanded and accelerated by the Reagan administration.

President Ronald Reagan was an arch-anticommunist who embraced the Munich analogy to explain Soviet behavior, but he was also sensitive to the Vietnam War's impact on public and congressional attitudes toward U.S. use of force overseas, especially in the Third World. His presidency was, therefore, marked by a significant disparity between its strident anticommunist rhetoric (especially during Reagan's first term) and its relative political unwillingness to use force directly against what Reagan called the "evil empire" and its Third World clients. His administration did use force against Libya and in Lebanon and Grenada, but anticommunism was a motivating factor only in Grenada. Moreover, Reagan knew that he could use force with virtual impunity against Libya, and there was never a chance that the invasion of that Caribbean spice island could turn into even the tiniest replication of Vietnam. Bashing Libya with air power and invading Grenada were cheap and easy enterprises.

Indeed, the very use-of-force doctrine that bears Reagan's name testifies to the domestic political imperative during the 1980s of confining U.S. responses to the Soviet Union's expanding power and influence in the Third World to indirect military assistance. Reagan also conducted a limited naval intervention in the Persian Gulf on behalf of Iraq in the Iraq-Iran War. This was not, however, a Cold War–driven intervention; rather, it was aimed at preventing a conclusive Iranian victory.

Reagan's one unarguably disastrous misuse of force was his unwitting injection of a U.S. Marine Corps "peacekeeping" force into a fierce Lebanese civil war. Colin Powell called that intervention "goofy from the beginning."[6] The intervention began with the best of humanitarian intentions, but slowly and inexorably the U.S. military was drawn directly into the strife, provoking deadly retaliation by those opposed to the American presence. Lebanon seemed to validate the Vietnam analogy, and it clearly contributed to Secretary of Defense Caspar Weinberger's determination to speak out on the issues of when and how force should be used.

The failed intervention in Lebanon is an important milestone in presidential uses of force since 1945. It seemed to repeat the mistakes of Vietnam, and it sparked a renewed national debate on the use of force overseas that continues to this day. The long-standing personal feud between Weinberger and Secretary of State George Shultz escalated into a sharp dispute over using force in Lebanon and elsewhere. Weinberger, backed by the Joint Chiefs of Staff, opposed sending U.S. marines to Lebanon, while Shultz pushed for their initial deployment and opposed their withdrawal even after the disastrous terrorist attack on the marine barracks in Beirut on October 23, 1983. It was a clash between two basic arguments: that force should be used only for a major war and only when diplomacy had failed versus the view that force was a necessary tool of diplomacy and should be threatened or used for precisely that purpose. Although the Munich analogy played no role in Lebanon, the Pentagon's opposition to intervention was based on the view that Lebanon was another Vietnam in waiting. Weinberger, whose attention was focused on the growing military power of the Soviet Union, believed that intervention in Lebanon was a distraction that could interfere with the Reagan administration's massive rearmament program.

The immediate albeit unstated aim of U.S. intervention in August 1982 was to restrain an ally—Israel—whose government, led by Prime Minister Menachem Begin, seemed to have lost control of its own strategically myopic invasion of Lebanon, led by the extremist Ariel Sharon.[7] The Israelis misled the Reagan administration into believing that the invasion would be limited to southern Lebanon—i.e., that it was designed to create a defensive buffer zone—whereas in fact Sharon's agenda was to destroy all Palestinian Liberation Organization (PLO) forces in Lebanon and establish a Christian, pro-Israeli government in Beirut. The invasion provoked both U.S. and Syrian intervention and ultimately led to the disintegration of central political authority in Lebanon. It turned Lebanon into Israel's Vietnam; Israeli forces remained in southern Lebanon for eighteen years fighting a costly and ultimately futile war of attrition. The invasion also set the stage for a U.S. military intervention that was, if possible, even more ill-considered than the decision to fight in Vietnam.

The general long-term U.S. aims in Lebanon were to secure the withdrawal of Israeli and Syrian forces and to establish a strong central government in Beirut. The problem from the very beginning was to establish clear and attainable intermediate political and military objectives and to match the military force and its rules of engagement to those objectives; this the Reagan administration never accomplished. "The experience in Lebanon," observed Richard Haass in his book *Intervention: The Use of American Force in the Post–Cold War World*, "underscores a critical point: having foreign policy objectives—in this case, a peaceful and independent Lebanon free of all foreign forces—is not the same as having objectives for a particular use of military force."[8] In Lebanon, as in Vietnam, translating general political goals into specific and attainable military objectives proved impossible. The urge to act overwhelmed considerations of feasibility.

History vindicates the wisdom of the Pentagon's opposition, if not the soundness of Weinberger's views on the utility of force (discussed in chapter 9). To be sure, the initial U.S. intervention did secure a cease-fire and the withdrawal of beleaguered PLO forces from West Beirut, where they had been hemmed in and pounded by Israeli aircraft and artillery. But U.S. reintervention in the wake of Israel's occupation of West Beirut and complicity in the Christian militia massacres of Palestinian civilians in the Sabra and Shatilla refugee camps was plagued from the start by a divided Reagan administration's inability to define clear political objectives attainable by military means. In fact, Haass suggested, "the U.S. decision to re-enter Lebanon was less a considered policy decision than an impulse to 'do something' to demonstrate U.S. concern (and assuage American guilt) over what had taken place in the refugee camps despite U.S. promises that Palestinians would be safe after the PLO's departure."[9]

During and after the seventeen months following the redeployment of U.S. marines back to Beirut, Reagan and other administration spokesmen cited at least a dozen different political objectives, some incompatible with each other and others clearly beyond the reach of the intervention forces and their rules of engagement. These declared objectives included guarding the Beirut airport, protecting Palestinian civilians in West Beirut, freeing the Lebanese army to pursue antigovernment militias and warlords, creating a democratic and unified Lebanon, advancing the Arab-Israeli peace process, preventing Lebanon's domination by Syria and the Soviet Union, stopping an Israeli-Syrian war, facilitating the mutual withdrawal of Israeli and Syrian forces, demonstrating that the United States could not be intimidated by terrorist attacks, and, above all else, providing "presence"—simply being there to show that the United States cared. To confuse matters even further, Reagan insisted, even after it had become clear to almost everyone else in his administration that the U.S. intervention was no longer politically or militarily tenable, that "we have vital interests in Lebanon."[10] The suicide terrorist attacks on the U.S. Marine Corps contingent in Beirut proved, he said, that the force "was doing the job it was sent to do in Beirut."[11]

The ultimate goal of a peaceful Lebanon free of all foreign forces was a noble one, to be sure, but facilitating the withdrawal of foreign forces presumed the willingness of the Israelis and the Syrians to withdraw. In fact, the Syrians refused to leave, and the Israelis conditioned their withdrawal on Syria's. As Weinberger correctly pointed out, "Our whole policy, including the [U.S.] military presence and the buildup of the Lebanese Armed Forces[,] was premised on . . . an agreement that would *require* both Israelis and Syrians to withdraw. Absent this, there was no *military* action that could succeed, unless we declared war and tried to force the occupying troops out of Lebanon." The marine contingent "had been correctly sized to act only as an interposition force, as a buffer between the withdrawing armies. It was not sized or structured to perform other actions."[12]

The multiplicity, vagueness, and infeasibility of the missions assigned to the marines would have been an intervention killer even in a simple target country. But consider the condition of the Lebanese "state" during the U.S. reintervention period as accurately depicted by the Defense Department commission assigned to determine responsibility for the terrorist attack on the marine barracks:

> A country beset with virtually every unresolved dispute afflicting the peoples of the Middle East. Lebanon has become a battleground where armed Lebanese factions simultaneously manipulate and are manipulated by foreign forces surrounding them. If Syrians and Iraqis wish to kill one another, they do so in Lebanon. If Israelis and Palestinians wish to fight over the land they both claim, they do so in Lebanon. If terrorists of any persuasion wish to kill and maim American citizens, it is convenient for them to do so in Lebanon. In a country where criminals involved in indiscriminate killing, armed robbery, extortion, [and] kidnapping issue political manifestos and hold press conferences, there has been no shortage of indigenous surrogates willing to do the bidding of foreign governments seeking to exploit the opportunities presented by anarchy in Lebanon.[13]

By comparison, Vietnam in 1965 was a model of simplicity; the war there was a two-sided affair within a single nation, and both sides sought the same objective—namely, political control of South Vietnam.

Lebanon's descent into civil war and even worse, outright anarchy, began with the assassination of President-elect and Christian Phalange militia chief Bashir Gemayel, which sparked the Israeli army's occupation of West Beirut. Anarchy, coupled with the Reagan administration's steadily expanding support of the increasingly beleaguered Lebanese government and army, transformed an initially benign and welcomed U.S. Marine Corps presence into an inviting target for Iranian- and Syrian-sponsored terrorists. It also made the United States a witless participant in a civil war in which Reagan's own national security adviser later conceded no important U.S. security interests were at stake.[14]

Making matters worse was Reagan's failure—and, more inexplicably, George Shultz's—to grasp the growing dangers posed by U.S. alignment with the Lebanese government against both its domestic militia enemies and Syria, which in response to Israel's invasion of Lebanon had occupied Lebanon's Bekaa Valley. The small U.S. marine contingent had been placed in militarily indefensible positions around the Beirut airport on the assumptions of limited duration, a relatively benign environment, provision of security by the Lebanese army in areas where the marine contingent would operate, and evacuation in the event of attack.[15]

Yet by the deadly day of October 23, 1983, all of these assumptions had dissolved. Terrorists had blown up the American embassy six months earlier, and the marines had been subjected to constant sniper fire that had killed several of them. A subsequent House Armed Services Committee investigation stated the obvious: "The bombing of the U.S. embassy on April 18, 1983, should have given warning that terrorism directed at the United States was a fully emerged threat."[16] Reagan himself confided to his diary at the time that the situation was worsening, although it apparently never occurred to him that action was in order.[17] The marines, for their part, were understandably confused as to what exactly their mission was. "From the beginning, the mission of the Marines was unclear," wrote military analyst Richard Gabriel in a devastating critique of U.S. intervention in Lebanon. "Officially, they were to provide a 'presence' and to act as 'peacekeepers' by staying neutral in any factional strife that developed. How this was actually to be achieved was unclear and unstated. It was almost as if the U.S. military presence itself became the policy."[18]

Shultz tried to place some of the blame for the debacle on Weinberger and the Joint Chiefs of Staff: "The Pentagon restricted our marines to a passive, tentative, and dangerously inward-looking role in Beirut. Assad and others in the region could see that. The secretary of defense was reluctant to contemplate or cooperate with even a limited application of force to bolster our diplomacy."[19] Yet it is testimony to Shultz's own poor judgment—specifically, his dogged determination to reinforce what in the wake of the slaughter of 241 marines was by then a manifest foreign policy disaster—that he continued to oppose withdrawal from Lebanon even after a very reluctant Ronald Reagan finally concluded that there was no alternative. "It would be devastating, I felt, for us to cut and run," Shultz claimed in his memoirs, because "our staying power under pressure would come into question time and again—and not just in the Middle East."[20] (Shultz's concern was not unjustified. The humiliating U.S. military withdrawal from Lebanon encouraged Saddam Hussein to believe that the United States would not forcefully contest his conquest of Kuwait.)[21]

Weinberger's pronouncement of the use-of-force doctrine that bears his name came just a month after the attack on the marine barracks, and Lebanon unquestionably was the catalyst. Reagan, in his memoirs, declared that "our experience in Lebanon led to the adoption by the administration of a set of principles to guide America in the application of force, and I would recommend it to future presidents." [22]

The failed U.S. intervention in Lebanon bore more than a surface resemblance to the intervention in Vietnam; indeed, it reinforced the Vietnam analogy. In both cases the United States intervened in an intractable foreign civil war; official declarations of the presence of vital interests proved false; military objectives were opaque, elusive, or both; enemy forces proved capable of sidestepping or negating U.S. conventional military strength; and public and congressional support, never enthusiastic, became unsustainable once the costs were perceived to outweigh the benefits. In both situations the United States misjudged the character of the war it was entering and failed to appreciate the great asymmetry of interest separating itself from the local warring parties. Lebanon was proof that even a post–Vietnam War administration could blunder militarily into an overseas political quagmire, although the scale and consequences of the Lebanon mistake were comparatively minor.

Perhaps the fact of defeat in Vietnam encouraged the Reagan administration to cut its losses in Lebanon far earlier than did Lyndon Johnson and Richard Nixon in Vietnam. Reagan believed that America had a powerful stake in creating a stable Lebanon, but he seemed to recognize, in the wake of the Beirut disaster, that continued U.S. military intervention was not the solution to what was essentially an intractable local political problem. This had also been the case in Vietnam, but the outcome of that war proved that a prolonged lost war is a far worse foreign policy outcome than an early decision to back out of a bad intervention. Wars of choice involve not only choosing to intervene but also choosing to halt a mistaken intervention in progress. Reagan did in Lebanon what Johnson could not bring himself to do in Vietnam.

✳ ✳ ✳

Reagan's invasion of Grenada was both a rescue operation to secure the safety of American students on the island who were believed to be in danger and a cheap and minor Cold War victory.[23] President Reagan and his senior foreign policy lieutenants believed that the almost eight hundred American medical students on the island were potential hostages to a virulently anti-American regime, even though it remains unclear whether or not they actually were ever in imminent danger. Indeed, Haass proposed that the "motivation behind the use of force seems more the result of perceived opportunity: to replace a government friendly toward Cuba and the Soviet Union with one more pro-Western and democratic, to prevent the use of Grenada and its airport by either Cuba or the Soviet Union to further their peacetime or wartime interests in the region, and to show that the United States could still act effectively in the aftermath of the Beirut debacle."[24] (In retrospect, George Shultz hailed the invasion of Grenada as "a shot heard round the world" because it demonstrated, as did Great Britain's invasion of the Falkland Islands the year before, that "some Western democracies were again ready to use the military strength they had harbored and built up over the years in defense of their principles and interests.")[25]

There was ample evidence in October 1983 that Grenada's political leadership was becoming a surrogate for Cuban ambitions in the Caribbean. It was also clear that the island was being converted into an air base for likely Soviet use and a storehouse for quantities of weapons and ammunition greatly in excess of the requirements of Grenada's tiny military. Reagan was not much off the mark in contending that "the Soviet Union and Cuba had been bankrolling the Marxists on Grenada as part of a scheme to bring communism to the entire region."[26] Eighteen months earlier, Reagan had publicly warned the leaders of the eastern Caribbean nations that Grenada "now bears the Soviet and Cuban trademark."[27] Cuban troops were in fact on the island in large numbers and were building an air base for military use; they were also supporting a radical Marxist military regime that had butchered its opponents in the streets. Neighboring Caribbean island states were worried that Grenada might attempt to subvert their own governments, and the Organization of Eastern Caribbean States not only called for U.S. military action but also participated in the invasion and occupation of Grenada. Under these circumstances, and with memories of the U.S. diplomatic hostages in Iran still vivid, it was not unreasonable to assume that the American medical students on the island were in danger and therefore needed immediate evacuation. There were thus both strategic and humanitarian reasons to take military action.

Grenada was, moreover, not Lebanon. It was a small nut that could be quickly and easily cracked, thereby avoiding the risk of protracted, bloody combat and significant adverse domestic political fallout.

Grenada was inherently defenseless against an American attack, and it did not hurt that the vast majority of Grenadans detested the regime that the United States overthrew. (Nothing succeeds like the invasion of a friendly country.) Indeed, as it turned out, Operation Urgent Fury, though hobbled by planning and coordination difficulties, played very well both in Grenada and back home in the United States, although some congressional skeptics suspected that the invasion was undertaken to deflect attention away from the disaster in Lebanon. It was the largest and first successful American use of force since the end of the Vietnam War.

Urgent Fury was also testimony to the Reagan administration's exceptional sensitivity to the taking, or prospective taking, of American hostages anywhere in the world. For Reagan, if there was an immediate and vivid historical experience he did not want to repeat, it was the specter of his predecessor being politically imprisoned by the Iranian hostage crisis of 1979–80. Ironically, this same obsession with hostage taking drove Reagan and his witless NSC staff advisers into authorizing secret U.S. arms transfers to the very same terrorist regime in Tehran that had helped drive Jimmy Carter from office. The power of historical analogies to warp presidential judgment should never be underestimated.

Reagan's refusal to provide advance notice of Urgent Fury to the congressional leadership stemmed in large measure from what he called the "post-Vietnam syndrome"—"the resistance of many in Congress to the use of force abroad for any reason, because of our nation's experience in Vietnam. . . . I understood what Vietnam meant for the country, but I believed the United States couldn't remain spooked forever by this experience to the point where it refused to stand up and defend its legitimate national security interests." Reagan believed "that if word of the rescue mission leaked out in advance, we'd hear this from some in Congress: 'Sure, it's starting small, but once you make that first commitment, Grenada's going to become another Vietnam.'"[28]

Reagan was right to reject the notion that small steps inevitably lead to big leaps. Grenada started small and ended small. There was no Vietnam waiting for the United States in Grenada. Yet Reagan took action against Grenada on the assumption that a communist takeover there would provide a base for the subversion of other Caribbean states. In this regard, Reagan in effect applied the Munich analogy to what was going on in Grenada: Grenada as an extension of the Cuban threat and the Cuban threat as an extension of the Soviet threat. Left uncontained, communism would claim other Caribbean dominoes.

Lebanon and Grenada were essentially sideshows in the much larger drama of the Cold War, which heated up during the Reagan presidency in part because of the conservative Californian's uncompromising opposition to the spread of communism anywhere, and in part because of Soviet aggressiveness in southwestern Asia and Africa. In her superb study of the Reagan presidency, Frances Fitzgerald observed that on more than one occasion Reagan compared his predecessor's policy of attempted détente with the Soviet Union to appeasement of Hitler, as when he said of Carter's efforts: "I believe we are seeing the same situation as when Mr. Chamberlain was tapping the cobblestones of Munich."[29] Lou Cannon, Reagan's best biographer, noted that Reagan "viewed the world through World War II eyes, and he had learned his generation's lesson that unwillingness to prepare for war invites aggression. For Reagan, the word 'appeasement' carried connotations of 'surrender.'" But Cannon also observed that "Reagan's picture of a golden, patriotic past was filtered through the dark distorting lens of Vietnam," a war that Reagan believed was a noble cause but doomed because of political interference in military operations.[30] President Reagan was clearly a member of the victory-was-self-denied explanatory school of U.S. defeat in Vietnam.

Reagan's attitudes on using force in specific situations were also influenced by often sharply divided counsel from his secretaries of state and defense. Indeed, George Shultz and Caspar Weinberger openly waged a rhetorical duel against one another on the issue of use-of-force criteria, a duel highlighted in 1984 by the proclamation of the Weinberger Doctrine. Weinberger was very averse to using force, a reflection of his assessment of what had gone wrong for the United States in Vietnam, whereas Shultz, like most secretaries of state, considered force as indispensable a tool of coercive diplomacy as it was of war itself. Weinberger was dismayed by public hostility toward the military in the wake of the Vietnam War, and he once said, "You can't fight Congress and public opinion and the enemy at the same time. That's why Vietnam was the crime of the century."[31] (As opposed to the Holocaust, Mao's "Great Leap Forward," and Stalin's perpetual mass slaughters and purges?) Weinberger's aversion to using force also stemmed from a felt need to protect the Reagan administration's massive military buildup from being dissipated in small-scale conflicts.

The impact of Munich on Reagan's foreign policy outlook is indisputable. Reagan's views on communism, the Soviet Union, and events in

Nicaragua, El Salvador, Afghanistan, Angola, Mozambique, and Ethiopia during his presidency were very much shaped by the failure of the democracies to stop Hitler until it was too late and by the assumption that the kind of strategic challenge posed by the Soviet Union in the 1980s differed little in its essentials from that posed by Nazi Germany in the 1930s. Throughout his presidency, Reagan made repeated public references to the lessons of the 1930s and World War II. In a March 1981 interview with Walter Cronkite he cited the isolationists' attack on Franklin Roosevelt's 1937 Chicago speech calling on the democracies to "quarantine" fascist aggression. "Can we honestly look back now and say that World War II would have taken place if we had done what [Roosevelt] wanted us to do back in 1938 [sic]? I think there's a very good chance it wouldn't have taken place."[32] In a subsequent speech Reagan returned again to the subject of appeasing Hitler, citing not only Winston Churchill's pleas to his countrymen "to recognize and arm against" the "expanding totalitarian war machine," but also the young John F. Kennedy's book *Why England Slept*.[33] Indeed, Reagan justified his administration's military buildup on the basis of the lessons of appeasement. "One of the great tragedies of this century was that it was only after the balance of power was allowed to erode and a ruthless adversary, Adolph Hitler, deliberately weighed the risks and decided to strike that the importance of a strong defense was realized," he argued in a 1983 radio address.[34]

Reagan also shared the convictions of his earlier and no less stridently anticommunist Democratic predecessors that not only were communism and nationalism incompatible but also that communist expansion in the Third World was centrally directed from Moscow. He once told the *Wall Street Journal,* "Let's not delude ourselves. The Soviet Union underlies all the unrest that is going on. If they weren't engaged in this game of dominoes, there wouldn't be any hot spots in the world."[35] Like Nixon in Vietnam, he dismissed the presence in the Third World of violent nationalist passions and the occasional success of communist elements in harnessing those passions for their own purposes. For example, he saw the Sandinistas in Nicaragua not as the product of popular reaction to decades of the Somoza family's corrupt dictatorship, but rather as little more than stooges of Cuba, which in turn was a henchman for Moscow. Reagan also interpreted the threat the Sandinistas posed in domino-like terms, describing the "malignancy in Managua" as a "strategic threat," a potentially "mortal threat to the entire New World," "another Cuba," and "a privileged sanctuary for terrorists and subversives just two days' driving time from Harlingen, Texas."[36] At a news conference in 1981, Reagan defined the objective of U.S. policy in El Salvador, which was confronting a Sandinista-supported insurgency: "What we are doing is to try to halt the infiltration into the Americas by terrorists, by outside interference and those who aren't just aiming at El Salvador, but, I think, aiming at the whole of Central and possibly South America—and I'm sure, eventually North America." The United States, he continued, was "trying to stop this destabilizing force of terrorism and guerrilla warfare and revolution from being exported in here backed by the Soviet Union and Cuba."[37] Indeed, Communists everywhere had as their "self-proclaimed goal . . . the domination of every nation on earth," and their "extension of totalitarianism" had "been accomplished . . . by military force or by subversion practiced by a tiny revolutionary cadre whose only real ideal is the will to power."[38]

Reagan portrayed the Sandinistas in El Salvador and Nicaragua as Central American analogues to the Viet Cong and their North Vietnamese sponsors and warned, as had the Johnson administration two decades earlier, that failure to stand and fight would both invite further aggression and threaten the credibility of American security commitments around the world. "Very simply, guerrillas, armed and supported by and through Cuba, are attempting to impose a Marxist-Leninist dictatorship on the people of El Salvador as part of a larger imperialistic plan. If we do not act promptly and decisively in defense of freedom, new Cubas will arise from the ruins of today's conflicts. We will face more totalitarian regimes tied militarily to the Soviet Union."[39] The effect of El Salvador's loss on America's reputation as a guarantor of its allies' security was clear: "If we cannot defend ourselves [in Central America], we cannot expect to prevail elsewhere. Our credibility would collapse, our alliances would crumble, and the safety of our homeland would be put in jeopardy."[40] This was precisely the same argument—indeed, almost exactly the same language—that Lyndon Johnson and Dean Rusk had used in 1965 to justify U.S. intervention in Vietnam.

If Reagan employed and deployed the Munich analogy in his Central America policy, he rejected the relevance of the Vietnam analogy. He often cited the relative proximity of Central America to the United States and repeatedly declared that his administration had no intention of dispatching U.S. combat troops to El Salvador. A small military advisory presence would not, as in Vietnam, be permitted to metamorphose into a mammoth combat presence. The absence of U.S. combat troops, however, did not prevent opponents of aid to the contras, who were waging an anticommunist insurgency against the Sandinista regime in Nicaragua, from deploying the Vietnam analogy on behalf of their case. Indeed, the fight over the issue became at times a duel of analogies. Robert Kagan's definitive account of the history of U.S. policy toward Nicaragua during the Sandinista period crisply sums up the perceived differences between the Carter and Reagan administrations. "If Carter officials were guided by the lessons of Vietnam," Kagan observed, "the new Republican administration, like Truman's decades before, believed the most important lessons were learned at Munich in 1938. Reagan and his advisors saw themselves as Churchill to the Carter administration's Chamberlain."[41]

Congressional critics and others opposed to Reagan's policies in Central America argued that providing assistance to the contras and the presence of even a few dozen U.S. military advisers in El Salvador constituted the first step down a slippery slope that would lead to the commitment of U.S. ground combat forces. After all, they argued, modest aid to South Vietnam and a few hundred American military advisers soon became massive aid and thousands of advisers, and then escalated to the bombing of North Vietnam (analogously Cuba), the deployment of ground combat forces to protect U.S. air bases, and finally to the commitment of 500,000 U.S. troops and the Americanization of the war. Secretary of State George Shultz later complained that "we had a Congress whose most active members saw the specter of another Vietnam and seemed determined to prevent such an outcome by denying the United States the ability to use any aspect of national power to deal with Communist advances in Central America."[42] Indeed, the Iran-contra affair, which exposed Reagan to the very real possibility of impeachment, was rooted in the bitter struggle between Congress and the White House over U.S. policy in Central America.

Munich clearly instructed Reagan in his attitudes toward the Soviet threat, although as the president of a country for whom the Vietnam War was still a fresh and very painful memory, he understood that the best insurance against a Central American Vietnam and the certain congressional revolt it would spark was to keep U.S. combat troops out of the fight. Whether he would have committed troops in the absence of congressional opposition remains unknown, although on several occasions he complained, as did Nixon before him, that the Vietnam War–traumatized Congress did not sufficiently appreciate "the need for a military element in foreign policy and its own responsibility to deal with that element."[43]

Reagan's realization that public and congressional tolerance for U.S. military intervention in the Third World was lacking was not only validated in Lebanon but also underlay a policy that became known as the Reagan Doctrine (a term coined by columnist Charles Krauthammer).[44] The doctrine, though never specifically enunciated, boiled down to a *practice* of undermining Soviet expansion in the Third World by providing assistance to anticommunist insurgencies that had arisen in Afghanistan and in such other newly acquired Soviet client states as Nicaragua, Angola, and Mozambique. Soviet overextension in the Third World provided the Reagan administration with the opportunity to pursue a policy of aggressive containment, even rollback, without exposing U.S. forces to the risks of direct intervention. In its essence, the Reagan Doctrine reflected, in James Scott's words, "the domestic constraints on the use of American forces imposed by the lesson learned in Vietnam: it stated that the United States would only *aid* those trying to liberate their own soil from Soviet half-baked regimes."[45] In this respect, the doctrine was a corollary of the Nixon Doctrine, which called for reliance on local surrogates to do most of the actual fighting.

The Reagan Doctrine was applied in various places, with varying levels of commitment, and with varying results. At the top of the list in terms of effort made and results achieved was Afghanistan, which seemed the ideal place to apply the doctrine. The rebels in that country were skilled and determined, and they were fighting Soviet troops who had invaded their country. They could be easily supplied through Pakistan, and most important of all, because Afghanistan was a clear-cut case of direct cross-border Soviet aggression, the administration could muster sufficient public and congressional support for assistance to the rebels. There was never any chance that American troops would be sent to fight in Afghanistan because the Afghan people were willing and able to provide the manpower for their own defense. In contrast to its support for the Reagan Doctrine in Afghanistan was the powerful resistance the Congress mounted against the administration's program to assist the Nicaraguan contras, who were neither militarily impressive nor victims of direct Soviet aggression. If Reagan was afraid of appeasement in Central America, congressional critics of Reagan's policy were more worried about slipping into a quagmire there.

How useful was the Munich analogy in informing the Reagan administration's policies in Central America and Afghanistan? With respect to the latter, precisely because Afghanistan was a manifest case of overt

Soviet aggression across an internationally recognized border, and because Russia had a long history of territorial expansion in Central Asia and an urgent need for warm-water ports, a strong case could be made that failure to prevent the Soviet Union from consolidating its hold on Afghanistan would sooner or later tempt Moscow to undertake further southward expansion. On this matter there was essentially no disagreement between Carter and Reagan, both of whom viewed the Soviet invasion as portending a direct military threat to vital U.S. interests in the Persian Gulf. Munich, in short, was quite relevant.

As for Central America, the Reagan administration was hardly the first to regard communist regimes in the Western Hemisphere as extensions of the Soviet threat. The Kennedy administration's perception of a Soviet-Cuban "axis" and of Cuban ambitions in the hemisphere also drew heavily on the Munich analogy. Castro sought, with Soviet assistance, to expand communism in the Americas, and in 1962 permitted the attempted transformation of Cuba into a base for Soviet nuclear missiles aimed at the United States. The subsequent *Cuban* missile crisis was resolved by dealing directly with *Moscow*, not Havana. During the 1970s and 1980s, Castro also permitted the Soviet Union to hire out the best units of the Cuban army for operations in Africa aimed at establishing and consolidating Soviet client states on that continent.

To be sure, preoccupation with Cuba as a stalking-horse for Soviet ambitions in Latin America often tended, as in Nicaragua and El Salvador, to deflect attention from indigenous sources of social unrest. Kennedy, at least, understood the connection between communism's appeal and local economic and social grievances, which he sought to address with his Alliance for Progress program. Indeed, the very concept of "nation building" was aimed at reducing developing states' vulnerability to communism via economic, political, and social reconstruction. Secretary of State Alexander Haig's conviction that "there was not the slightest doubt that Cuba was the source and supply and the catechist of the Salvadorian insurgency" ignored the degree to which that insurgency thrived on the brutality of El Salvador's reactionary regime.[46] Reagan himself seemed to perceive little if any connection between communism and local political, social, and economic conditions. Nor did he appear to grasp the mileage communist movements always got by riding the horse of anti-American nationalism. This was especially true in Central America and the Caribbean, the objects of repeated U.S. military interventions on behalf of unpopular local dictatorships.

On the other hand, the presence of Cuban troops in Grenada, Angola, and Ethiopia and Cuba's military and political advisory presence in Nicaragua were hardly accidental. The Sandinistas relied heavily on Cuban advice, and Cuba served as a transshipment point for the massive deliveries of Soviet arms to Nicaragua, whence some of them made their way to communist insurgents in El Salvador. The Sandinistas were much more dependent on their Soviet and Cuban benefactors than were the Vietnamese Communists on external support in 1965, the year the United States Americanized the war in Indochina.

The Munich analogy was hardly irrelevant to Central America in the 1980s, though the Reagan administration, as administrations are wont to do in selling a war or foreign policy for which public and congressional support is unenthusiastic, painted excessively dire consequences of failure. Whatever the fate of the contras, no hostile force in Central America was ever going to push on through Mexico and lay siege to Harlingen, Texas. As dominoes, the Central American countries except for Panama were small potatoes, and their "fall" would hardly have toppled the rest of North America. The Cold War allegiances of Central American governments were never strategically critical for the United States unless those governments threatened the Panama Canal or permitted the establishment of Soviet military bases on their territory. Moreover, the United States was in an unassailable military position to defend the canal against external threats and to thwart transformation of any Central American state into a forward Soviet base.

The Munich analogy was to some degree relevant in Central America in the 1980s, even if the threat and strategic stakes were hardly comparable to those in Europe in the late 1930s. The Sandinistas' freedom of military action, like that of Kim Il Sung's in Korea in 1950, was almost wholly a function of Soviet largesse and advice, which in Nicaragua's case was transmitted through Cuban intermediaries. Sandinista leader Daniel Ortega did not spend a lot of time in Moscow because he enjoyed the nightlife there. Moreover, although the Sandinistas did have a political base in Nicaragua's urban areas, the regime was detested in the countryside. It never commanded the allegiance of a Nicaraguan majority, as the Sandinista leadership learned to its surprise in 1990 when it was decisively defeated in free elections it had been shamed into holding by the international community.

Yet those who looked at Central America through the lens of the Vietnam War rather than that of Munich were guiltier of questionable reasoning by historical analogy. Central America in the 1980s bore only the most superficial resemblance to Indochina in the 1960s. Unlike Indochina, Central America was not strategically remote and culturally unfamiliar; it bordered Mexico, contained the strategically important Panama Canal, and had a long history of U.S. military intervention (especially Nicaragua). The United States was also in a position to isolate Nicaragua geographically as it never could isolate South Vietnam from North Vietnam and North Vietnam from Soviet and Chinese assistance. There was never any doubt, even among the Sandinistas, that the United States, should it so choose, could invade and occupy Nicaragua. And in terms of quality of leadership, the Ortega brothers could not hold a candle to Ho Chi Minh, Vo Nguyen Giap, and Le Duan. Most important, the very experience of the Vietnam War exerted decisive military restraint on the American political leadership. As journalist Don Oberdorfer remarked at the time, "We're not going to have another Vietnam [in Central America] now because we've already had Vietnam."[47]

Nor did the Sandinistas display a military prowess and capacity for political ruthlessness remotely comparable to that of their Vietnamese communist brethren. Hanoi's awesome fighting power drove the United States out of Indochina, and North Vietnam's political leadership was prepared to kill large numbers of ordinary Vietnamese to impose communism in their country. In contrast, the Sandinistas never consolidated control over Nicaragua, dissipating their initial popularity—a function of their displacement of the hated Somoza regime—by rejecting democracy in favor of converting the country into a Soviet client state. This left them friendless even among their Central American neighbors and ultimately made them unpopular in Moscow, which by the end of the decade was rapidly withdrawing from the Cold War and cutting its imperial burdens in the Third World.

Better than some of his congressional critics, President Reagan sensed that the public and Capitol Hill would not tolerate direct U.S. military intervention against the Sandinistas; the contras and the CIA's covert operations against Nicaragua were substitutes *for* American troops. In the hands of Reagan's policy opponents, the Vietnam analogy served much more effectively as a tool of advocacy than as one of diagnosis. The Vietnam analogy misled in Central America just as the Munich analogy had done in Southeast Asia.

7

Bush in Panama,
the Persian Gulf,
and Somalia

George Bush was the fourth post–Vietnam War president and the last president for whom Munich and World War II were the dominant foreign policy referent experiences. He was also exceptionally well qualified in foreign policy and self-assured when it came to using force, certainly when compared with his immediate Democratic predecessor and successor. "He had been raised in the austere tradition of public service of former Secretary of State and Secretary of War Henry L. Stimson," Steve Ropp wrote of Bush. "Like Stimson, Bush was steeped in the values of militant Republican internationalism that traced its origins to the foreign policies of Theodore Roosevelt. The president's views on the use of force were further shaped by his own generation's experience in world affairs during the 1930s and 1940s. Leaders had a right, even a duty, to use force against international aggressors, a perspective that led Bush to enlist in the military when World War II began and to become the navy's youngest fighter pilot."[1]

The one-term Bush administration launched two major military interventions: the first, in 1989, against the regime of Manuel Antonio Noriega in Panama, and the second, a year later, to reverse Iraq's conquest of Kuwait. Less than two months before he left office, Bush also ordered U.S. forces into Somalia to provide humanitarian relief to the starving population. None of the three interventions was motivated by Cold War considerations; the Cold War was rapidly crumbling by the time the Bush administration took office, and it effectively ended in 1989–90 with the dissolution of the Soviet empire in Eastern Europe and Germany's reunification within NATO.

Operation Just Cause, the invasion of Panama in December 1989 that destroyed the Noriega regime and its military prop, the Panama Defense Force (PDF), was the largest use of U.S. force since the Vietnam War—twenty-five thousand troops were committed—and a swift and clear military success.[2] It was motivated by a deterioration in U.S. relations with Noriega, beginning in the mid-1980s, that culminated in Noriega-inspired attacks on U.S. military personnel and their dependents in Panama. Both the Reagan administration and then the Bush administration tried to remove Noriega by means short of force, including economic sanctions, highly publicized U.S. military exercises in the Canal Zone, a federal court indictment of the Panamanian dictator on a host of drug-trafficking charges, and support—albeit weak—of an attempted coup against Noriega on October 3, 1989, by one of his henchmen. These measures, however, served only to increase Noriega's defiance, driving him into such increasingly reckless behavior as securing from Panama's puppet legislative body a declaration of war on the United States and encouraging increased attacks by goon-squad "dignity battalions" on exposed American citizens. The straw that broke the camel's back was the murder of Marine Corps lieutenant Robert Paz and the detention of a U.S. Navy officer and sexual abuse of his wife. "That was enough," declared Bush in his address to the nation explaining the reasons for military action. "Noriega's reckless threats and attacks upon Americans in Panama created an imminent danger to the 35,000 American citizens in Panama. As President, I have no higher obligation than to safeguard the lives of American citizens. And that is why I have ordered our Armed Forces to protect the lives of American citizens in Panama and to bring General Noriega to justice in the United States."[3]

The United States also sought "to defend democracy in Panama, to combat drug trafficking, and to protect the integrity of the Panama Canal treaty."[4] But there were other factors at play as well. Bush personally detested Noriega, who had spent many years on the payroll of the Central Intelligence Agency, which Bush once directed. Moreover, by mid-December 1989, Bush's seeming *un*willingness to use force had become a domestic political liability, with conservative Republicans and even some Democrats charging that the administration was both timid and incompetent in dealing with Noriega.[5] Bush's sensitivity to what had become known in the press as the "wimp factor" was evident in a presidential press conference held the month before Operation Just Cause was launched. In response to a question from a Latin American journalist about domestic criticism of his administration's failure to back the failed coup against Noriega in early October, Bush, who for months had been calling for Noriega's removal, replied: "We've got a lot of hawks out there; we've got a lot of macho guys out there that want me to send somebody's else's kid into battle. And what I will do is prudently assess the situation at the time. . . . [W]e are not going to imprudently use the force of the United States."[6]

Several features of Bush's decision to use force against Noriega merit at least brief discussion. First, both Colin Powell and his predecessor as JCS chairman, Adm. William Crowe, were reluctant to use force in Panama; Crowe opposed a military option altogether, and Powell backed force only when the murder of Paz gave the United States no choice. Neither Powell, who served as Ronald Reagan's last national security adviser, nor Crowe saw another Vietnam in the making, but neither saw the stakes at hand as worth a war, at least until the threat to American citizens became clear and immediate. Powell and Crowe represented the Vietnam-seared generation of military professionals who strongly believed, as Ropp put it, "that politicians and their organizational supporters in other Washington bureaucracies were all too willing to initiate conflicts for which the nation's soldiers would be blamed if they failed."[7]

Second, there was never any question of the military feasibility of overthrowing the Noriega regime quickly and at low cost. U.S. military forces had been stationed in Panama for almost a century and could be easily augmented to provide overwhelming force against any Panamanian resistance. Additionally, domestic political support for Operation Just Cause was strong, in part because, as Powell subsequently observed, "Noriega was rich villain material,"[8] and in part because the vitality of at least one U.S. interest at stake—the safety of threatened American citizens in Panama—was unquestionable. The fact that most Panamanians welcomed the invasion also contributed to its popularity.

Third, Bush was encouraged by the public's response to President Reagan's invasion of Grenada and his 1986 punitive bombing of Libya. The popularity of both actions suggested that the public, if less so Capitol Hill, was prepared to back U.S. use of force overseas as long as it was quick, successful, and conducted on behalf of interests believed to be worth the risks of combat. "Libya and Grenada taught Bush and his team of advisors that both the American public and Congress would support military interventions when they were swift, when vital national interests were perceived to be at stake, and when they were conducted on a pragmatic 'one time only' basis," Ropp observed in his analysis of the Panama invasion.[9] Moreover, military action against Grenada and Libya incurred only light U.S. casualties (sixteen dead in Grenada, two pilots fatally shot down over Libya), an accomplishment upheld in Operation Just Cause, which incurred twenty-four U.S. military dead out of twenty-five thousand troops committed.[10] America's military leadership during the decade of the 1980s may have been skittish about using force for fear of failure, but there simply was no analogy to Vietnam in either Grenada or Panama; on the contrary, for Operation Just Cause, Grenada itself was the most relevant analogy.

Fourth, threats of force before the invasion failed as tools of coercive diplomacy because Noriega apparently did not take them seriously. For several years prior to the invasion, the United States had been openly seeking Noriega's ouster and employing a host of pressures, including threatening military exercises in Panama and reinforcement of the U.S. garrison there. Noriega responded to these pressures by becoming even more defiant. He apparently did not believe the United States would use military force to unseat him, a belief undoubtedly reinforced by the Bush administration's failure to provide effective support for the attempted coup of October 3.[11] Did Noriega ignore the precedents of Grenada and Libya? Did he believe, as did many of George Bush's domestic political critics, that the president was afraid to use force in Panama? Did he believe that the Vietnam War still paralyzed the United States? Answers to these questions remain unavailable.

Finally, the success of Operation Just Cause accounted in significant measure for the Bush administration's subsequent confidence in the domestic political viability of a much larger use of force in the Persian Gulf the following year. Secretary of State James Baker believed that "in breaking the mind-set of the American people about the use of force in the post-Vietnam era, Panama established an emotional predicate that permitted us to build public support so essential to the success of Operation Desert Storm thirteen months later."[12] Powell also saw Panama as a use-of-force precedent: "The lessons I absorbed from Panama confirmed all of my convictions over the preceding twenty years, since the days of doubt over Vietnam. Have a clear political objective and stick to it. Use the force necessary, and do not apologize for going in big if that is what it takes. Decisive force ends wars quickly and in the long run saves lives."[13]

✳ ✳ ✳

The Munich analogy would play just as big a role as the Vietnam analogy in determining the Bush administration's response to Iraq's conquest of Kuwait in 1990. Like his predecessor, Bush believed in the lesson of Munich, to which he analogized Saddam Hussein's invasion of Kuwait in 1990. At the same time, however, he was also very conscious of the Vietnam War's impact on public and congressional attitudes about using force in the Third World.

For Bush, the Munich analogy answered the question of whether to use force, if necessary, to overturn Iraq's aggression against Kuwait, whereas the Vietnam War analogy, specifically the lessons of the war *as embodied in the Weinberger-Powell Doctrine*, instructed him in how to go about doing so.[14] Indeed, with Powell at his side as chairman of the Joint Chiefs of Staff, Bush engineered a military resolution of the Gulf crisis that more or less satisfied all the Weinberger-Powell use-of-force criteria, including those of vital interests, public and congressional support, clear and achievable political and military objectives, and overwhelming and last-resort employment of force. In this effort Bush was assisted immensely by the self-defeating behavior of a politically isolated and strategically incompetent Iraqi adversary. Bush also profited by the presence of vital U.S. interests in the Persian Gulf, and by, as did Reagan in Afghanistan, the unambiguous nature of the enemy's aggression.

Bush was and has remained candid about viewing the conquest of Kuwait as another Munich. During the crisis, the Bush White House orchestrated a major public relations campaign to demonize Saddam Hussein, with the president himself publicly comparing Saddam to Adolf Hitler and reiterating the results of appeasing fascism in the 1930s. He continued doing so even after his national security adviser, Brent Scowcroft, cautioned him against using the Hitler analogy because it suggested that the United States would settle for nothing less than the destruction of Saddam Hussein and his regime.[15] But the Munich analogy also genuinely informed Bush's reasoning. In 1998, he recounted his first reaction on learning of the Iraqi invasion: "I was keenly aware that this would be the first post–Cold War test of the [United Nations] Security Council in crisis. I knew what had happened in the 1930s when a weak and leaderless League of Nations had failed to stand up to Japanese, Italian, and German aggression. The result was to encourage the ambitions of those regimes."[16] During the prehostilities phase of the crisis, he told Turkish president Turgut Ozal that a possible Iraqi withdrawal in exchange for what amounted to Kuwaiti extortion payments "is not another solution but another Munich."[17] And in drafting his first major address to the nation about the crisis, Bush later recalled that he "tightened up the language to strengthen the similarity I saw between the Persian Gulf and the situation in the Rhineland, when Hitler defied the Treaty of Versailles and marched in."[18] On New Year's Eve, 1990, he wrote his sons, asking, "How many lives might have been saved if appeasement had given way to force earlier on in the late '30's or earliest '40's? How many Jews might have been spared the gas chambers, or how many Polish patriots might be alive today? I look at today's crisis as 'good' vs. 'evil'—Yes, it is that clear."[19]

Bush has also acknowledged that during the first weeks of the Gulf crisis he was reading historian Martin Gilbert's best-selling 1989 book, *The Second World War: A Complete History.* "I saw a direct analogy between what was occurring in Kuwait and what the Nazis had done, especially in Poland," he noted in his memoirs.[20] Additionally, in part because he had little regard for the Iraqi army, Bush did not see any Vietnam parallels in the Gulf crisis, even though Secretary of State James Baker "worried . . . that we could get bogged down in another Vietnam, lose public support, and see the Bush presidency destroyed."[21] More than Baker, and much more than Powell, Bush correctly sensed that he was up against nothing remotely comparable to the communist military threat in Vietnam a quarter of a century earlier. In effect, he rejected, in terms of enemy fighting power, the relevance of the Vietnam analogy in the Persian Gulf while at the same time proceeding to act on the perceived lessons of that war.

The Vietnam analogy does seem relevant to the administration's abrupt termination of the war and quick military withdrawal from Iraqi territory. Despite pressure to drive on to Baghdad and unseat Saddam Hussein, Bush declared a unilateral cease-fire once Kuwait had been liberated; he also refused to provide any assistance to the war-sparked Shia and Kurdish uprisings in Iraq. "Here," historian Yuen Foong Khong noted, "the first lesson of 'no more Vietnams'—no more involvement in other people's civil wars—had an impact on the Bush administration. It would have been messy and there would be no assurance of victory in fighting alongside the Kurds and Shiites against Hussein's army and his supporters, however much the Bush administration wanted to unseat Hussein. Vietnam showed that such civil strifes are difficult to control and win."[22]

Munich, however, remained the dominant analogy, with Bush dismissing the prospect of a Vietnam in the desert. Throughout the Gulf crisis, Bush continued to compare Saddam Hussein to Hitler and frequently referred to the lesson learned from appeasing fascism in the 1930s. Clearly, he not only believed in the Munich analogy but also sought to use it as a means of creating public support for the war to come. Less than a week after Iraq's invasion of Kuwait, Bush told the nation that "if history teaches us anything, it is that we must resist aggression or it will destroy our freedoms. Appeasement does not work. As was the case in the 1930s, we see in Saddam Hussein an aggressive dictator threatening his neighbors."[23] Ten days later, on August 20, 1990, Bush declared that "August 1990 has witnessed what history will judge one of the most crucial deployments of allied power since World War II. . . . Half a century ago, the world had a chance to stop a ruthless aggressor and missed it. I pledge to you: We will not make that mistake again."[24] On October 28, Bush told a military audience that "in World War II, the world paid dearly for appeasing an aggressor who could have been stopped. Appeasement leads only to further aggression and, ultimately, to war. And we are not going to make the mistake of appeasement again." Bush then noted that "Harry Truman understood this lesson" when "he, too, spoke to the Nation" about his decision to fight in Korea, "and he could almost have been talking about Kuwait."[25] A few days later, Bush cited "an awful similarity" between Iraqi behavior inside Kuwait and "what happened when the [Nazi] Death's Head regiments went into Poland."[26]

As war drew nearer, however, Bush began reassuring the public that it would not be "another Vietnam."[27] In his announcement that military action against Iraq was finally under way, Bush declared: "I've told the American people before that this will not be another Vietnam, and I repeat this here tonight. Our troops will have the best possible support in the entire world, and they will not be asked to fight with one hand tied behind their back. I'm hopeful that this fighting will not go on for long and that casualties will be held to an absolute minimum."[28] A week into the war, Bush repeated his pledge: "This will not be another Vietnam. Never again will our Armed Forces be sent out to do a job with one hand tied behind their back. They will continue to have the support they need to get the job done, get it done quickly, and with as little loss of life as possible."[29]

Bush's conduct of the Gulf War conformed to the injunctions of the Weinberger-Powell Doctrine. He made the case for the vitality of American interests in reversing the aggression of a nuclear-aspirant Arab Hitler in a region of incontestable importance to the entire Western economy. He worked hard and successfully at mobilizing initially unenthusiastic public and congressional opinion and painstakingly exhausted every nonwar alternative to get the Iraqis out of Kuwait. He laid out clear and achievable political and military objectives and harmoniously married military means to political goals.

He also gave a loose, though not free, rein to the military professionals. As he confided to his personal journal on the eve of the Coalition's ground assault in the Gulf War, "I have no qualms now about ordering a ground war—none at all. . . . I have not second-guessed [the military]; I have not told them what targets to hit; I have not told them how much ordnance to use or how much not to use, or what weapons to use and not to use. I have learned from Vietnam."[30] In George Bush the Pentagon enjoyed a president who believed U.S. military power had been disastrously mishandled in Vietnam by civilian authority and whose behavior during the Gulf crisis displayed a keen appreciation of the requirements for political and military success as laid out in the doctrine. After the war, Bush remembered that he "did not want to repeat the problems of the Vietnam War (or numerous wars throughout history), where the political leadership meddled with military operations. I wanted to avoid micromanaging the military."[31] Shortly after the U.S. victory, Bush triumphantly if prematurely declared that "we've kicked the Vietnam syndrome once and for all" because the "specter of Vietnam has been buried forever in the desert sands of the Arabian peninsula."[32] Indeed, Arnold Isaacs concluded, "it was hard to escape the impression that laying the Vietnam syndrome to rest was itself a major administration goal, perhaps even equal in importance to the goal of defeating Iraq."[33]

Yet, for better or for worse, the Vietnam syndrome had not been discarded; on the contrary, it governed the Bush administration's conduct of the war. Indeed, Bush's senior military adviser himself was the living embodiment of that syndrome, and his performance throughout the crisis reflected a dread of stumbling into another Vietnam. Colin Powell not only opposed going to war over Kuwait, but also encouraged the premature U.S. termination of hostilities that may have stripped an impressive military victory of much of its potential strategic effect.[34] From the outset of the crisis Powell favored defensive U.S. military deployments to

Saudi Arabia and reliance on sanctions to compel Iraq's withdrawal from Kuwait.[35] The evidence suggests that the shrewd JCS chairman tried indirectly to scare off his more hawkish civilian superiors by submitting war plans that he believed, or at least hoped, would deter the White House from deciding for war. National Security Adviser Brent Scowcroft, in his joint memoir with Bush published in 1998, recounted that the "initial plan for retaking Kuwait, briefed to President Bush in October [1990], had not seemed designed by anyone eager to undertake the task. Similarly, the force requirements for a successful offense given to him at the end of October were so large that one could speculate that they were set forth by a command hoping their size would change his mind about pursuing a military option."[36] During much of the crisis Powell was also surreptitiously confessing his doubts to the legendary Bob Woodward, who recorded them in his book *The Commanders*. The book was published right after the war ended and was widely regarded as Powell's "I-told-you-so" insurance policy against an American battlefield disaster in the desert.

If Powell opposed going to war because he feared another Vietnam, he was certainly not alone in seeing the prospect of another Vietnam even after the Iraqi army had been broken in Kuwait and was fleeing northward. The haste with which the Bush administration terminated the war and pulled U.S. ground forces out of the Gulf reflected a Vietnam-driven dread of involvement in postwar Iraq. This fear of getting sucked into a bloody Arab quagmire drove the Bush administration to end the war prematurely with little thought given to how it should most advantageously be terminated. With the Iraqi army on the run, the administration took the extraordinary step of declaring a unilateral cease-fire in the absence of any request for terms from Baghdad. It then sent Gen. Norman Schwarzkopf, *without* political instructions, to Safwan, a place in allied-occupied Iraqi territory that was not even under U.S. control at the time of the cease-fire, to negotiate cease-fire terms with a bunch of Saddam's military lackeys. (It apparently occurred to no one that the Iraqis should have been *summoned* to appear at *Schwarzkopf's* headquarters and told that a cease-fire required, among other things, a public acknowledgment of defeat by Saddam himself.) Thus, almost the first thing the administration did was to discard potentially decisive leverage for forcing Saddam's ouster. Without any subsequent objection from his civilian superiors, Schwarzkopf declared the U.S. intent to evacuate Iraqi territory taken and held by U.S. ground forces. Again without a peep from Washington,

Schwarzkopf also allowed himself to be snookered into permitting the Iraqis to continue flying their attack helicopters, which they promptly used to crush the subsequent Shia rebellion in southern Iraq as U.S. forces stood by and watched.

Adherence to the Weinberger-Powell injunctions produced a heady military victory at a stunningly low cost in American lives, but it also restricted that victory's potential strategic effects. At Safwan, the Bush administration got what it wanted: a cheap and clean military win followed by a speedy exit from the Gulf. But Saddam also got what he wanted: survival. Operation Desert Storm dealt with the symptoms of Iraqi aggression but left its source intact.

But if the administration's termination of the war left much to be desired, President Bush's employment and deployment of the Munich analogy was by and large justified, as was his apparent confidence that the risks of immersion in a Vietnam-like quagmire could be avoided—even if the price of assured avoidance was, as it turned out, the continuation of Saddam Hussein's regime. Although Iraq was hardly a great power in 1990, it was the local military giant in a region of indisputably vital importance to the West. Saddam, moreover, had nuclear ambitions as well as visions of territorial empire in the Gulf that threatened U.S. interests there. If he was not a replica of Hitler, he was a pretty close facsimile in terms of the brutality of his dictatorship and his willingness to wage wars of conquest to achieve his imperial ambitions. He was a personally as well as politically vicious man who began his career as an assassin, started a war with Iran, and used poison gas against his own people. His conquest of Kuwait, had it been allowed to stand, would have given him control of one-quarter of the world's proven oil reserves. It also would have placed him in a position to easily invade Saudi Arabia's oil-rich Eastern Province, or at a minimum to coerce Saudi concessions on oil and security issues. Saddam's military power in 1990 had no local equal and dwarfed that of Saudi Arabia, a U.S. client state for whose survival past U.S. presidents had declared a willingness to fight. Whatever judgment may be made of the Bush administration's termination of the war, the decision to fight was strategically justified, perhaps even imperative.

Bush avoided any real chance of a Vietnam in the Gulf by laying down limited, clear, and achievable political and military objectives, which included Kuwait's liberation, its monarchy's restoration, and the destruction of Iraq's offensive military capacity. U.S. war aims did not explicitly encompass Saddam's removal and Iraq's political reconstruction, although the dictator's known residences were attacked and the Iraqi people were urged to get rid of him. Bush's task in the Gulf was enormously facilitated by an incompetent Iraqi military relative to its American counterpart and an enemy leader who displayed a remarkable capacity for strategic misjudgment. Iraq under Saddam Hussein in 1990 was close to being, in the words of one analyst, "the perfect enemy."[37]

The Iraqi military was large but had little experience against a first-class Western military establishment, and it was up against U.S. armed forces at the peak of their Cold War military effectiveness. The Iraqi army in 1990 was isolated from external support, and its rank and file consisted largely of sullen conscripts, many of them reservists recalled after only a short respite from up to eight years' service in the hellish Iraq-Iran War. Additionally, Saddam himself lacked any professional military training and picked his generals on the basis of political loyalty rather than professional competence. In short, the United States was hardly facing a major league military opponent, notwithstanding the Pentagon's significant prewar overestimation of Iraq's fighting power, particularly the vaunted Republican Guard.[38] Certainly there was no useful comparison with communist forces in Vietnam, which, unlike the Iraqis, did not try to ape industrial models of conventional warfare but instead practiced an asymmetric style of fighting designed to neutralize U.S. superiority in firepower and technology. For Hanoi, the protraction of hostilities was the key to victory because it pitted an ultimately superior communist political will against an inferior American will. Nor was there any similarity in the quality of political and military leadership; Iraq had no equivalent to the charismatic, politically astute, internationally respected Ho Chi Minh or to Vo Nguyen Giap, one of the most brilliant and accomplished military minds of the war-torn twentieth century.

Ironically, Saddam Hussein appears to have been a much stronger believer in the Vietnam syndrome than anyone in the Bush administration, including Powell. Saddam drew his own lessons from the Vietnam War (and its subsequent reinforcement in Lebanon), which boiled down to the twin conclusions that U.S. technological superiority was not necessarily decisive and that Americans were casualty-averse to the point of strategic paralysis. After all, had not the technologically inferior Vietnamese Communists driven the Americans out of Indochina? Did not a single truck bomb drive the Americans out of Lebanon? And what about Iraq's own bloody eight-year war with Iran? Did that not prove that grinding attrition on the ground was, as in Vietnam, the key to victory in war?

Saddam seems to have completely ignored both the recovery of America's strategic self-confidence during the 1980s and the profound changes in U.S. military doctrine and technology that made it possible for the United States by 1990 to use military power against a second-class conventional enemy with greatly reduced risk.

A conviction that the United States lacked the political will for war is the only convincing explanation for Saddam's invasion of Kuwait, his subsequent failure to keep going and seize port facilities and air bases in the Eastern Province, his continued military passivity as the United States began to pour fighting forces into Saudi Arabia, and his refusal to evacuate Kuwait as the UN's deadline for evacuation approached. Even after the Coalition air campaign began, he still seemed to believe that the United States lacked the guts for ground combat.[39] (And what must Saddam have made of the unilateral American cease-fire other than lack of political will to do what was necessary to bring his regime down? Saddam certainly would never have given decisive respite to a fleeing enemy.)

Indeed, America's premature unilateral cessation of hostilities dictated by a lack of will to strike at the source of Iraqi aggression ended up saddling both Bush and his successors (including Bush's son) with the task of repeatedly using force to enforce tough peace terms (UN resolutions mandating Iraq's substantial disarmament and draconian economic sanctioning) on a recalcitrant regime determined to achieve their eventual elimination. The analogy to the harsh Versailles treaty of 1919 and Germany's ultimate overthrow of its provisions in the wake of weakening British and French determination to enforce them is an apt one. If the Munich analogy encouraged the Bush administration to go to war against Iraq in the first place, the Vietnam analogy produced a half-baked, politically inconclusive termination analogous to that of World War I, which simply postponed for two decades the day of reckoning with an angry and vengeful Germany. The "peace the victorious coalition imposed upon Iraq in 1991 bears a troubling similarity to the peace imposed on the Germans in 1919," concluded Donald and Frederick Kagan in *While America Sleeps*. "Its terms were harsh enough to engender resentment, hatred, and the desire for revenge in the hearts of the Iraqis without providing a satisfactory long term defense against a revived Iraq."[40] Bush himself conceded at the time of victory that he didn't share the "wonderfully euphoric feeling that many of the American people feel." "There was a definitive end to [World War II]," Bush said, but the Gulf War had ended with "Saddam Hussein still in power there—the man who wreaked this havoc upon his neighbors."[41] As of this writing, Saddam Hussein is still in power, and he has managed, like Germany in the 1920s and early 1930s, to loosen or cast off altogether key military and economic sanctions imposed on Iraq at the end of the Gulf War. With his freedom of action increasing, he may soon, like the same Hitler to whom George Bush compared him, plunge his region into a second war.

✳ ✳ ✳

If the Bush administration was in a hurry to depart the Persian Gulf, it was no less eager to vacate the premises in Somalia. Exactly what prompted the lame-duck president to intervene in Somalia in December 1992 remains unclear. Perhaps it was a combination of genuine humanitarian concern and a desire to divert the attention of domestic political critics of his administration's Vietnam syndrome–driven inaction in the face of mounting atrocities in Bosnia. But the decision, in late 1992, to put U.S. forces on the ground in that starving, anarchic African country to facilitate the delivery of humanitarian relief supplies laid the foundation for a subsequent American foreign policy humiliation on the order of the Lebanon debacle in the 1980s.

Defenders of the Bush administration claim that its successor administration essentially messed up a perfectly simple and safe intervention by permitting it to cross the line between humanitarian relief/peacekeeping to nation building/peace enforcement.[42] But surely it was naïve of Bush to believe that the United States could simply dart into Somalia, pass out some food, and then leave without at least attempting to deal with the primary source of starvation, which was political, not meteorological or logistical. Mark Bowden, in his gripping account of the intervention-ending firefight in downtown Mogadishu in which eighteen American soldiers were killed and seventy-five wounded, observed that "President Bush committed the United States to the mission, and the decision to nation-build once the famine ended was the perfectly logical outgrowth of that policy. The famine in Somalia had not been caused by a natural disaster; it was man-made, a result of cynical, feuding warlords deliberately using starvation as a weapon. It would not have made much sense to simply walk away after delivering food for a few weeks or months and allow the crisis to renew."[43]

But that is exactly what President Bush thought he could do.[44] The plan was to go in quickly, secure Somali ports and airfields, open up roads and escort relief convoys, and then, having halted starvation, turn responsibility for continued administration of humanitarian relief and provision of whatever security it required over to the United Nations. Although fear of getting sucked into the civil strife lay behind "the alacrity with which the United States would attempt to hand over the task to the UN," William Durch observed, the Bush administration ignored both the political sources of the starvation and the difficulties inherent in maintaining political neutrality in a place of anarchy.[45] As in Lebanon, even well-intentioned intervention aroused the hostility of those indigenous factions—most notably Mohammed Farrah Aideed and his Somalia National Alliance (SNA)—whose local interests the intervention threatened; and, of course, once the shooting started and U.S. soldiers returned fire, any pretense of neutrality disappeared. Moreover, the United Nations was manifestly incapable of providing the security necessary for its ever-expanding political agenda in Somalia, which ultimately included disarming the clans, creating a national police force, imposing peace throughout the country, and putting "quickly in place the broad institutional capabilities and resources needed to revitalize at least minimal elements of a functioning Somali society and government."[46] The United Nations, with the supporting vote of the United States as the leading permanent member of the Security Council, hoped to replace the United States in Somalia without sufficient American military cover. Yet the very presence of that cover exposed U.S. soldiers to precisely the kind of casualties that ended up driving the United States out of Somalia during the Clinton administration.

What is striking in retrospect is that such cautious and experienced decision makers as George Bush and Colin Powell (Brent Scowcroft was skeptical from the start) not only intervened in a civil war in a place of no strategic significance to the United States, but also seemingly failed to understand that even the simple provision of food to the Somali population by any external agency would automatically invite the hostility of those for whom withholding food was an effective political weapon. There is—and can be—no such thing as a politically immaculate military intervention in a failed state. Even the most benign external military intrusion affects the local balance of power. "There was a risk inherent in the American role," observed foreign policy expert and "realist" William Hyland, a role "which was mistakenly conceived and portrayed as a limited military effort that could be divorced from political reality."[47]

These judgments do not absolve the Clinton administration from witlessly embracing UN secretary-general Boutros Boutros-Ghali's ambition to rebuild the Somali state. President Clinton paid little attention to foreign policy in 1993, and almost none of his foreign policy principals in that year (the exception being Secretary of Defense Les Aspin) seemed to recognize the potential consequences of the expanding UN political agenda in Somalia. On the contrary, the U.S. ambassador to the United Nations, Madeleine Albright, "wanted to make Somalia a model exercise in multinational peacekeeping" and did not seem to understand that once Aideed and his SNA began to resist forcible disarmament there was no longer any peace left to keep in Somalia.[48] In her view, failure to disarm Aideed's forces would be "appeasement" and would prevent Somalia from being lifted from a "failed state to an emerging democracy."[49]

The failed U.S. intervention in Somalia is significant for two reasons. First, although neither the Munich analogy nor the Vietnam analogy had anything to do with the decision to intervene—no one even pretended that important U.S. interests were involved—the failure seemed to reaffirm the lessons of Vietnam and Lebanon, at least as those lessons were reflected in the tenets of the Weinberger-Powell Doctrine. Second, it provided conclusive evidence of the American political elite's extreme sensitivity to incurring casualties in small wars and of the potential strategic consequences of that sensitivity. A local and militarily primitive warlord managed to drive the mighty United States out of his country by killing eighteen American soldiers and parading one of the dead on CNN television. The chilling effect of the Mogadishu firefight on subsequent U.S. uses of force overseas prompted an accomplished American diplomatic troubleshooter to redefine the Vietnam syndrome as the "Vietmalia syndrome."[50] Somalia torpedoed any chance of subsequent U.S. military intervention in Rwanda to stop the slaughter of as many as 800,000 Tutsis, and it came close to crippling the U.S. will to use force in the former Yugoslavia.

✳ ✳ ✳

If the Bush administration saw little risk in its humanitarian intervention in Somalia, it envisaged risks aplenty in military intervention in the unfolding civil war in the former Yugoslavia. It stayed out of Bosnia for the same reason it stayed out of post–Gulf War Iraq. The war in Bosnia bore obvious similarities to Vietnam. It was a brutal civil war in a place of relatively low strategic importance to the United States, and the utility of U.S. conventional military power seemed questionable in an operationally unconventional environment in which elusive irregular forces did much of the killing. The *New York Times* quoted Bush as declaring, "I do not want to see the United States bogged down in any way into some guerrilla warfare [in Bosnia]. We've lived through that once already."[51]

Coming off the clean and stirring victory in the Persian Gulf and facing a budgetary crisis and soft economy at home, the Bush administration had no incentive to intervene in a place it regarded as a Balkan Vietnam in waiting. Additionally, there was little or no public support for intervention, and the Pentagon was openly opposed to any military action in the Balkans. Indeed, during the last month of the 1992 presidential election campaign, JCS chairman Colin Powell wrote an op-ed for the *New York Times* in which he warned that intervention would violate the lessons of the Bay of Pigs, Vietnam, and Lebanon, notably the necessity for clear and attainable political and military objectives.[52]

The Bush administration found itself in 1992 in a situation analogous to that confronting the Eisenhower administration in 1954 with respect to prospective intervention in French Indochina: arguments against intervention simply swamped arguments for it. Both Eisenhower and Bush believed in the Munich analogy, although Eisenhower believed— rightly, as it turned out—that he could limit both the strategic and the domestic political damage of a communist victory in Indochina. Bush apparently rejected the Munich analogy as pertinent to the Milosevic "threat" in the former Yugoslavia, seeing instead an analogy with Vietnam. Bush did, however, deploy a small U.S. "tripwire" force to Macedonia because Serbian aggression against Macedonia could have set in train a series of events resulting in war between Greece and Turkey, two NATO allies. For the same reason, on December 24, 1992, Bush warned Milosevic via cable that "in the event of conflict in Kosovo caused by Serb action, the US will be prepared to employ military force against Serbians in Kosovo and in Serbia proper."[53] Seven years later, Bill Clinton acted on that threat.

Clinton in Haiti

and the Balkans

President Clinton was the first president born after World War II, and the first for whom the Vietnam War was the dominant foreign policy referent experience. Comparing the Vietnam War generation with the older generation of Vietnam War decision makers, former national security adviser Zbigniew Brzezinski observed: "The leadership of the sixties was always thinking about Munich. Now there is a generation worried about Vietnam, with the consequences of self-imposed paralysis, which is likely to be costlier in the long run."[1]

Clinton was also the first president to take office after the end of the Cold War, and the first since Franklin Delano Roosevelt who had never performed personal military service. Additionally, unlike his predecessor, Clinton was far more interested in domestic policy than he was in foreign affairs. Clinton presidency analysts James Burns and Georgia Sorenson concluded that his "first instinct was to debate rather than act," and that he "often blundered" when "military action was required" because such action mandated "decisiveness, bold action, and no backpedaling."[2]

Paradoxically, Clinton ended up using force more often than any of his post–World War II predecessors—in Somalia, Haiti, the Balkans (twice), and against Iraq (numerous times), Afghanistan, and Sudan. But all of these cases involved the use of force as a tool of coercive diplomacy and punishment, not a means of full-scale war. Force was, moreover, always used as a last resort, and all too often after the bluffs of previously threatened force had been called. Additionally, with the exception of operations in Somalia and Haiti, the use of force was restricted to air power.

The Clinton administration's initial foreign policy team drew heavily from the second tier of Jimmy Carter's team. Former Kissinger aide and later editor of *Foreign Affairs* William G. Hyland noted that such appointees as Warren Christopher, Anthony Lake, Strobe Talbott, and Madeleine Albright all believed, with Clinton, that the Vietnam War was at best a strategic disaster and at worst a moral abomination. They also believed, at least initially, that the Cold War's demise enabled the United States to shift from primarily an interest-based foreign policy to one that rested more on such values as democracy, market economics, humanitarian relief, and genocide suppression. At the same time, Clinton's chief foreign policy lieutenants served a president whose interest in foreign affairs derived almost entirely from domestic political considerations and who, at least in the early years of his presidency, did not seem fully prepared to accept the legitimacy of force in international politics.[3] Where Bush had displayed determination in using force, Clinton seemed hesitant and indecisive. This combination of being "a prisoner of his own instinctive aversion to the use of military force" and a no less instinctive "tailor[ing of] his foreign policy to popular opinion, which," Hyland suggested, "he mistakenly believed was the foundation of legitimate foreign policy," worked against swift and conclusive uses of force during the Clinton presidency.[4]

Indeed, force was alien to Clinton and his political persona. A compulsive desire to please people governed his presidency, and as an optimist and a lawyer, Clinton strongly believed that even acutely conflicting interests could be reconciled through compromise and patient negotiation. He seemed, at least during his first term, not to understand, perhaps not even to want to understand, that civil wars are inherently intractable, and that the parties' competing interests in the fight are almost always irreconcilable. Clinton seemed surprised by the savagery of the civil wars in Somalia, Rwanda, and the Balkans, and did not appear to grasp fully that the stakes for those engaged in such wars are inherently much greater than those of intervening external powers. This was as true in the Balkans as it had been in Vietnam. Power-sharing arrangements among parties seeking one another's political and even physical extermination are by their nature difficult to negotiate and almost impossible to sustain absent an external police force—a fact of international political life the Clinton administration learned the hard way in Somalia and the Balkans.

Clinton equivocated even on whether the Gulf War was justified. When asked during the 1992 election campaign how he would have voted had he been in the Senate when it took votes on whether or not to support a presidential decision to go to war, candidate Clinton replied, "I guess I would have voted with the majority if it was a close vote. But I agree with the argument the minority made [in favor of sanctions rather than war]."[5]

The lesson of Munich does not appear to have exerted a significant influence on Clinton's attitude toward the role of force in foreign policy. On the eve of the fiftieth anniversary of the Allied landings in Normandy, he told an interviewer that "yes, maybe [Americans] were a little, slow, you can argue in hindsight, to respond to Hitler's aggression."[6] (In this one sentence, Clinton hedged his judgment on Munich four times: "maybe," "a little slow," "you could argue," and "in hindsight.") A year later he told a military audience that the "World War II generation truly saved the world."[7] But for Clinton, the 1930s and early 1940s were history, not personal experience, and while he accepted, also in hindsight, America's Cold War policy of containment, he obviously opposed its application in Vietnam. Indeed, his own avoidance of military service during the Vietnam War became a political liability during the 1992 presidential election campaign, and undoubtedly contributed to his great reluctance, once in office, to discuss the Vietnam War or its lessons unless the press raised the issues. Clinton did once volunteer, however, that "the only lesson [of] Vietnam is that you can't fight someone else's fight for them. You can't do that. There is a limit to what you can do for someone else."[8] In this declaration Clinton essentially restated the essence of the Nixon Doctrine. But he also implied that if the Vietnam War was instructive on the issue of whether to fight, it contained no lessons on how best to employ force once a decision was made to use it. Certainly his own uses of force reflected no appreciation of what the Vietnam War might have taught about how—and how not—to use force.

Clinton's threatened and actual uses of force in the former Yugoslavia during the 1990s revealed unwillingness to risk significant military means to achieve declared political objectives. One observer commented that Clinton's "primary goal" in Bosnia "was not sending U.S. troops to Bosnia."[9] Clinton was never self-confident when it came to using force, and both he and the Pentagon viewed the collapsing former Yugoslavia as a beckoning potential quagmire. Both were convinced, and not without reason, that even light U.S. casualties would politically torpedo any U.S. military intervention. Indeed, following the American debacle in

Somalia and the terrorist attack on Khobar Towers, a billet for U.S. military personnel in Saudi Arabia, the Pentagon became so "force protection"–minded that by the end of the 1990s it seemed to be placing the safety of U.S. troops above the success of their military missions. Accordingly, in the former Yugoslavia, force was either not threatened at all, threatened without the will to use it, or used with such caution as to jeopardize the achievement of political objectives. As two critics characterized the Clinton approach in the wake of the war over Kosovo, "Using force in small amounts to send messages, deflect domestic political pressure, or attempt to affect the course of a difficult negotiation in progress is generally ill-advised. It conveys weakness rather than strength—a sense that the use of force is based on the *hope* that it will be effective rather than on the *certainty*."[10]

The most prominent advertisement of U.S. military timidity was the administration's restriction of force to air power alone. Throughout the wars in the former Yugoslavia, Clinton repeatedly declared that U.S. ground forces were off the table as a tool of U.S. military intervention except as posthostilities peace enforcers. Predictably, this encouraged compensatory Serbian ground action and defiance of U.S. and international ultimatums.

As the United States approached war against Serbia, the Clinton administration and the professional military leadership regarded deployment of ground troops to combat as a Rubicon not to be crossed under any circumstances. Public and congressional support even for aerial bombing was always problematic (in part because of weak presidential leadership), and Capitol Hill was resolutely opposed to putting U.S. ground troops in harm's way in the Balkans. The parallels with Vietnam seemed apparent to all concerned: the former Yugoslavia was strategically peripheral to core U.S. security interests, and the commitment, unless immediately successful, of even a small U.S. ground force to the fighting in what amounted to a messy civil war would generate irresistible pressure to commit reinforcements.[11] Those who were resisting Serbian aggression on the ground—Bosnian Muslims, Croatians, and, later, Albanian Kosovars—could have served as potential surrogates for U.S. ground troops, but the Clinton administration, notwithstanding its genuine outrage over Serb atrocities, was not prepared, absent allied consent, to arm and train them. Until 1995, the Clinton administration was politically boxed in by NATO allies, who had lightly armed and ridiculously irrelevant "peacekeeping" forces in Bosnia. Bombing the Serbs, lifting the arms embargo against Bosnia, or both would have exposed those forces to Serb retaliation. U.S. military action became possible only when the allies' peacekeeping contingents were reinforced. Even in Kosovo, where a friendly peacekeeping presence was not an obstacle, the United States kept the Kosovo Liberation Army (KLA) at arm's length.

The Clinton administration thus fell between two stools when it came to using force in the Balkans. On the one hand, it was extremely reluctant to expose U.S. forces to danger there; on the other hand, it was equally reluctant to develop local surrogate forces that in the end might have obviated the need for the U.S. bombing campaigns that it did launch in 1995 and 1999. The Nixon Doctrine also sought to limit U.S. liability by curbing U.S. ground forces' exposure to combat on behalf of clients who were supposed to shoulder the primary manpower burden for their own defense. But the Nixon Doctrine called for the deliberate cultivation of local surrogates through arms transfers and training programs as well. How differently might events in the former Yugoslavia have unfolded had the Clinton administration been prepared to provide the Bosnian Muslims and the Kosovo Liberation Army with even a tiny fraction of the military assistance the Nixon administration lavished on the shah of Iran?

The Clinton administration in 1993 inherited both a savage war in Bosnia and a JCS chairman, Colin Powell, doggedly opposed to any U.S. military involvement in the former Yugoslavia.[12] Indeed, the Pentagon was constantly serving up to intervention proponents on Capitol Hill and elsewhere grossly inflated estimates of the number of U.S. troops required to stop the Serbs and avoid another Vietnam.[13] Powell subtly warned President-elect Clinton in his *Foreign Affairs* article that "if force is used imprecisely out of frustration rather than clear analysis, the situation can be made worse," adding: "We should always be skeptical when so-called experts suggest that all a particular crisis calls for is a little surgical bombing or a limited attack."[14] Yet the war continued for two more years not only because the United States and its European allies refused to use the necessary force but also because they lacked the will to use force effectively. Serbian forces literally got away with murder—indeed, genocidal acts on a scale not witnessed in Europe since the Holocaust— mainly because America's political and military leadership viewed the conflict through the lens of Vietnam, not Munich. In his exhaustive examination of the West's dismal diplomatic performance in the former Yugoslavia during the first half of the 1990s, James Gow concluded: "If there was an overall policy failure, its central feature was the absence of armed force as a bottom line. The reason for that absence was a lack of 'political will' to act forcefully in a transitional situation that appeared to be both laced with risk and not absolutely indispensable." The lack of will was attributable to Western politicians' fear that what lay waiting for them in the Balkans was "another Northern Ireland, Dien Bien Phu, or broader Vietnam," and "particularly critical in this respect was the shadow of Vietnam hanging over U.S. political and military leaders."[15]

Richard Holbrooke, the American diplomatic troubleshooter who brokered the 1995 Dayton Accords that ended the Bosnian War, also remarked on the cause-and-effect relationship between memories of Vietnam and the professional military's aversion to any Balkan intervention: "Vietnam was, of course, the seminal event of our generation. By 1995, its shadows were lengthening, but they had marked almost every contemporary official and politician in Washington—some as student radicals, others as Vietnam veterans; some as doves, others as hawks." In recounting the military's opposition to extra bombing to force the Serbs to negotiate a settlement, Holbrooke continued, "There was irony in my support of air strikes. As a young Foreign Service Officer working in Vietnam, I had disagreed with the air campaign against North Vietnam." But Holbrooke recognized that military opinion failed—or chose not—to recognize key differences between Vietnam and Bosnia. "The comparison was dangerously misleading. While we had to learn from Vietnam, we could not be imprisoned by it. Bosnia was not Vietnam, the Serbs were not the Vietcong, and Belgrade was not Hanoi. The Bosnian Serbs, poorly trained as bullies and criminals, would not stand up to NATO air strikes the way the seasoned and indoctrinated Vietcong and North Vietnamese had. And . . . Belgrade was not going to back the Bosnian Serbs the way Hanoi had backed the Vietcong."[16]

The one senior administration official who from the beginning saw events in the former Yugoslavia more through the lens of Munich than Vietnam was UN ambassador and later secretary of state Madeleine Albright. "My mindset is Munich, not Vietnam," she often told people.[17] An insightful study of her approach to diplomacy observes that Albright "missed one of Vietnam's crucial lessons for modern policymakers: the ability of relatively weak countries or groups to defy the powerful, to reject the collective advice or instruction of the big powers, and to use unconventional methods to gain their objectives."[18] Albright apparently had more confidence in the U.S. military's potential effectiveness in the Balkans than did the Pentagon itself. She certainly lamented the Vietnam syndrome, which she believed made the United States "afraid to use power. The tragedy of Vietnam is that there . . . [were] people . . . in the [Clinton administration] who felt that the use of power was something alien to America, because it had been misused [in Vietnam]. I think that what we needed to do was to get at the selective use of power instead of saying 'We can't do that.'"[19] Yet dismissing the "we can't do that" view implied that U.S. military power, backed by sufficient determination to use it, was irresistible. The inherently limited political effectiveness of conventional military power against enemies practicing unconventional, asymmetrical warfare and having a far greater strength of interest in the fight seems to have escaped her. "We can't do that" can be a code for "We don't *want* to do that," or it can reflect a genuine appreciation of the limits of U.S. military power in a specific set of circumstances.

The Vietnam War did not discredit U.S. military power per se; rather, it underscored the limited utility of conventional Western military power in a revolutionary or otherwise unconventional Third World setting. The secretary of state might have taken note of this fact in Somalia, where a low-technology but slippery adversary inflicted a failed intervention on the Clinton administration.

By the time the Kosovo crisis erupted, she and others within the administration had come to see Slobodan Milosevic as a Balkan Hitler bent on toppling dominoes in the former Yugoslavia and in the process destabilizing Europe and jeopardizing the very integrity of NATO. Albright, who as a Czech refugee was forced to flee her homeland when the Nazis arrived in Prague in 1939 and again nine years later when the Soviets overthrew the noncommunist government, "saw events through the prism of the pre-world war disaster of appeasing dictators, i.e., the Munich syndrome," William Hyland observed.[20] Certainly she seemed to see a link between Milosevic and Hitler. At one point in the fruitless negotiations over Kosovo at Rambouillet in 1999, Albright responded to an aide's suggestion of compromise with, "Where do you think we are, Munich?"[21]

Indeed, in the months leading up to the war over Kosovo, both Albright and Clinton raised the specter of falling dominoes. Declared Clinton, who may or may not have employed the Munich analogy to interpret Serbian behavior but who certainly saw it as a means of mobilizing public and congressional opinion: "What if someone had listened to Winston Churchill and stood up to Adolph Hitler earlier? How many people's lives might have been saved? And how many American lives might have been saved?"[22] Clinton also spoke of the need to "defuse a powder keg in the heart of Europe" because "all the ingredients of a major war are present," noting that World War I began in Sarajevo.[23] Clinton subsequently referred to the "tinderbox of the Balkans," concluding that "the time to put out a fire is before it spreads and burns down the neighborhood."[24] For her part, Albright told an audience at the U.S. Institute for Peace that "twice before in this century, American soldiers in huge numbers have been drawn to Europe to fight wars that either began in the Balkans or that sparked bitter fighting there." She also declared the lesson of Bosnia to be that "we can pay early, or we can pay much more later . . . in dollars lost, in lost credibility, and in human lives."[25] In their biography of Milosevic, Dusko Doder and Louise Branson postulated that the Serbian dictator "became for Albright a metaphor for the same evil that had forced her family to flee their native Czechoslovakia . . . after Munich in 1938."[26]

Only in 1995 was there an intersection of events in Bosnia that produced a firm U.S. use-of-force decision that broke the political will of the Bosnian Serbs. First came the UN-NATO failure to protect the UN-declared "safe area" of the town of Srebrenica, where Bosnian Serb forces committed the worst act of genocide in Europe since Auschwitz. Then came the CNN-filmed carnage of a Serb mortar shell explosion in Sarajevo's marketplace. For both the Clinton administration and other NATO governments, the political and moral embarrassment of continuing to do nothing decisive was no longer acceptable. Clinton himself recognized that his administration's policy of making idle threats was "doing enormous damage to the United States and to our standing in the world. We look weak."[27] The administration and NATO finally decided to act by authorizing major air strikes against Bosnian Serb military targets, which began August 30 under the name Operation Deliberate Force. Third, a few days before air strikes began, the Milosevic regime in Belgrade decided to cut its losses in Bosnia and negotiate for the Bosnian Serbs—not in their interests but in Serbia's. Fourth, and probably most important, was the collapse of the Bosnian Serb military position on the ground. A Croatian invasion supported by a Bosnian Muslim offensive (followed by NATO bombing) broke the back of Bosnian Serb military power. These offensives accomplished what the United States and its NATO allies were never prepared to do: change the military facts on the ground by direct means *on* the ground.

Yet even with the painful experience of Bosnia so recently behind it, the Clinton administration displayed no greater fortitude in dealing with the subsequent Kosovo crisis. In his book on the war over Kosovo, Michael Ignatieff observed: "Military force is credible only to the extent that the will that uses it is credible. Since self-doubt is always obvious to an enemy, it can negate the effect of [military] superiority. If an opponent doubts our commitment to use force, we are then forced to use force, not in service of a strategic objective of our own choosing, but because our bluff has been called. Such was the case in Kosovo."[28] During the war over Kosovo, Milosevic himself declared, in a television interview that was shown to American audiences, that NATO's crushing military superiority was offset by the fact that "you are not willing to sacrifice lives to achieve our surrender; but we are willing to die to defend our rights as an independent sovereign state."[29]

Indeed, U.S. behavior before and during Operation Allied Force constituted the most dramatic display to date of the Vietnam syndrome at work and its operational and political consequences for American foreign policy. Initial threats of force were made, only to have Belgrade call the bluff. Right down until the last few days before the first U.S. bombs hit Serbian targets, Milosevic apparently did not believe that the Clinton administration would use force—certainly major force—against him because of America's well-established reputation for military timidity in the Balkans and elsewhere. When the use of force finally came, it was immediately evident that the Clinton administration, with the full support of the Pentagon and NATO, was prepared to place the safety of U.S. troops above that of their most important mission: halting the ethnic cleansing of Kosovo. The administration publicly renounced any ground combat option and restricted air operations to fifteen thousand feet and above. These conditions not only made it impossible to interfere with ethnic cleansing; they encouraged its acceleration. Thus, obsession with protecting the military means precluded satisfaction of the immediate political end.

It was, in fact, evident at the time, and is indisputable in retrospect, that the Clinton administration believed that the *Serbs* were bluffing, that a couple of days of token bombing would force Milosevic to throw in the towel. Moreover, it is apparent that neither Clinton nor the extremely hawkish Albright fully recognized that an immediate and savage Serb response on the ground in Kosovo was the logical—indeed only— response to the launching of a NATO air campaign on behalf of the Albanian Kosovars. Ignatieff's analysis makes the administration's responsibility in the massacre clear: "Faced with war from the air, [Milosevic] decided to finish his war on the Kosovars. NATO's war provided perfect cover for his war."[30] Eliot Cohen's judgment is harsher still: "It was absurd to think that the stylized air operations that began this conflict could prevent bands of men with automatic weapons from driving off or shooting civilians in Kosovo. Secretary of State Madeleine Albright rightly resents the notion that she and the administration are morally responsible for the predictable slaughter that occurred; but they were appallingly naïve if they expected anything else."[31]

The accelerated ethnic cleansing of Kosovo sparked by Operation Allied Force had a potentially decisive—and catastrophic—strategic payoff: it flooded neighboring countries with hundreds of thousands of refugees, whose presence in turn threatened to destabilize southeastern Europe and even to split the NATO alliance on the wisdom of pursuing further military action against Serbia. On this score, though, Milosevic greatly miscalculated. Television coverage of the terrified refugees being driven out of Kosovo backfired on Belgrade. The program of accelerating ethnic cleansing was a public relations disaster that hardened, not weakened, NATO's resolve. People being rounded up, beaten, stripped of their belongings, and sent off on terrible journeys evoked memories of the Holocaust caused by the democracies' failure to stand up to Hitler in the 1930s.

A comparison of the Clinton administration's approach to using force against Serbia with the Johnson administration's approach in Vietnam is revealing.[32] The Johnson administration in 1965, unlike the Clinton administration in 1999, selected military means consistent with the political objective sought: to prevent South Vietnam's takeover by communist ground forces. When it became clear that air power alone could not satisfy that objective, Johnson committed U.S. ground combat forces. Moreover, those ground forces succeeded, albeit at great cost in blood and domestic political dissension, in preventing a communist victory until they were finally withdrawn. Indeed, in 1965 the Johnson administration was at an enormous disadvantage vis-à-vis the Clinton administration in 1999: the Munich-seared policy makers of the former did not have the experience of Vietnam to inform their decision making. They had instead the great victory of World War II and the half victory of Korea; the painful lessons of Vietnam were yet to be learned. Nor did the Johnson administration have available the experience of the Gulf War. The Vietnam and Gulf Wars bulged with instruction on how to use—and how not to use— force effectively, and the availability of both experiences imposed on the

Clinton White House an especially heavy burden to get it right against Serbia.

Yet President Clinton, determined to avoid a Balkan Vietnam and constrained in any event by like-minded and even more fainthearted NATO allies, opted for a no-ground–limited-air use of force aimed at coercing Serbia into accepting the terms declared at the failed prewar negotiations at Rambouillet. This choice of military means was irrelevant to the immediate goal of stopping the Serbian rampage in Kosovo; it also ignored a discouraging record of air power's employment in the past as a means of diplomatic coercion.

The Johnson administration did have the record of the World War II U.S. strategic bombing campaigns against Germany and Japan available for examination and policy guidance. But since those campaigns were hardly examples of coercive diplomacy, their relevance to the decision initially to employ air power as a means of coercing Hanoi to cease its support for revolution in the south was highly questionable. By the time Operation Allied Force was launched some thirty-four years later, however, there was no basis, at least in Washington, for confidence in bombing alone as a tool of coercion. The Clinton administration had for guidance not only the Johnson and Nixon administrations' experience in Vietnam, but also the experience of the Gulf War and the following decade's coercive air and cruise missile attacks against Iraqi targets, as well as the experience of Bosnia, where air strikes succeeded in coercing only in combination with a major Croatian and Bosnian Muslim offensive on the ground. It is not unreasonable to assume, in fact, that Milosevic's prewar refusal to buckle over Kosovo in the face of threatened U.S. air action was encouraged by Saddam Hussein's survival of Operation Desert Fox in December 1998. Desert Fox was a U.S.-British bombing campaign aimed at forcing the Iraqi dictator to stop obstructing UN arms inspections monitors. Yet seventy hours of bombing failed to force the return of the monitors. Milosevic could only have been encouraged by the example.[33]

In the end, the United States and its NATO allies even fudged on the settlement terms. At Rambouillet the United States had demanded a NATO-authorized and NATO-only occupation force in Kosovo and on-demand NATO inspections of suspect military sites in the remainder of Serbia. Additionally, Serbia was to agree to a plebiscite in Kosovo within three years to determine Kosovo's political future—which would have meant a certain vote for independence. Yet representatives from the G-8 countries (the Group of Seven plus Russia), who served as the negotiating team for NATO, cut a settlement that substituted a UN-authorized occupation force that included Russian and other non-NATO forces. The G-8 negotiators also dropped the insistence on NATO inspections inside the rest of Serbia and made no provision for a self-determination vote. Moreover, Serbian army forces in the field survived the war virtually unscathed by hunkering down in caves and beneath concrete and camouflage, and above all by not moving. Thus the army emerged from the war not only capable of further aggression but also understandably convinced that it had not been defeated. These facts are not altered by Milosevic's political overthrow seventeen months later.

Exactly what role the bombing played in Milosevic's decision to accept NATO's terms remains unclear, a fact conceded by the U.S. Defense Department's own report to the Congress on the war. Unquestionably, the mounting damage inflicted on Serbia's infrastructure and specific "regime" targets and Serbia's inability to damage NATO forces affected Milosevic's decision. Yet "other extremely important factors were also at work in precipitating Milosevic's capitulation," the report concludes, including NATO's own intensifying political solidarity, Russia's diplomatic defection to the G-7 (making it the G-8), mounting KLA attacks on Serb forces, and growing indications that NATO was reconsidering its abjuration of ground combat options.[34] There was, too, the G-8's softening of the original Rambouillet terms.

The Vietnam syndrome's governance of U.S. behavior during the Kosovo crisis of 1999 continued after the hostilities ceased. As in Bosnia, the Pentagon recoiled from assuming any peace-enforcement tasks beyond those of maintaining a cease-fire. It shunned involvement in any activities, such as hunting down war criminals and policing civil disorder, related to political and social reconstruction for fear that involvement would suck U.S. forces into renewed hostilities. Indeed, the primary mission of the U.S. peace-enforcement contingents remained the same as that of U.S. combat forces during Operation Allied Force: self-protection. Unlike other national contingents, which were stationed in small units among the population of Kosovo, most of the sixty-three hundred troops of the U.S. contingent lived apart in relative luxury. In an expression of "force protection and casualty aversion run amuck," they were based at 775-acre, heavily fortified Camp Bondsteel, and were permitted to venture outside only with body armor and Kevlar helmets and only in helicopters or convoys of armored fighting vehicles.[35] By comparison, British troops, with their long experience in imperial policing operations, were widely dispersed among the civilian population, with small groups billeted in apartments and houses in tense neighborhoods. They patrolled on foot in small numbers without armored vests or helmets, which put them in much closer touch with local residents and events. The Pentagon's obsession with force protection, epitomized by Camp Bondsteel, the largest U.S. military base constructed since the Vietnam War, quickly became the butt of jokes by other peace-enforcement contingents.[36]

How influential and useful were the Munich and Vietnam War analogies in shaping the Clinton administration's policy in Bosnia and Kosovo? Clearly, fear of another Vietnam played a stronger role than fear of the consequences of not stopping Serbian aggression. Had it been the other way around, the United States would have used decisive force against Milosevic much earlier than it did. Only Madeleine Albright seems from the very beginning to have regarded Serb aggression in the former Yugoslavia exclusively through the lens of Munich. She was consistently in the forefront in arguing for force and seemed completely free of Vietnam syndrome infection. Yet, in both Bosnia (1995) and Kosovo (1999), the Clinton administration finally resorted to major force for the very same reason that the democracies should have acted against Hitler in 1938: the need to preserve strategic credibility in order to prevent worse things from happening. For the United States and its NATO allies, Serbian aggression was not the ultimate issue in Bosnia and Kosovo. In terms of the scope of his ambitions and his capacity to act on them, Milosevic was no Hitler; and at no time did his actions threaten to provoke a repeat of the Balkan-sparked great powers clash that became World War I. (The Clinton administration's deployment of the 1914 analogy in 1999 was ludicrous. In 1999, all but one of Europe's great powers were in alliance with each other, and the odd power out, Russia, lacked the desire and capacity for military intervention in the Balkans.) The ultimate issue was the fate of the Atlantic alliance itself. Failure to act decisively against Belgrade's bloody bid for a greater Serbia would have raised fundamental questions about NATO's very purpose and relevance in the post–Cold War era, and no member of NATO was prepared to countenance the alliance's dissolution in order to avoid risk in the former Yugoslavia. Thus NATO itself was the domino threatened by alliance inaction against Serbia.

Yet if the Munich analogy played a belated role in the decision to use force in Bosnia and over Kosovo, once those decisions were made, the Vietnam analogy produced a timid application of force. Those who regarded the decision to intervene in Vietnam as a disastrous mistake seemingly failed to recognize that the war that followed offered serious instruction on how—and how not—to use force.

Holbrooke was certainly right in dismissing comparisons between Ho Chi Minh and Milosevic, Serbia and North Vietnam, and Bosnian Serb forces and the Viet Cong. Nor can any legitimate comparison be made between the victims of Serbian aggression and the South Vietnamese whom the United States picked as clients in Indochina. The war in Vietnam was a war largely among Vietnamese, whereas Milosevic's wars were ethnically based and driven. Victims of genocide and ethnic cleansing do not need much political motivation to fight back; the Croats and Bosnian Muslims never lacked the will to fight, whereas will was always a problem for the far better equipped South Vietnamese military forces. And surely the Clinton administration's very self-prohibition of ground combat options in Bosnia and Kosovo rendered even a small-scale repetition of Vietnam in the Balkans impossible.

On the other hand, the "quagmire" fear—the most powerful metaphor for the Vietnam War—cannot be easily dismissed in terms of the political and military obligations imposed by intervention in the former Yugoslavia. Although virtually bloodless for the Pentagon, Operations Deliberate Force and Allied Force incurred open-ended obligations to maintain the absence of war in Bosnia and Kosovo. Moreover, since neither military operation addressed the underlying political sources of the violence (which would have required, among other things, replacing the Milosevic regime in Belgrade), the United States set itself up for an indefinite drain on its already overtaxed military resources in a region peripheral to traditional U.S. security interests. Worse yet is the prospect of military humiliation à la Lebanon and Somalia: given the fragility of public and congressional support for a continued U.S. military presence in the Balkans, even a small attack on U.S. forces that draws blood may prompt a unilateral American withdrawal.

✳ ✳ ✳

The term *quagmire* was also enlisted by congressional and other opponents of the Clinton's administration's 1994 invasion of Haiti. Operation Restore Democracy removed a venal, drug-trafficking military dictatorship and restored the democratically elected government the junta had overthrown in 1991. It was primarily a value-driven intervention, although removal of the despotic Raoul Cedras regime was also intended to staunch the flow of unwanted Haitian refugees into the United States.

The invasion was bloodless, but it commanded little domestic political support beyond that of liberal Democrats and the Congressional Black Caucus. Because the U.S. occupation of Haiti passed virtually without violence, however, it was tolerated on Capitol Hill.

Characteristically, in John Sweeney's view, Clinton's decision to move on Haiti was the product of domestic political pressures and concerns. He "wanted to get the Congressional Black Caucus and African-American leaders off his back, he hoped to stop the flood of Haitian boat refugees who were undermining the gubernatorial prospects of Florida's governor Lawton Chiles, and he was determined to show a skeptical American public that he was a tough and decisive leader—albeit after months of waffling and being humiliated by the thugs who had ousted [President Jean-Bertrand] Aristide."[37] In William Hyland's analysis, Clinton paid attention to foreign policy only when he had to, and never "displayed strong convictions about what American foreign policy should accomplish, 'except to please the voters.'"[38] Moreover, he unwittingly allowed his policy of economically sanctioning the Cedras regime to paint the United States into the corner of military action; the sanctions accelerated the very flow of Haitian refugees into the United States that made the absence of military action a growing domestic political liability.

The Munich analogy was neither employed nor deployed on behalf of the invasion because it was manifestly irrelevant. Nor was the Vietnam War analogy of much assistance even to Clinton's critics. The Haitian military was a professional joke, and its unpopularity at home was obvious. There was never any prospect of effective military or popular "guerrilla" resistance to U.S. occupation.

Yet the Vietnam War—and its most recent analog, the debacle in Somalia—significantly influenced the crisis behavior of both the Clinton administration and the Cedras regime. As in the Balkans, U.S. military action was belated, hesitant, and launched in the wake of repeated declarations of threats that turned out to be bluffs. The spectacle of an American warship—the *Harlan County*—turning tail before a dockside mob of regime thugs in Port-au-Prince (eight days after the deadly shootout in Mogadishu) exquisitely captured the degree to which the Clinton administration was infected by the Vietnam syndrome.[39] Also as in the Balkans, the target of U.S. military action was quite skeptical of American will to use force. Cedras was convinced that the United States meant business only after two days of intense discussions in Port-au-Prince with former president Jimmy Carter, former chairman of the Joint Chiefs of Staff

Colin Powell, and Senate Armed Services Committee chairman Sam Nunn, all of whom warned Cedras that invasion was a certainty unless he left the country immediately.[40]

The Vietnam syndrome was further evident in the narrowness of the military postinvasion occupation mission. The Pentagon had opposed Operation Restore Democracy from the start,[41] and once Aristide had been restored to power it essentially confined the U.S. military mission to force protection pure and simple. Eschewed were any tasks that could be remotely tagged "nation building," including disarming the Cedras regime's police and goon squads, who continued to terrorize the population. Thus the underlying political and economic sources of Haiti's seemingly perpetual misery were left undisturbed, inviting further U.S. military intervention in the future. "You might think that when a magnificent army invades and, with nary a shot fired, conquers, they would then at least *imagine* themselves in control of a society they now occupied, but that was not the case here," observed Bob Shacochis in *The Immaculate Invasion,* his devastating and highly critical portrayal of events in Haiti. "U.S. soldiers had invaded Haiti for the primary purpose of protecting themselves. Stopping the brutality wasn't in the mission. The Haitian military was supposed to police itself while the agencies and departments and Aristide himself sorted everything out."[42]

The Clinton administration's uncertain approach to the use of force was the product of some combination of presidential personality, generational change, and the disappearance of the Cold War. His successor, George W. Bush, has quite a different personality but is of Clinton's political generation. Bush, moreover, must make his use-of-force decisions, as did Clinton, in a post–Cold War era of great strategic ambiguity and in the absence of domestic political consensus on the organizing principle of American foreign policy.

9

Legacies of Munich
and Vietnam for the
Post–Cold War World

"As awful as Kosovo is now," wrote former secretary of defense Robert McNamara during NATO's war against Serbia, "the odds of a long-term tragedy will be far greater if we don't apply the lessons the Vietnam conflict taught us. In fact, my greatest concern is that we and our adversaries may have already made mistakes that might have been avoided had we learned from experience. Studying the lessons of the Vietnam War may allow us to end this war earlier; ignoring them may result in catastrophe."[1]

McNamara's judgment on NATO's air assault on Serbia testifies simultaneously to the continuing influence of the Vietnam War analogy and the poor reasoning that analogy can promote and has promoted. McNamara's statement together with his two anguished books on the Vietnam War exhibit not only a remarkable inattention to the great differences separating U.S. use of force in Indochina in the 1960s and in the Balkans in the late 1990s, but also a continuing befuddlement over the sources of the U.S. defeat in Vietnam.[2]

There never was a Balkan Vietnam lying in wait for the United States, although opponents of intervention in the former Yugoslavia invoked the specter of a bloody morass. Precisely because of the experience of Vietnam, American policy makers from the start limited U.S. military liability in southeastern Europe in a way that Lyndon Johnson did not in Southeast Asia. They did so at considerable cost in military effectiveness, but it was a price the Clinton administration was willing to pay. But even if the

United States had not been burdened by the Vietnam syndrome, the objective strategic and operational circumstances it faced in the Balkans were dramatically more favorable to success than were those thirty years earlier in Indochina. Not the least of America's relative advantages in the Balkans was a Serbian military that could not hope to match the awesome fighting power of the Vietnamese Communists. Indeed, given American air supremacy and the coercive intent of Operation Allied Force, the United States did not even have to directly engage Serbian forces in the field in order to compel Belgrade to accept NATO's terms. Hanoi, in addition to its superior combat experience and willingness to sacrifice, enjoyed powerful political and military support from the Soviet Union and China, whereas Serbia was diplomatically and territorially isolated. North Vietnam also was a more effective police state than Serbia, and it had less regime-sensitive infrastructure that could be bombed effectively.

The Vietnam War was thus not a particularly useful guide to policy makers grappling with events in the former Yugoslavia, although it exerted a powerful influence on decisions of when and how to use force. Indeed, the instructiveness of the Vietnam War's lessons, certainly as those lessons are enshrined in the Weinberger-Powell Doctrine, is questionable on several counts in the post–Cold War era of small wars of choice (as opposed to the earlier large wars of necessity).

First, to the extent that the doctrine purports to be a warning against another Vietnam, it is almost certainly unnecessary. The very experience of the Vietnam War remains the greatest obstacle to its repetition. And even if it were not, there are probably no more Vietnams—certainly on the scale of U.S. intervention in Southeast Asia in the 1960s—lying in wait for the United States anywhere in the world. The Cold War's end has reduced the strategic importance to the United States of most of the nonindustrial world, thereby eliminating a critical condition promoting *major* use of force there. Even if one accepted George Kennan's judgment in 1946 that the Third World was of little value in the U.S.-Soviet global struggle, successive administrations nonetheless made commitments to Third World countries and in so doing made America the guarantor of their security.

More to the point, there is probably no nonindustrial state or faction, now or in the foreseeable future, that could replicate the remarkable performance of Vietnamese communist forces in Indochina from 1945 to 1975. Iranian Pasdaran, Nicaraguan Sandinistas, Lebanese militia, Iraqi Republican Guards, Somali "technicals," and Serbian gunners may be strategically vexing and tactically dangerous, but in skill, tenacity, and discipline none of them hold a candle to North Vietnamese army regulars and the main force Viet Cong of the 1960s. Additionally, the United States, in part because of its experience in Vietnam, is generally more selective in picking new clients in the Third World. Indeed, the very phenomenon of peasant-based insurgencies of the kind the United States confronted in the early 1960s in Vietnam is receding with the Third World's rapid urbanization and the defeudalization of its remaining rural populations. Even in Colombia, where U.S. military advisers are working with government forces waging war against a drug-financed insurgency, the likelihood of a slide down the slippery slope to direct U.S. ground combat intervention is low. There is no sentiment for such intervention because of the Vietnam experience, because the war in Colombia is manifestly a civil conflict, and because no president since Theodore Roosevelt has argued that Colombia or events in that country pose any threat to core U.S. security interests. Illegal drug use is an internal threat to public health, not an external threat to the security of the American state.

Second, the doctrine's injunctions that vital interests must be at stake and that the United States should fight only wars it intends to win beg the question of criteria for "vital" and "winning." Beyond the defense of U.S. territory and citizens, there is no consensus on what constitutes vital U.S. interests. In fact, since the end of the Second World War, few areas of the world have escaped presidential declarations of vitality; for obvious reasons, presidents contemplating military intervention have displayed a penchant for pronouncing the stakes at hand to be vital. Were Quemoy and Matsu, Vietnam, and Lebanon really vital to U.S. interests? Did Europe, in confronting Serbia in 1999, really stand on the same precipice that it stood on in 1914? NSC-68 was explicitly indiscriminate in weighing the consequences of a single defeat in the global struggle against communism: "In the context of the present polarization of power a defeat of free institutions anywhere is a defeat everywhere."[3] But was every square meter of noncommunist territory, be it in Germany, Japan, Botswana, or Paraguay, really equal in value? Weinberger's own support of the 1983 U.S. invasion of tiny Grenada, hardly a country capable of passing the vital interest test, suggests that, as Michael Handel put it, "whenever political and military leaders feel certain of success and are ready to commit troops to combat, they will always find a convincing explanation as to why the contemplated action protects and enhances the vital interests of their country."[4]

Michael Kinsley argued that "if you wish to claim world leadership—which we do—you have to be willing to use your strength for something other than self-protection."[5] With power comes responsibility. Great powers are in the business of protecting others as well as maintaining the stability of the international system that serves their power and interests. Great powers are therefore in the business of defending allies and others who look to them for security. They are also in the business of policing instability in situations in which instability, if unchecked, might ultimately become a direct threat to their security. A great power cannot restrict its use of military force to the defense of its territory and population and expect others to follow its lead in the dangerous and unpredictable arena of international politics. Munich epitomized the abdication by Great Britain and France of their great power responsibilities to maintain the European order. The consequence was World War II. In contrast, President George Bush's reaction to Iraq's invasion of Kuwait reflected an understanding of America's responsibilities as the world's sole remaining superpower. On August 2, 1990, Kuwait was a stridently anti-Israeli sheikdom to which the United States had no defense commitment. Yet U.S. acceptance of Iraq's conquest of Kuwait would have encouraged other nations to violate the established principle of nonaggression and would have placed Saddam Hussein in a position to create an even greater threat to the United States and its indispensable Gulf ally, Saudi Arabia.

None of this is meant to argue for indiscriminate U.S. military engagement overseas. Strength of interest, considerations of feasibility, and both quantitative and qualitative limits on U.S. military power dictate selective engagement. The fact that containment was indiscriminately applied in Vietnam on behalf of a feckless ally with disastrous results is not a convincing argument for refusing force in every circumstance not involving direct threats to the United States, its citizens, and its declared allies.

Except in total war, "winning" is an elusive concept. Most wars are limited in their political and military objectives, and it is difficult—the Vietnam War being an excellent case in point—to translate political goals into military ones. It is also quite possible to win militarily but to lose, or at least not win, politically. Wars that successfully reverse aggression but leave the aggressor in place to fight another day can be hollow victories. Winning wars is not the same as ending them. The victors of World War I threw away the possibility for an enduring peace by imposing the Treaty of Versailles on the losers. Additionally, the course of hostilities itself can dramatically alter war aims. As Colin Gray so rightly pointed out, "the strategic fact of historical experience is that once the dice of war are rolled, policy achievement is largely hostage to military performance."[6] Military success encourages inflation of war aims, while failure can impose contraction of those aims and even complete capitulation to the enemy's terms for war termination. In Korea, U.S. war aims gyrated, as America's military fortunes moved from near-defeat to spectacular success to eventual stalemate, from restoration of South Korea's territorial integrity to reunifying the whole peninsula under American auspices to a willingness to settle on the status quo ante. Moreover, new aims can emerge during a war that simply could not have been anticipated at the beginning of hostilities. The Truman administration's refusal to forcibly repatriate Chinese prisoners of war was the major sticking point in the Panmunjom negotiations during the last year of the Korean War, but this war aim arose only after Truman's decision to fight in Korea. Mapping out prehostilities "exit strategies" is fine as long as there is recognition that war's dynamics can alter and even wreck such strategies.

Powell's call for "overwhelming force" is another way of formulating Weinberger's insistence on a determination to win. Overwhelming force was employed in Grenada, Panama, and the Persian Gulf against enemies either too small and weak to offer much resistance or too short-sighted to try to prevent the assembling of such force. But crushing military superiority is not something that can be simply dialed up when desired; on the contrary, it is a rare commodity against determined and intelligent enemies, who can be counted on to resist its mustering. If George Washington had insisted on the certainty of swift victory via over-whelming force, the Union Jack might still be flying in the capital city that today bears his name. Additionally, greatly superior conventional military power can be offset by unconventional styles of warfare. In Korea, Chinese night infiltration tactics stalemated U.S. conventional military superiority. In Indochina, Hanoi's revolutionary warfare and superior political will ultimately drove the United States out of South Vietnam. It is easy to beat up the helpless and incompetent; the challenge lies in pre-vailing over first-team enemies, or at least those clever enough to make it a real contest.

In any event, "winning" may not entail the destruction or even the significant damaging of enemy military forces. NATO defeated Serbia in 1999 without inflicting serious losses on Serbian ground forces in Kosovo, which remained more or less intact during the seventy-eight-day war

and subsequently evacuated Kosovo defiantly and in good order. Likewise, the United States won the forty-year Cold War without ever engaging Soviet military forces. The foundation of that victory was successfully
threatened uses of force (such as contained, for example, in the NATO
treaty and President Kennedy's Cuban missile crisis speech of October
22, 1962, and implicit in post-1950 levels of U.S. defense expenditure)
that deterred a hot war. Indeed, threatened and even actual uses of force
to coerce an adversary usually take place outside the boundary of war
precisely because their very object may be to deter war rather than to
wage it. In his rejoinder to Weinberger's famous speech on the use of
force, Secretary of State George Shultz conceded that "nations must be
able to protect themselves when faced with an obvious threat," adding
that "we learned the lesson of the 1930s—that appeasement of an aggressor only invites aggression and increases the danger of war." "But," won-
dered Shultz, "what about those gray areas that lie somewhere between
all-out war and blissful harmony? How do we protect the peace without
being able to resort to the ultimate sanction of military power against
those who seek to destroy peace?"[7]

Third, the Weinberger-Powell Doctrine's insistence on public support
ignores both the influence of military performance (an exhilarating victory is likely to generate enthusiastic public support) and the irrelevance
of public support to swift military enterprises (e.g., the invasion of Grenada). Even unpopular, more time-consuming interventions (e.g., the invasion and occupation of Haiti and the deployment of U.S. peace enforcement contingents to Bosnia and Kosovo) can be sustained as long as they
entail little or no blood cost. Military action need not be popular as long
as it is perceived to be necessary; and if not seen as necessary, action can
still be sustained as long as domestic political opposition to it remains
tolerable to the White House. The problem in Vietnam was not the state
of public and congressional opinion at the beginning of U.S. intervention: there was near consensus, reflected in the editorial pages of even
the *New York Times* and *Washington Post*, that intervention was necessary because of the perceived threat to U.S. vital interests. The problem was
sustaining public and congressional support after years of increasingly
bloody combat with no apparent satisfactory end. Ultimately, the cost of
the war was seen to greatly exceed its benefits.

Fourth, the Weinberger-Powell Doctrine's implicit rejection of force as
an instrument of diplomacy is irreconcilable with the reality of war as an
extension of politics. For Weinberger, the only purpose of the U.S. milita-

ry was to win big wars, not to be "sent on endless assignments to such places like Bosnia, Kosovo, and Haiti, where there is no chance of 'winning' because there are no clear-cut objectives or exit strategies. Many of these operations are what are delicately termed 'operations other than war,' meaning they do not help train our forces in their principal task of winning wars."[8]

Yet to enshrine force as a substitute for diplomacy is to gut diplomacy as an indispensable tool of statecraft. The doctrine essentially stands Clausewitz on his head; war becomes a substitute for politics rather than its extension by other means. Shultz hit the nail on the head in his counter to Weinberger: "Americans have sometimes tended to think that power and diplomacy are distinct alternatives. This reflects a fundamental misunderstanding. The truth is that power and diplomacy must always go together or we will accomplish very little in this world. . . . [T]he hard reality is that diplomacy not backed by strength will always be ineffectual at best, dangerous at worst."[9]

Small wonder it is that presidents and secretaries of state have denounced the doctrine and routinely ignored its explicit cautions, especially in crises not involving the prospect of major war with another well-armed state. President Reagan made his disastrous decision to intervene in Lebanon's civil war against the strong objections of Secretary of Defense Weinberger and the Joint Chiefs of Staff; President Bush chose to go to war over Kuwait notwithstanding the grave reservations of JCS chairman Colin Powell; President Clinton launched an invasion of Haiti in the face of considerable congressional opposition. Whatever occasional rhetorical obedience presidents have paid to various tenets of the Weinberger-Powell Doctrine, they have not hesitated to exercise the president's authority as commander in chief to place U.S. military forces in harm's way. They have used force on behalf of nonvital interests, in the absence of public and congressional support, and not always as a last resort.

Presidents, secretaries of state, and even secretaries of defense seem to regard the doctrine as both an implicit intrusion on presidential authority in making national security policy and, more important, an enemy of flexibility in crises, especially crises calling for possible uses of force short of full-scale war. In his 1985 book, *No More Vietnams*, retired president Richard Nixon delivered a comprehensive critique of the Weinberger Doctrine, although he did not mention it by name. He clearly regarded the doctrine as a dangerously restrictive philosophy that threatened to turn the United States into a "diplomatic dwarf."[10] The "reluctance of our military leaders to be bogged down in another Vietnam is understandable," he conceded, but he warned against defining "our vital interests too narrowly solely out of fear of getting involved in another Vietnam."[11] Nixon noted that "every military operation cannot be a sure thing," and that "we must take risks" to protect our interests.[12] He then paid homage to the goal of using force as a last resort, but cautioned that "the capability and will to use force as a first resort when our interests are threatened reduces the possibility of having to use force as a last resort, when the risk of casualties would be far greater."[13] Nixon concluded his critique by observing that "the outstretched hand of diplomacy will have a very weak grip unless the President holds the scepter of credible military power in his other hand."[14]

Even McNamara was troubled by the Weinberger-Powell Doctrine. The "U.S. military and the American people may have learned the wrong lesson from the war," he wrote in his analysis of the Vietnam War, namely that "American military forces should be used only where our firepower and mobility can be directed with overwhelming force against a massed enemy." He lamented that "'No More Vietnams' . . . has become the watchword for the military as well as for those generally opposed to U.S. military intervention anywhere."[15] Another former secretary of defense, James Schlesinger, also opposed "the emerging belief that the United States must fight only popular, winnable wars. The role of the United States in the world is such that it must be prepared for, be prepared to threaten, and even be prepared to fight those intermediate conflicts that are likely to fare poorly on television."[16]

Shultz pilloried the doctrine in his memoirs, calling it "the Vietnam syndrome in spades, carried to an absurd level, and a complete abdication of the duties of leadership" because it excludes the use or threatened use of force in "situations where a discrete assertion of power is needed or appropriate for limited purposes." Weinberger, he continued, believed that "our forces were to be constantly built up but not used: everything in our defense structure seemed geared exclusively to deter World War III against the Soviets; diplomacy was to solve all other problems we faced around the world."[17] The U.S. ambassador to the United Nations at the time, Madeleine Albright, had the same complaint about Colin Powell's aversion to deploying U.S. troops to Bosnia. "What's the point," she asked Powell in a White House meeting, "of having this superb military you are always talking about if we can't use it?"[18] The late Secretary of Defense Les

Aspin also condemned the Weinberger-Powell Doctrine as "the 'all-or-nothing' school [which] says if you aren't willing to put the pedal to the floor, don't start the engine."[19]

Certainly the mantra that force should be used as a last resort promotes an inflexibility that can make its ultimate use inevitable. "Preserving force as a last resort implies a lockstep sequencing of the means to achieve foreign policy objectives that is unduly inflexible and relegates the use of force to in extremis efforts to salvage a faltering policy," wrote Jane E. Holl in a paper entitled "We the People Don't Want No War."[20] The democracies' appeasement of Hitler in the 1930s brought upon them a much larger and longer war with Germany than they would have risked had they stood firm in the Rhineland, Austria, or Munich. It is no less clear that an early and sharp NATO use of force against the Serbs—perhaps when they began shelling Dubrovnik in October 1991—would have been far more preferable, and probably decisive, than standing idly by for three more years as the Serbs ravaged Bosnia. "The refusal of the Bush administration to commit American power early was our greatest mistake of the entire Yugoslav crisis," concluded Richard Holbrooke. "It made an unjust outcome inevitable and wasted the opportunity to save over a hundred thousand lives."[21] Wayne Bert, in his key study of U.S. policy in Bosnia, agreed: "If the West was to intervene effectively after the war had begun, it was important to move to stop Serb advances early rather than attempt to roll back their gains later. As the war went on, the Bosnian Serbs formed an increasingly more complete view of U.S. will and intentions, and it took stronger threats to get their attention as they constantly validated their assumption that the U.S. was not willing to intervene."[22]

But when does it become apparent that one has expended all available alternatives to force? Chamberlain did not approach his meetings with Hitler assuming that the only alternative to appeasement was war; in 1938, he still believed that war with Germany was avoidable because he believed that Hitler's territorial ambitions were limited to Germanic Europe. Likewise, a significant body of public and congressional opinion opposed going to war with Iraq in 1991, favoring instead the alternative of continued economic and diplomatic sanctioning. "Unless the United States is physically attacked, the 'last resort' test will remain highly subjective," observed Eric Alterman. "In Vietnam, for instance, the war came gradually, and so this test . . . was never applied. The question remains whether this test is taken seriously by political and military leaders."[23]

The doctrine does stand on firm ground in its insistence on having clear political and military objectives and on reassessing those objectives during the course of combat. Clarity of purpose is indispensable to success in both war and coercive diplomacy, and the penalties of haziness were evident in both Vietnam and Lebanon. U.S. military objectives in Vietnam were multiple and in some cases disconnected from one another, and the political and military missions of U.S. Marine Corps "peacekeeping" forces in Lebanon were never clear, even in President Reagan's own mind. In Korea, the problems during the first few months of the war were initially the casual official attention paid to the political objective and then its subsequent dramatic subordination to MacArthur's seemingly conclusive counteroffensive in the wake of the Inchon landing.

Military success should not preclude an expansion of original political objectives, even an expansion of military objectives (the dreaded "mission creep"), but the possible consequences of such expansion must be carefully considered. They were not in Korea, and the penalty exacted was Chinese intervention and disaster along the Yalu. Much the same thing happened in Somalia. Political and military objectives were expanded in almost willful ignorance of the likely dangerous consequences. (Great care, in contrast, was displayed in defining military objectives during World War II. Germany's and Japan's unconditional surrender, for example, was not a realistic war aim until the strategic tide had turned decisively against the Axis powers. Thus the proclamation of unconditional surrender came only in January 1943, *after* the battles of Stalingrad, El Alamein, Midway, and Guadalcanal.)

Having clear objectives, however, does not mean sticking to them regardless of the course of events. Objectives cannot be insulated from the effects of friendly and enemy military performance. Nor does clarity mean setting departure deadlines. "The 'Vietnam syndrome' continues to paralyze American leaders as the memory of the trenches [of World War I] did the British [in the 1920s and 1930s]," concluded Donald and Frederick Kagan in their comparison of British defense policy in the 1920s with U.S. defense policy in the 1990s. "The notion of 'mission creep,' rooted in the belief that the gradual expansion of America's role caused that loss, defeats any solid understanding of the relationship of politics and war. The notion that a state can enter a war with a clearly defined mission and 'end-state' and pursue the war without changing either, whatever circumstances arise, and arrive, thereby, at the desired outcome, is absurd and impossible in the real world. Things change and missions will creep—or shrink—and sometimes they must be allowed to do so. *There is no escape from the responsibility of judgment and no reason to believe that inaction is safer than action.*"[24] A good example is the Vietnam War. The U.S. "entrance" objective in 1965 was to prevent a communist takeover of South Vietnam; by 1973, when the Paris agreement was signed, the objective had dwindled to extricating a strategically exhausted United States from its Indochinese quagmire with a minimum of humiliation.

Americans prefer short, clean, and decisive wars in which the objective is *military* victory, preferably including destruction of the enemy's political regime and military forces. They like their foreign policy, Wayne Bert noted, "nice and neat with well-defined goals, costs, strategies, and starting and ending points."[25] Neither war nor peace, however, can be managed with such clarity and precision. Especially messy is the post–Cold War world, "where limited conflicts will be fought for limited and often shifting objectives, and with strategies that are difficult to formulate, costs that are uncertain, and entrance and exit points that are not obvious."[26]

Americans' obsession with exit strategies—how to get out, when, and at what cost—is an unfortunate legacy of the Vietnam War. Pre-Vietnam presidents and military leaders were not so afflicted. They took the use of force in stride in part because they had no vivid examples of disastrous failure to caution them; and for those for whom the 1930s and World War II were the dominant foreign policy experiences, Munich was about entering wars, not getting out of them. The blunder of intervention in Vietnam did not prove the need for exit strategies; on the contrary, it demonstrated their impossibility. Vietnam was a reminder that the timing, course, and outcome of a use of force cannot be predetermined or controlled during hostilities, especially against a skilled and determined enemy. Insistence on exit strategies and timetables is an insistence that the use of force be freed from friction and the iron law of unintended consequences. It is also an insistence that the United States can and should walk away from the residual political and military responsibilities that success in war inevitably incurs. The United States made this mistake after World War I but did not repeat it after World War II. Should the United States have politically and militarily exited Europe and Japan in 1945? Korea in 1953? The Persian Gulf in 1991? Bosnia in 1995? Kosovo in 1999? If war were simply a sport, it could be waged as a politically immaculate enterprise. But war is not a sport; it is inherently a politically consequential undertaking, and consequences, intended or not, entail responsibilities.

The Weinberger-Powell Doctrine may be essentially irrelevant to many security challenges of the post–Cold War era.[27] The doctrine seems most relevant to precisely the kind of conflict—large-scale interstate warfare requiring full and sustained national political and military engagement—that is receding as a threat to U.S. security. To be sure, any president contemplating this kind of war would be a fool to ignore the cautions of the doctrine. President Bush went to war in the Persian Gulf only after he had successfully conveyed the vitality of American interests at stake, mobilized public and congressional opinion, and exhausted all economic and diplomatic alternatives to war. He also conducted the war on behalf of clear and achievable objectives, and he used overwhelming force because a rare combination of circumstances—the Soviet Union's sudden disappearance as a military threat to Western Europe and Saddam Hussein's inaction in the face of the massive U.S. buildup in the Persian Gulf—made such force available.

But the Gulf War appears to be the exception that proves the rule. Large-scale interstate warfare—the collision of big conventional armies—has hardly vanished forever, yet its scope and incidence have declined dramatically since 1945. In the post–Cold War world, which so far lacks another great power capable of politically and militarily challenging the United States, the primary security demands on the Pentagon have been small wars and "military operations other than war" in places traditionally peripheral to core U.S. security interests. Since the Gulf War, the Pentagon has been called on to deal with humanitarian crises around the world, to deter war in Korea and across the Taiwan Strait, to hunt down a warlord in Somalia, to coerce Bosnian Serbs and then Serbia itself into halting ethnic cleansing in the former Yugoslavia, to police cease-fire agreements in Bosnia and Kosovo, to maintain a punitive air occupation of Iraq, to destroy suspected terrorist sites in Sudan and Afghanistan, and to assist other national military establishments attempting to deal with the chaos created by failed states.

Indeed, intrastate warfare seems to be displacing interstate warfare as the principal source of violence in the world, with much of that violence erupting in such failed states as Yugoslavia, Somalia, Rwanda, Sri Lanka, Angola, Sierra Leone, and Haiti. "The core problem," observed Leslie Gelb, "is wars of national debilitation, a steady run of uncivil civil wars sundering fragile but functioning nation-states and gnawing at the well-being of stable nations."[28] A growing body of international political analysis is concluding that "the chief threat to international security in the post–Cold War world is the collapse of states, and the resulting collapse of the capacity of civilian populations to feed and protect themselves, either against famine or ethnic warfare. In a world in which nations once capable of imperial burdens are no longer willing to shoulder them, it is inevitable that many of the states created by decolonization should prove unequal to the task of maintaining civil order."[29] No one has put it more succinctly than Philippe Delmas, a former military analyst for the French Foreign Ministry: "Wars today are caused not by the strengths of States but by their weakness. The primary problem of security today is not the desire for power and expansion, but rather the breakdown of States."[30] The problem is a legacy not just of the dissolution of European colonial empires in the aftermath of World War II but also of the more recent disintegration of the Soviet Union and other former communist states in Europe. The problem the world faces now is not expanding totalitarian empires but scores of imploding states. It is the Lilliputians, not the Brobdingnagians, that threaten world stability.

The Weinberger-Powell Doctrine, except for its insistence on clarity of political and military purpose, does not provide much useful instruction in dealing with a world of small wars waged largely within established state boundaries by irregular forces practicing unconventional warfare. On the contrary, the doctrine essentially proscribes U.S. intervention in such wars. This is not to gainsay the powerful influence of the Vietnam War analogy on post-Vietnam U.S. foreign policy, or the Vietnam syndrome's positive service as a formidable though not impermeable barrier to casual military intervention. Where else might the United States have intervened in the 1980s and 1990s had it not been for fear of stumbling into another Vietnam. Angola? Cuba? Central America? Rwanda? East Timor? Sierra Leone? The defeat in Vietnam could not have had anything less than a chilling effect on America's approach to using force overseas, and the syndrome it produced contributed mightily to the architecture and low blood cost of the U.S. victory in the Gulf War.

At the same time, however, the Vietnam analogy, reinforced by Lebanon and Somalia, contributed to the emergence of a powerful myth that has already compromised U.S. military effectiveness and may cripple it in the future. Chilling effects can be healthy or degenerative, and in this case they are the latter. The myth that the American people are intolerant of incurring casualties in situations not involving a clear and present danger to the United States and its allies runs strong in America's political and military elites, especially the latter. And it threatens the ability of the United States to act as a great power, to say nothing of the world's sole remaining superpower. If the Munich analogy encouraged early use of force, the Vietnam analogy's corollary of what I have elsewhere chosen to call "force protection fetishism" encourages military timidity, even paralysis.[31]

To put the issue of force protection fetishism in perspective, consider the differences between two notable American military commanders: George Armstrong Custer and George Brinton McClellan. Custer was a glory hunter who recklessly exposed his command to slaughter at the hands of the Sioux in 1876. Custer's lust for celebrity was greater than his concern for the lives of his troops. In contrast, McClellan was so afraid of exposing the Army of the Potomac and himself to possible defeat at the hands of Robert E. Lee that he forgot why there *was* an Army of the Potomac. Lincoln finally sacked him because McClellan placed force protection above mission accomplishment. Yet, somewhere between the poles of foolhardiness and faintheartedness lies the proper ground of willingness to accept the risks necessary to accomplish the mission for which force is employed. The choice between Custer and McClellan is a false choice, yet this does not seem apparent to senior U.S. political and military leaders.

Consider the joint statement made by Secretary of Defense William Cohen and JCS chairman Gen. Henry Shelton shortly after the conclusion of the war against Serbia: "The paramount lesson learned from Operation Allied Force is that the well-being of our people must remain our first priority."[32] Consider further the postwar caution of NATO's supreme allied commander, Gen. Wesley Clark: "In an air campaign you don't want to lose aircraft" because when "you start to lose [them] the countdown starts against you. The headlines begin to shout, 'NATO loses a second aircraft,' and the people ask, 'How long can this go on?'"[33]

To repeat, a distinction can and must be made between the moral and political imperatives of shielding one's military forces from risks that are superfluous to the accomplishment of the mission at hand, and subordinating that mission to the ideal goal of bringing every soldier, sailor, airman, and marine back home alive. Casualty aversion is one thing, casualty phobia is quite another. Casualty-phobic timidity can be just as self-defeating as bloodthirsty recklessness. One Matthew B. Ridgway is worth a dozen Custers and McClellans because Ridgway gets the job done without undue risk. Ridgway, the 18th Airborne Corps commander in Europe during World War II and MacArthur's impressive successor in Korea, had both an ego and a strong sense of caution, but he never let either get in the way of his professional responsibilities on the battlefield. If protection of one's own troops has top priority, then they should never be exposed to combat in the first place; they should be kept at home. Or, at a minimum, as in Operation Allied Force, policy makers should confine America's enemies to those incapable of shooting back in the air while at the same time offering those enemies nothing to shoot at on the ground.

The casualty phobia that has infected U.S. political and military elites represents a perhaps deliberately misperceived lesson of the Vietnam War (and of Lebanon and Somalia). The lesson in question is not the public's absolute intolerance of casualties, but rather the need for flexibility *contingent* on such reasonable criteria as perceived strength of interests at stake and prospects for success. Casualties incurred in protracted, inconclusive wars for unconvincing goals are not the same as those taken on behalf of decisive military action launched for a compelling cause.[34] Americans will not accept the same blood risk in order to prevail in strategically inconsequential civil wars in Lebanon and Somalia that they willingly accepted in defeating Japan and Nazi Germany and in containing the Soviet Union. They can and have, however, accepted modest casualties in such "gray area" interventions as the U.S. invasions of Grenada and Panama and the attempted hostage rescue mission in Iran.

Furthermore, public attitudes toward casualties are malleable. Casualty tolerance depends on circumstances, and those circumstances include not only presidential success or failure in mobilizing public opinion but also the enemy's behavior. The Japanese attack on Pearl Harbor instantly dissolved the America First movement as a domestic political obstacle to President Franklin Roosevelt's foreign policy, and the manifest personal and political evil of Saddam Hussein greatly facilitated George Bush's successful demonization of him. In contrast, Ronald Reagan could never explain to the American people exactly what the U.S. military intervention in Lebanon's civil war was all about, nor did Bill Clinton ever make a convincing case for invading Haiti. Unfortunately, although the contingent nature of the public's tolerance for casualties is supported by a substantial body of data, such studies seem to make no impression on the White House and the Pentagon.[35]

Twentieth-century America has been prepared to expend the lives of more than half a million of its sons and daughters to defeat totalitarian aggression in Europe and East Asia. Only during the Vietnam War did public support crack, and even then only after the shock of the Tet Offensive, four years of apparent stalemate on the battlefield, and mounting evidence of official war policy duplicity in Washington. It is amazing in retrospect that public support remained as strong as it did for as long as it did given the war's geographic remoteness and abstract U.S. war aims. Even after the Cold War ended, President Bush mobilized substantial public and congressional support for going to war on behalf of an undemocratic country—Kuwait—that most Americans had never heard of and to which the United States had no prior defense commitment. Although American casualties were miraculously low (148 killed in action), both the public and Capitol Hill were prepared to accept a much higher death toll.[36] Indeed, Operation Desert Storm was planned by the Pentagon and authorized by the president on the assumption of American war dead numbering in the low thousands.[37]

Recent polling data marshaled by the Triangle Institute for Security Studies' Project on the Gap between Military and Civilian Society confirms that the "mass public says it will accept casualties" in a variety of scenarios.[38] The data further reveal that civilian policy makers, and even more so senior military officers, are much more casualty intolerant than the average American citizen.[39] The project surveyed forty-nine hundred Americans drawn from three groups: senior or rising military officers, influential civilians, and the general public. Among the questions asked were how many American military deaths would be acceptable to (a) stabilize a democratic government in the Congo, (b) prevent Iraq from obtaining weapons of mass destruction, and (c) defend Taiwan against an invasion by China. For the military elite, civilian elite, and general public, the numbers of acceptable military dead for each scenario were, respectively, as follows: Congo—284, 484, and 6,861; Iraq—6,016, 19,045, and 29,853; and Taiwan—17,425, 17,554, and 20,172.[40]

Why do the elites seem to lack the nerve of the people they serve? Is it because the assumption that the public will not tolerate casualties excuses presidents and generals from taking the kind of battlefield risks that might invite casualties? Because casualty avoidance offers an alibi for mission frustration and even failure? Because casualty phobia reinforces the argument against using force as a tool of coercive diplomacy? The authors of the Triangle Institute study speculated that senior military officers may lack confidence in the reliability of civilian leaders to stay the course of intervention if casualties mount. They also posited that "casualty aversion may be an aspect of a growing zero-defect mentality among senior officers, in which casualties are not only deaths—they are an immediate indication that an operation is a failure."[41] This proposition seems convincing; when force protection becomes the primary mission, casualties by definition become the primary standard of success or failure. (By this standard, the U.S. Marine Corps's amphibious assaults on Guadalcanal, Tarawa, Kwajalein, Saipan, Iwo Jima, and Okinawa would have to be reclassified as defeats precisely because they entailed substantial losses of American lives.)

The consequences of casualty phobia—i.e., of the Vietnam War's most potent legacy for American statecraft—include a penchant for military half measures, encouragement of enemies, irritation of allies, and degradation of the warrior ethic. "The argument is not that commanders should avoid unnecessary casualties—duty demands no less," observed Charles Hyde. "The issue is the impact of excessive casualty aversion on planning and the military ethos."[42] Putting the safety of one's troops ahead of the civilians they are supposed to protect—as the United States did in the war over Kosovo—makes a mockery of genuine warrior values, the most important of which is willingness to die on behalf of something greater than oneself. "Troops are supposed to be willing to die so that civilians do not have to," Peter Feaver and Christopher Gelphi insisted in a *Washington Post* article, yet this axiom seems to be changing.[43] Indeed, Charles Dunlap suggested that military "professionals need to ask themselves whether the military's altruistic ethos, axiomatic to its organizational culture, is being replaced by an occupationalism that places—perhaps unconsciously—undue weight on self-preservation over mission accomplishment."[44]

Damage to the warrior ethos is damage to reputation, and reputation is as important to great powers as it is to individuals. Dozens of other states and hundreds of millions of people around the world look to the United States for peace and security. But the United States in the end can provide neither if it is unwilling to place its military power in circumstances that risk death and even defeat. The Vietnam War, followed by Lebanon, taught Saddam Hussein that he could face down the United States over his conquest of Kuwait. Manifest U.S. military timidity encouraged Slobodan Milosevic to believe that he could get away with the four wars he started in the former Yugoslavia. Indeed, even though the United States finally went to war over Kosovo, noted Vincent Gould-ing Jr., the "world's only superpower sent the strongest possible signal that, while it is willing to conduct military operations in situations not vital to the country's national interests, it is not willing to put in harm's way the means necessary to conduct these operations effectively and conclusively." Continued Goulding, referring both to the war over Kosovo and to postwar force protectionism as embodied in Camp Bondsteel, "The portrait of U.S. ground forces becomes complete in the eyes of future enemies: too valuable to be risked in combat, too soft and coddled to bear the rigors of peacekeeping."[45]

The lesson of Vietnam is not that force is evil or that force is such an inherently unstable commodity that it should not be used except in the gravest of circumstances. The lesson of Vietnam is that disaster awaits military intervention that violates Carl von Clausewitz's admonition to first establish the kind of war that is to be fought and to understand its nature before proceeding.[46] The United States in 1965 mistook rev-olutionary nationalism in Vietnam for a case of traditional international aggression, and then proceeded to fight the conventional war it wanted to fight rather than the war at hand. In so doing, it sowed the seeds of a disaster whose shadow still darkens American statecraft.

If the Vietnam War analogy is an unreliable, even dangerous, guide to using force in the post–Cold War era, is that also true of the Munich anal-ogy? Munich would seem to remain instructive as long as there are aggressive states with agendas of territorial conquest in places the United States and its allies value. It does matter whether the aggressor state's imperial ambitions are global, regional, or local; Hitler's goals dwarfed those of Ho Chi Minh, Saddam Hussein, and Slobodan Milosevic. An aggressor state's ability to act on its ambitions also counts heavily in any calculus, and here again, Nazi Germany trumps all competitors except the Soviet Union in the wake of the Vietnam War. No less important is whether the aggressor state's ambitions endanger interests for which the United States is prepared to fight. Saddam Hussein's ambitions were regional in scope; he possessed the military ability to act on those ambi-tions; and when he acted against Kuwait, he threatened established strategic interests long deemed vital to the United States and its major allies in Europe and East Asia. The Bush administration accordingly fol-lowed the lesson of Munich and overturned Iraq's invasion of Kuwait, leaving Iraq in no military position to repeat it anytime soon, much less to provide Saddam Hussein hegemony in the Persian Gulf.

The challenge in applying the Munich analogy is making sure that the enemy state in question really seeks territorial expansion and has the means to effect it. An even greater challenge is being able to sort out the importance of interests being threatened versus the potential costs of defending them militarily. In the 1960s, the United States misread the nature of the conflict in Vietnam, overestimated the strategic consequences of a communist victory there, and underestimated the price of preventing such a victory. The Vietnamese Communists were fighting for themselves, not for Moscow or Beijing, and their ambitions did not extend beyond the confines of old French Indochina.

Most wars are not like prairie fires. They do not start small and automatically grow until they burn out. Local aggression does not habitually expand into regional aggression and then into global aggression. Had Slobodan Milosevic succeeded in creating a greater Serbia from the ashes of Yugoslavia, it does not follow that he would next have tried to conquer the rest of southeastern Europe and then invaded Germany. "The one important lesson to be learned from Bosnia," argued Wayne Bert, "is the need to be flexible, to give up the preconceived notions that involvement inevitably proceeds from one stage of escalation to another in a linear path, and that taking one step toward intervention inevitably leads to the next one if the desired results are not obtained."[47] It was simply not the case, as Secretary of State Lawrence Eagleburger argued in defense of U.S. inaction in Bosnia, that the only alternative to doing nothing was another Vietnam.[48] The first step in Bosnia (and for that matter in Lebanon, Somalia, and Kosovo) did not in fact escalate into a new Vietnam.

Then there is the issue of when and where to make a stand. Munich teaches that, in dealing with a territorially aggressive state, an early and convincing use of force is always better than appeasement because appeasement simply postpones the final day of reckoning and raises its price. (The exception would be appeasement aimed at buying time to rearm.) Reversing Hitler's occupation of the Rhineland in 1936 could have spared Europe both Munich and the war that followed, yet how many European governments in 1936 really saw the occupation for what it was—i.e., the first installment of an ambition to conquer all of Europe? Would Saddam Hussein really have moved into Saudi Arabia's oil-rich Eastern Province had his aggression against Kuwait been allowed to stand? Was it ever really possible, even without NATO military intervention, for Slobodan Milosevic to create and maintain a greater Serbia in the former Yugoslavia?

Clearly, the Munich analogy is most instructive in dealing with aggressive great powers operating in places of uncontestable strategic vitality to the United States such as Europe and East Asia. Nazi Germany and Imperial Japan fit this bill, as might China someday. Indeed, nothing could guarantee the Munich analogy a more thriving life extension as an informant of U.S. foreign policy than the emergence of a hostile, militarily competitive China seeking to reclaim "lost" territories and ocean spaces in East Asia. Such a possibility cannot be discounted; a number of observers have already concluded that China is destined to be America's next great enemy by virtue of its internal political governance, the hostility to the United States within the Chinese military and much of its political leadership, and Beijing's declarations of sovereignty over Taiwan, the South China Sea, and other areas in Asia.[49]

China's political system is certainly hostile to American values, and it is ridiculous to talk of China as a strategic partner of the United States in the wake of the Soviet Union's disappearance. There is also no denying the potency of the Taiwan issue as a potential war starter. Americans should not forget that U.S. miscalculation drove the United States into a bloody, unwanted war with China in Korea back in 1950. But neither should they rush to the judgment that China is destined to be America's next strategic rival and therefore needs to be "contained" just as the Soviet Union had to be contained during the Cold War.

China is not an impressive military power and is not likely to become one anytime soon because military modernization is not among Beijing's top priorities. China, moreover, has substantial internal security demands in Tibet and Xinjiang, and it faces multiple potential adversaries along its borders—India, Vietnam, Mongolia, Russia, and at some point a united Korea. China's land borders with Vietnam and India remain unresolved and have occasioned war in the past. China's military also serves as the ultimate enforcer of the regime's writ against political democratization.[50]

Postulation of China as the next *qualified* military competitor of the United States—i.e., as a replacement for the Soviet Union—rests on several assumptions, all of them speculative. First, it presupposes sustained high annual GDP growth rates. Yet China's spectacular double-digit rates of the early 1990s have declined to single digits, and much of China's industrial production is of economically worthless state-owned goods. Massive corruption also pervades the economy, as does staggering and potentially destabilizing unemployment and underemployment. There is also the issue of whether China's socialist statistical system can even provide reliable data on economic change. Many independent economists believe that the official statistics are inherently unreliable and overstate China's growth.[51] In terms of its overall economic performance, "China remains a classic case of hope over experience, reminiscent of de Gaulle's famous comment about Brazil: It has great potential and always will," concluded Gerald Segal.[52]

Second, China-as-the-new-Soviet-Union assumes the presence of global Chinese ambitions, when in fact the imperial aims of post-Mao China are strictly regional in scope. China may indeed someday challenge America's strategic position in the Far East, but it will not do so in Europe, the Middle East, and the Western Hemisphere. Even in the Far East, China has few friends precisely because of regional apprehension over Beijing's long-term strategic intentions and because, Segal observed, "it abhors the very notion of genuine international interdependence."[53] In contrast, the United States is rich in East Asian friends and allies, including Japan, South Korea, Taiwan, Thailand, Singapore, Australia, and New Zealand.

A third assumption is continued autocracy in Beijing. Dictatorship in most areas of the world, including East Asia, has been in retreat for decades, and both the history of Europe and recent political events in Taiwan, South Korea, and Indonesia suggest that economic democratization exerts a powerful and ultimately often irresistible pressure for political democratization. Whether China will follow this pattern remains to be seen, and violence often attends the transition from dictatorship to democracy. But it is reasonable to assume that a fair chance exists for a democratic China, and that such a China would be less likely than an autocratic China to risk war with the United States by pursuing imperial ambitions.

A fourth assumption is that China would be prepared to sacrifice its large and growing stake in the international capitalist trading order, including massive trade surpluses with the United States, for the sake of its imperial ambitions. The Soviet Union never had to make this choice because it shunned participation in that order. Yet China has no choice but to participate if it is to become a modern, economically viable state, even though participation fosters a dreaded dependence on other states that would make war even more ruinous than it otherwise would be. China's admission to the World Trade Organization is far more of a strategic plus for the United States than an economic one.

For the foreseeable future, China will be preoccupied with managing enormous internal economic change. Never before has any regime tried to move so many people so far into economic modernity so quickly, and it is far from certain that the autocrats in Beijing can pull it off without revolutionary upheaval, which in fact has been the norm for China in the twentieth century. The late 1990s crackdown on the Falun Gong spiritual movement underscores the regime's insecurity and its preoccupation with preserving its own legitimacy, which since the advent of Deng Xiao-ping has rested on economic progress. Obviously, economic disaster or the disintegration of central political authority in China would torpedo China's emergence as a strategic rival.

None of this is to argue against the possibility of China's emergence *someday* as America's next great strategic rival. China and the United States have conflicting interests in East Asia, and China has never been kind to democratic impulses. China certainly has the intellectual and physical resources to create a competitive military threat to the U.S. strategic position in East Asia. Surely, however, it is premature for the United States to start acting as if China is predestined to be America's next big enemy. Even if China does become a qualified threat, it will be decades in the making, and the United States will have plenty of time to begin containing China's imperial ambitions—just as it did those of the Soviet Union for forty years.

One final note on the subject of China: using force against China in East Asia would differ markedly from the way the United States approached the challenge posed by Nazi Germany and the Soviet Union in Europe. On the continent of Europe, the United States has been and remains willing to wage major and sustained ground warfare against adversaries seeking continental domination. In both world wars and against the Soviet Union during the Cold War, the United States and its allies were compelled to deal directly and in kind with enemies rich in ground power. But the United States does not have to do that in East Asia against China. In fact, avoidance of involvement in a large land war on the Asian mainland has been a long-standing strategic injunction of American force planning, an injunction whose wisdom was validated by the U.S. military's defeat in Indochina.

The sound reasoning behind the injunction is as follows: the strategic consequences of hostile domination of the Asian mainland are tolerable as long as Japan and the rest of offshore and peninsular Asia—namely,

South Korea, Taiwan, the Philippines, Malaysia, Singapore, and Indonesia—remain beyond hostile reach. This basic concept of America's "defense perimeter" in East Asia, first enunciated by Gen. Douglas MacArthur in the late 1940s, remains sustainable precisely because it exploits America's strengths—sea and air power—while rendering a mainland Asian hegemon's advantage in land power more or less irrelevant. The United States can tolerate and has tolerated a hostile China, and even Japanese control of Korea and Manchuria; what it cannot tolerate—and in Imperial Japan's case did not tolerate—is an Asian power that attempts to control both China and offshore Asia. Indeed, the United States performs a great strategic service for China by enmeshing Japan in a security relationship that precludes repetition of Japanese behavior in China during the 1930s and 1940s.

In sum, the usefulness of the Munich and Vietnam War analogies as informants on using force in the post–Cold War era is not yet clear because that era's ultimate contours themselves are not yet clear. Munich remains instructive in dealing with aggressive dictators seeking territorial expansion in areas of strategic interest to the United States. Vietnam remains instructive as a caution against intervening in foreign civil wars where U.S. intervention is likely to be ineffective or its costs are likely to exceed the perceived benefits. But how many clear-cut cases of either continue to emerge? In the Balkans, the United States intervened in a civil war in a failing state because that war produced a dictator bent on a regionally destabilizing course of aggression. Which analogy applied? They both did. During the Cold War, policy makers tended to treat the Munich and Vietnam War analogies as mutually exclusive as informants of action. Munich applied to traditional international aggression, whereas Vietnam applied to internal war. This distinction is fast vanishing in the post–Cold War world.

Moreover, a relatively new analogy is emerging as a possible competitor to the Munich and Vietnam analogies. Although the planning and implementation of Operation Desert Storm were in large measure products of lessons learned in the Vietnam War, the Gulf War itself offers lessons that have influenced subsequent U.S. uses of force (at least at the operational level of warfare) and may continue to do so for decades to come. Of special interest is a particular lesson that was seemingly revalidated in the Balkans: namely, the technological possibility of using force without risk of incurring significant casualties. This possibility has been advanced most vocally by proponents of the "Revolution in Military Affairs" (RMA), who believe that new technologies point to transparent battlefields, information dominance, and remotely controlled combat. Specifically, according to a leading RMA proponent, today's technologies, whose precursors dazzled the world during the Gulf War, "can give us the ability to see a 'battlefield' . . . 200 miles on a side . . . with unprecedented fidelity, comprehension and timeliness." Advanced sensing and information-reporting technologies will enable the commander to "know the precise location and activity of enemy units—even those attempting to cloak their movements by operating at night or in poor weather, or by hiding behind mountains or under trees."[54] Such "battlefield awareness," when combined with ever more accurate and longer-range weapons, "cannot reduce the risk of casualties to zero, but it can keep that risk low enough to maintain the American public's support for the use of force."[55]

To be sure, U.S. military casualties during the 1990s were unprecedented in their scarcity. During the Gulf War, 148 U.S. military personnel were killed in action out of more than 500,000 committed. During the following decade, the United States conducted two aerial bombardment campaigns in the former Yugoslavia, including a seventy-eight-day air war against Serbia that involved almost one-half of the U.S. Air Force's deployable strength, that entailed no American loss of life. In all three cases—Operations Desert Storm (1991), Deliberate Force (1995), and Allied Force (1999)—U.S. ground forces were withheld from combat altogether or unleashed only at the very end, with air power assuming the dominant role in attacks on enemy forces and regime targets. And in each case, the key to successful casualty avoidance was the employment of ever-longer-range precision-guided munitions launched from aircraft, ships, and submarines. The 1990s also witnessed U.S. development of and investment in pilotless aircraft for the purposes of reconnaissance and surveillance. By the end of the decade plans were afoot to explore the possibility of developing drones that could assume some, perhaps most, of the combat roles now shouldered by piloted planes.

The combat precedents of the 1990s and the promise of new technologies have encouraged public, congressional, and media expectations about American casualties in future combat that may prove profoundly optimistic. The high benchmark established by the Gulf War carried into the 1995 and 1999 air campaigns in the former Yugoslavia, in which the downing of a single U.S. pilot and the capture (in Macedonia) of three U.S. soldiers provoked a national media fixation and political trauma at the White House. Indeed, news of the recovery of the pilot by a search-and-rescue team was received in the White House as if it were a strategically decisive victory.[56]

Both the Munich and Vietnam analogies implicitly associate war with great danger, uncertainty, and sacrifice. The Munich analogy focuses on when to fight, whereas the Vietnam analogy addresses the issues of when and how to fight. In contrast, those who see the Gulf War and the Balkan air campaigns as harbingers of American wars to come are wont to envision a future warfare stripped of risk and pain. But riskless and painless war trivializes the injunctions of Munich and Vietnam; if technology can make war essentially cost-free for the United States, then less care needs to be given to the questions of whether to fight and how. Target management replaces strategy. War becomes formula and technique. If the United States can use force to coerce or defeat its enemies at little or no price in blood and treasure to itself, then why bother with exacting standards for using force? Such standards arise only on the presumption of war as an inherently perilous and bloody enterprise. If this painless war becomes the primary use-of-force message drawn from the Gulf War and subsequent military operations in the Balkans, then the Munich and Vietnam analogies may have to cede some of their "turf" to a newcomer analogy that challenges the very nature of war itself.

Yet the Gulf War analogy as an expression of the possibility and desirability of war without danger or sacrifice raises two fundamental questions: Is it possible for the United States to eliminate (at least for itself) danger and sacrifice from war? If so, what are the implications for the use of force?

The answer to the first question depends on whether war is best characterized as an art or a science.[57] Clearly, it might be a science but for the participation of fallible human beings, but it is precisely the human presence that denies reduction of war's conduct to a set of universal prescriptions. War is no more a science than is politics, of which it is an extension. Although war contains elements of science, it is first and foremost a human enterprise. Sun Tzu and Carl von Clausewitz understood this, even if Antoine Henri Jomini and Alfred Thayer Mahan did not. Clausewitz's "fog" and "friction" are inherent in war, regardless of the technological sophistication of one side or the other.[58] Science has become a very important tool of war, but it should not be confused with war itself. War's intangibles continue, more often than not, to outweigh its measurable indexes in determining outcomes—how else to explain the U.S. defeats in Indochina and Somalia, and Russia's defeats in Afghanistan and Chechnya?

Those who believe that science can transform war into an enterprise free of chance, danger, and uncertainty are not just naïve. In embracing a vision of essentially riskless war they are also embracing a world in which the United States could use force with impunity. Such a world would be good neither for the United States nor for the rest of the planet. Why? Because in such a world America would be tempted to use force in circumstances that otherwise might impose caution. Why would the United States bother with complicated and time-consuming remedies short of force if it could use force effortlessly and successfully? And why should the United States care about enemy losses when inflicting them would require so little sacrifice? If the United States could use force casually, without the accountability imposed by the risk of death and defeat, might it not become the arrogant global bully that its enemies today accuse it of being? And what of the warrior ethic? How does it survive warfare without risk?

For better or for worse, because war is still more an art than a science, enemies incapable of competing against the United States at the conventional level of warfare—the arena in which RMA zealots believe that war-as-science can minimize danger and death for America—can employ asymmetrical responses that either sidestep or altogether negate their conventional military impotence. Such responses are hardly new; they were on display in Korea, Vietnam, Beirut, and Mogadishu. Indeed, potential asymmetrical responses are growing in number and lethality. Increasingly sophisticated and well-financed efforts by "rogue" states and nonstate actors (e.g., Colombian drug lords) point to their eventual acquisition of weapons capable of inflicting massive American civilian casualties both at home and abroad. The very fact of U.S. conventional military supremacy compels intelligent and dedicated adversaries to seek supra- and subconventional counters; and such counters, which include terrorism, cannot be readily defeated by RMA technology. As Lawrence Freedman observed, such adversaries will pick "alternative strategies reflect[ing] those that the weak have consistently adopted against the strong: concentrating on imposing pain rather than winning battles; gaining time rather than moving to closure; targeting the enemy's domestic political base as much as his forward military capabilities; relying on his intolerance of casualties and his weaker stake in the resolution of the conflict; and playing upon his reluctance to cause civilian suffering."[59]

It thus seems unlikely that the Gulf War analogy as discussed here will compete effectively with, much less displace, the influence of the Munich and Vietnam War analogies. The latter are associated with bloody and soul-searing foreign policy disasters. Accordingly, they have had a much more profound effect on subsequent presidential uses of force than has the relatively cheap and easy victory over a doomed Iraqi army. The message of Munich was serious, as were the messages of Vietnam, notwithstanding continuing disagreement over exactly what those messages are. The problem was and remains recognizing circumstances relevant to the analogies' application, and here the record of presidential judgment has been mixed. In the case of the Gulf War, however, if the message is that decisive war can be had on the cheap (in terms of lives lost), then it is a message that at best still awaits confirmation in future war, and at worst is a dangerous fantasy.

Using Force,

Thinking History

Past employment and deployment of the Munich and Vietnam analogies suggest that they can teach effectively at the level of generality, but that they are insensitive to differences in detail. Historical events do not repeat themselves with an exactitude permitting accurate prediction of what will or will not happen if one chooses this or that course of action. In any case, every president's knowledge of past events is different and is subject to political bias. Human imperfection renders misjudgment a permanent and prominent feature of human endeavor, and that misjudgment includes poor reasoning by historical analogy. "Reasoning by analogy is probably essential," concluded Wayne Bert in *The Reluctant Superpower: United States Policy in Bosnia, 1991–1995*. "But reasoning by analogy . . . is also inadequate. Since a given event is almost never the same as a past event, and the environment in which events take place is changed and conditions are different, it is risky to assume that a past event or outcome can be used as an accurate model for the present one."[1]

The examples of Munich and Vietnam reveal the strengths and limits of reasoning by historical analogy. Munich constituted a legitimate lesson in how not to deal with a powerful aggressor seeking regional or global domination. Stopping Hitler in 1936, 1937, or 1938 would almost certainly have averted World War II. And the subsequent American decision to contain rather than appease post–World War II Soviet expansion probably—although no one can say for sure—prevented Europe's domination by a hostile power and may even have forestalled a third world war. Even so, the differences between Nazi Germany and the Soviet Union were probably critical (along with the presence of nuclear weapons) in making the Cold War cold. Hitler was reckless and impatient and did not fear war; indeed, his Nazi ideology glorified war. In contrast, the Soviet leadership—Khrushchev in 1961–62 being the exception—was cautious and unhurried, and all Soviet leaders who lived through World War II feared war.

But the differences between Europe of the 1930s and Southeast Asia of the 1960s were so profound as to make Munich an enemy of sound American judgment on Vietnam. Indeed, Paul Kattenburg suggested, reasoning by the Munich analogy "became a virtual ritual in the United States under Secretaries of State Acheson (1949–52), Dulles (1953–58) and Rusk (1961–68), who very early persuaded themselves that the Soviet Union under Stalin and Khrushchev, the Chinese under Mao, as well as the Vietnamese Communists under Ho, behaved similarly, in all important aspects of external policy, to the Nazi Reich under Hitler, fascist Italy under Mussolini, and Japan under the militarists." The "ritual" persisted, moreover, notwithstanding "the conservatism of Stalin in foreign policy, the rise of polycentrism in world communism with the emergence of Tito, Communist China, and Communist Vietnam, and the Sino-Soviet conflict, [which] were tearing the Sino-Soviet bloc asunder."[2]

For U.S. policy makers in the 1960s, the relevant historical knowledge about Indochina was not Franco-British behavior toward Hitler in the 1930s, but rather knowledge of the long history of Vietnamese nationalism and military performance. In no other major war in American history have so many policy makers been so ignorant of the foreign enemy they faced. They were as clueless as to what they were stepping into as Napoleon III was in his half-witted attempt to establish a Hapsburg dynasty in Mexico in the 1860s—a marvelously apt analogy made decades ago by historian Ernest R. May.[3] Policy makers embraced a set of convenient myths that even a modest amount of historical knowledge would have dispelled, among them: that Vietnamese communism was the enemy of Vietnamese nationalism (the two were married), that Hanoi was a surrogate for Chinese imperialism (it was, in fact, a perennial victim), that the French had been defeated in Indochina because they were militarily incompetent (which was false and also ignored the competence of the Vietnamese), that the struggle in Vietnam was a case of international aggression (Vietnamese fighting Vietnamese?), and that American military might was invincible.

The French-Indochinese War should have been of particular interest because France enjoyed two major advantages that the United States did not: the French knew much more about Vietnamese history and culture than the Americans ever would, and they fought their war in Indochina exclusively with seasoned professional troops serving twenty-six-month tours of duty, not with relatively ill-trained conscripts serving one-year tours. The French-Indochina War was, moreover, much closer in time and place than Munich, and the United States had indirectly participated in it by providing massive military assistance to the French. Additionally, although Munich may have seemed relevant to the decision on whether or not to fight in Vietnam, it provided no guidance on what the United States might expect in the way of resistance. As it turned out, the United States went on to repeat the French defeat (though without the dramatic ending of a Dien Bien Phu), and it was defeated by the very same Vietnamese political and military leadership that had driven out the French in 1954.

It seems astonishing in retrospect that the senior American policy makers, George Ball excepted, ignored the French experience. Yet Americans are notoriously ahistorical, and in 1965 policy makers were strategically arrogant to the point of dismissing the relevance of the French-Indochina War. After all, these were men for whom the glorious and total victory of World War II was the great referent experience for judging the likely outcomes of subsequent conflicts. Few believed that a piddling country like North Vietnam could stand up indefinitely to the awesome might of the United States. An America that had crushed Nazi Germany and Imperial Japan, that had kept the hordes of the Chinese People's Liberation Army at bay in Korea, could surely cow a small, impoverished, preindustrial state on the Asian mainland's periphery. "It seemed inconceivable," wrote Chester Cooper, who served as McGeorge Bundy's assistant for Asian affairs on the National Security Council staff, "that the lightly armed and poorly equipped Communist forces could maintain their momentum against, first, increasing amounts of American assistance to the [South] Vietnamese Army, and, subsequently, American bombing and [ground] forces."[4] That is, even if Vietnam's history were relevant—and it was not—American firepower would make it irrelevant. So what if the Vietnamese had spent an entire millennium fighting the Chinese? So what if they had beaten the French? Since when had the French won a war?

Advocates of intervention could justify their dismissal of the French-Indochina War analogy on the grounds that considerable differences separated France's chances for success in Indochina in the late 1940s and early 1950s and America's chances a decade later. France was, after all, a hated colonial occupier, and French forces lacked the firepower and tactical mobility of their American successors. In 1965, both the communist enemy and domestic political opposition were much less significant than what the French military and government, respectively, faced at the time of the Dien Bien Phu crisis of 1954. But there are always differences between historical events and those at hand; it is the strength of the similarities that counts the most in sound reasoning by historical analogy.

Probably the most compelling reason why the French experience was rejected was what Ernest May and Richard Neustadt called the phenomenon of "dodging bothersome analogies"—i.e., analogies that condemn the policy at hand.[5] For the Johnson administration to have taken the French-Indochina War seriously would have been to countenance U.S. abandonment of South Vietnam and the perceived domestic political disaster such a move would have entailed for a Democratic president in 1965. Thus, in its decision to commit U.S. military power to South Vietnam's defense, the Johnson administration not only employed an attractive but poor analogy, it also rejected a good albeit unpleasant analogy.

Much more attractive than the French analogy was the Korean War analogy, which is known to have greatly influenced the Johnson administration's deliberations on Vietnam. That war preserved an independent, noncommunist South Korea, and the analogy reinforced the Johnson administration's postulation of the war in Vietnam as a case of resisting international aggression rather than meddling in a local civil war. Korea proved that communist aggression could be reversed by American firepower, but placing the template of South Korea over South Vietnam obscured the Vietnam War's true character as a civil war. In Korea, the United States was primarily fighting another outside power—China— whose interests in the Korean War were, like those of the United States, limited and therefore *negotiable*. This paved the way for a negotiated settlement between the United States and China that overrode the interests of their respective Korean clients in Seoul and Pyongyang. In Vietnam, the United States was dealing with an indigenous adversary whose stake in the fight was total and therefore nonnegotiable. This meant that the United States was unlikely to attain its objective in Indochina absent a direct and determined assault on North Vietnam. But Johnson would never have attempted such an assault for fear that it might provoke a repetition of the Chinese surprise in Korea.

This discussion poses a broader question: Was it a mistake to militarize the doctrine of containment and extend it to the Asian *mainland*? After all, had militarized containment not been extended to the Asian mainland, the United States presumably would have been spared involvement in both the Korean and Vietnam Wars and the influence of their attendant analogies on subsequent U.S. use-of-force decisions.

Containment was originally conceived by George Kennan as a predominantly *non*military means of containing Soviet power and influence in *Europe* (Japan also was to be shielded). At a 1986 National Defense University symposium on containment, Kennan recalled that "in no way did the Soviet Union appear to me . . . as a military threat to this country. Russia was at that time [1946] utterly exhausted by the exertions and sacrifices of the recent war. . . . So when I used the word *containment* with respect to that country in 1946, what I had in mind was not at all the averting of the sort of military threat people are talking about today. What I *did* think I saw—and what explained the use of that term was what I might call an ideological-political threat." Kennan then proceeded to explain: "Great parts of the Northern Hemisphere—notably Western Europe and Japan—had just then been seriously destabilized, socially, spiritually, and politically, by the experiences of the recent war. Their populations were dazed, shell-shocked, uncertain of themselves, fearful of the future, highly vulnerable to the pressures and enticements of communist minorities in their midst. The world communist movement was at the time a unified, disciplined movement under the total control of the Stalin regime in Moscow. Not only that, but the Soviet Union had emerged from the war with great prestige" and was "in a position to manipulate these foreign communist parties very effectively in its own interests."[6]

But North Korea's invasion of South Korea in June 1950 was hardly an act of attempted political subversion, and it prompted the Truman and subsequent administrations to adopt a geographically much less discriminating approach to containment based primarily on military power. They did so because they viewed the North Korean attack and preceding communist victory in China through the lens of Munich—i.e., as an extension of *Soviet* power. The administration's decision to act on NSC-68's recommendations became the basis of a U.S. Cold War foreign policy that led straight to Vietnam because NSC-68 held that (1) the Soviet threat was primarily military, (2) the Soviet threat and the communist threat were more or less the same, (3) abandonment of any noncommunist state was intolerable, and (4) U.S. security rested as much on *per-*

ceptions of the balance of power between the United States and the Soviet Union as it did on the actual balance.

Kennan supported Truman's decision to repel North Korean aggression and to shield Formosa from attack by Communist China.[7] Yet he rejected the interpretation of the North Korean attack as "the first move in some 'grand design' . . . on the part of Soviet leaders to extend their power to other parts of the world by the uses of force." Such thinking, he argued, encouraged "the militarization of thinking about the cold war generally, and [served] to press us into attitudes where any discriminate estimate of Soviet intentions was unwelcome and unacceptable. In addition, it encouraged the military planners in another tendency against which I had fought long and bitterly but generally in vain: the tendency, namely, to view Soviet intentions as something existing quite independently of our own behavior. It was difficult to persuade these men that what people in Moscow decided to do might be a reaction to things we had done."[8]

On the other hand, NSC-68's redefinition of containment as primarily a military challenge blinded policy makers to the persistent strength of nationalism even within the communist bloc, to say nothing of its strength in the decolonizing Third World. Senator John F. Kennedy declared to a European newspaper in 1960 that "the final victory of nationalism is inevitable" and that "nationalism is the force which disposes of sufficient power and determination to threaten the integrity of the communist empire itself."[9] Yet as president he, like his predecessor and successor, interpreted decolonization of the Third World largely through East-West, Cold War lenses rather than North-South, nationalism-versus-imperialism ones. Indeed, "few American leaders cared to examine the nuances and subtle differences in the various ideologies that thrived under the label of communism," observed Robert Mann. "To most U.S. leaders, every Communist was a tool of a vast, monolithic Soviet conspiracy to rule the world. Most American foreign policy leaders believed that 'nationalism' was simply the fraudulent label that Asian Communists used to conceal Soviet designs on the region. They concluded that Ho's repugnant political ideology far outweighed his professed desire for Vietnamese independence."[10] Robert McNamara recalled that "we believed our interests were being attacked all over the world by a highly organized, unified communist movement, led by Moscow and Beijing, of which we believed, and I now think incorrectly, that the government of Ho Chi Minh was a pawn."[11]

To dismiss Ho Chi Minh as simply a Comintern agent, a flunky for the Kremlin's ambitions in Southeast Asia, was to dismiss the nationalism at the very core of the Vietnamese Revolution. In any event, communism could not triumph in Vietnam absent the mobilization of nationalism and the success of that mobilized nationalism in expelling the power and influence of the great capitalist United States. The substantial evidence now available suggests that, if anything, Ho Chi Minh's nationalist convictions were stronger than his communist ones. His best American biographer so argued, pointing out that neither Stalin nor Mao Zedong fully trusted Ho because both suspected that his commitment to liberating Vietnam from foreign domination exceeded his commitment to communism.[12]

The tendency to regard violent nationalism in the Third World as the product of a centrally directed international communist conspiracy was a strategic error of the first magnitude because it encouraged the use of force based on a fundamental misunderstanding of the nature of the war at hand. To be sure, both the Soviet Union and localized Communists embraced Third World wars of national liberation as a means of gaining power, and both the Soviet Union and China provided assistance to the Vietnamese Revolution and other communist revolutions elsewhere. But it was naïve to refuse to recognize the heavy nationalist content of Third World revolutions during the era of decolonization. And it was just as naïve, especially for the leaders of a country born in revolt against British colonial rule, to ignore the presence of legitimate economic as well as political grievances in the colonial and postcolonial Third World. Ngo Dinh Diem's South Vietnam was hardly the only American Cold War client whose repressive dictatorship and allegiance to a reactionary social order fueled the very internal revolutionary threat that so unnerved U.S. policy makers. Communist success required potentially revolutionary social conditions at the local level, which were present in South Vietnam in the early 1960s. Wars of national liberation were not solely enterprises, as Alexander M. Haig Jr. categorized them, "financed and catechized from Moscow."[13] Indeed, the grip of the communism-dissolves-nationalism myth on American Cold Warriors was evident in Haig's reaction in 1972 to Zhou Enlai's plea that the United States not lose in Vietnam. "I was startled by his frankness," recounted Haig. "How could a Communist want the United States to defeat a Communist insurgency? Chou explained the reasons for it, which should have been obvious in

Washington all along. The last thing China wanted was an armed and militant Soviet client state on its southern borders."[14]

Harry Truman's decision to fight in Korea triggered the creation of a national security state: the placement of the U.S. economy on a semiwar footing, the mobilization of science and education for war, the establishment of a large standing army in peacetime, the garrisoning of Western Europe and East Asia, and the government's persecution of "subversives."[15] Whether the creation of such a state was essential to defeat the Soviet Union in the Cold War is not subject to empirical validation. States at war, hot or cold, are driven to excesses both at home and abroad. Yet the evidence suggests that a containment policy devoid of strong military teeth would not have impressed the Kremlin. Truman's decision also led straight to Vietnam fifteen years later. But if Vietnam was a mistake, it was also just one battle in an ultimately victorious, forty-year war in which the most lethal scourge of the twentieth century—communism— was decisively defeated. The Soviet military threat to core U.S. strategic interests was powerful and real, and required the creation and maintenance of countervailing Western military power.

The mistake of extending militarized containment to mainland Asia was encouraged by NSC-68's elevation of the Cold War's military dimension over its nonmilitary dimensions. Truman's decision to rearm the United States following the outbreak of the Korean War was the correct one. But rearmament tended to divert attention away from the economic, political, and ideological dimensions of the Cold War, and in so doing encouraged resort to narrow military solutions. In his analysis of the Cold War, John Lewis Gaddis argued that "the way we calculated power during the Cold War years [was] almost entirely in monodimensional terms, focusing particularly on military indices, when a multidimensional perspective might have told us more. . . . [T]he Soviet Union collapsed, after all, with its arms and armed forces fully intact. Deficiencies in other kinds of power—economic, ideological, cultural, moral—caused the USSR to lose its superpower status . . . and a slow but steady erosion in those non-military capabilities had been going on for some time."[16] The U.S. military solution in Indochina ultimately failed because the problem in South Vietnam was at root political.

Yet if Munich argued strongly for intervention in Korea and later Vietnam, why did it not prompt intervention to prevent the great communist victory in China? China was a far greater strategic prize than South Korea or South Vietnam, and a Nationalist government victory in China after World War II would have been a tremendous strategic setback for both Kim Il Sung and Ho Chi Minh. Indeed, absent a *communist* China, North Korea could not have survived the war of 1950–53; Stalin might not even have permitted Kim Il Sung to attack South Korea in the first place. Absent a *communist* China, Ho Chi Minh would not have been able to defeat the French when and where he did, and might not even have been able to sustain his Democratic Republic of Vietnam. Had not Truman declared in 1947 that it would henceforth be the policy of the United States to assist states threatened externally or internally by communism?

Here again, as with Eisenhower's nonintervention in French Indochina in 1954, the influence of the Munich analogy on presidential decision making was overwhelmed by other considerations that argued against intervention. Analogies influence, but do not dictate, decisions. They often compete with each other, and always compete with nonanalogical considerations. In the case of China during the four years separating the Japanese surrender in 1945 and the Communists' victory over the Nationalist government of Chiang Kai-shek, the United States had neither the capacity nor the will for effective intervention. The United States had effectively disarmed itself after World War II, and even the harshest Republican critics of Truman's China policy opposed direct U.S. military intervention to save the Nationalist government. The American people were weary of war and preoccupied with domestic economic and social issues. It was, moreover, far from clear that the Nationalist cause in China was salvageable by any means. Chiang Kai-shek's corrupt and militarily incompetent regime had clearly lost its heavenly mandate, and the Truman administration saw no point in throwing good money after bad. It refused to escalate U.S. involvement beyond the provision of arms. Unlike the Johnson administration later in Vietnam, it was prepared to cut its losses rather than send troops.

The Vietnam analogy properly cautions presidents contemplating intervention in a foreign civil war or in circumstances in which intervention itself might spark civil war. The Vietnam War is ever a reminder to the national leadership that there are limits to what the electorate will bear in uses of American military power overseas. When it came to fighting communist aggression anywhere, the Johnson administration assumed that it had virtually unlimited drawing rights on the electorate's patience and pocketbooks—that the American people would pay any price and bear any burden in the twilight struggle against communism in the Third

World. If the Vietnam War was a military defeat, it was also a political disaster for the imperial presidency and its implicit arrogance toward the electorate.

But the Vietnam War—or at least some of its perceived lessons—continues to get in the way of sound thinking about using force. Presidential nominee George W. Bush declared at the August 2000 Republican National Convention: "A generation shaped by Vietnam must remember the lessons of Vietnam. When America uses force in the world, the cause must be just, the goal must be clear, and victory must be overwhelming."[17] This restatement of the Weinberger-Powell Doctrine may be the ideal, but it runs afoul of basic tenets of warfare. States do not always enter wars by choice, and against any genuine competitor there can never be a guarantee of victory, much less overwhelming victory. Real war is a messy and dangerous enterprise, and the experience of Vietnam provides no basis for believing that the United States can confine its uses of force to the circumstances of the virtuous, the viable, and the victorious.

The Gulf War waged by Bush's father was essentially an application of the Weinberger-Powell Doctrine that produced an impressive military—if an unsatisfying political—victory over an isolated and witless enemy who could think of nothing better to do than stare dully into his approaching and inevitable defeat. It was a war against an almost perfect enemy. As such, the Gulf War is hardly likely to be repeated. Quick and clean wars are exceptional, and nostalgia for them is a treacherous foundation for making use-of-force decisions. The Gulf War was analogous to nothing before it and is likely to remain so sui generis as to be of little analogical value to future policy makers except to those who believe that science can eliminate war's fog and friction.

Whatever the utility of reasoning by historical analogy as a tool of policy formulation and implementation, it is clear that policy makers will continue to be influenced by past events and what they believe those events teach. It is also clear that presidents' knowledge of history varies widely, and that reasoning by historical analogy is but one of a host of factors at play in presidential decision making. Presidents Theodore Roosevelt, Woodrow Wilson, Harry Truman, and John Kennedy were well read in history, whereas presidents Lyndon Johnson, Ronald Reagan, and George Bush displayed considerably less knowledge of history. Moreover, in analyzing a specific presidential use-of-force decision it is virtually impossible to determine the exact influence of reasoning by historical analogy in relation to such other factors as presidential personality, domestic political considerations, and the role of key advisers. Munich clearly weighed heavily on the minds of Truman in 1950, Johnson in 1965, and Bush in 1990, as did Vietnam on the mind of Clinton in the 1990s. But all the evidence suggests that, for better or for worse, some thinking about history attends all significant presidential uses of force, especially those that invite war.

Notes

Introduction

1. Harry S. Truman, *Memoirs*, 2:335.

2. Ibid., 1:121.

3. See Jeffrey Record, "Weinberger-Powell Doctrine Doesn't Cut It Anymore," 35–36.

4. Robert Jervis, *Perception and Misperception in International Politics*, 217.

5. Christopher Hemmer, *Which Lessons Matter?* 12.

6. See Howard Shuman and Cheryl Rieger, "Historical Analogies, Generational Effects, and Attitudes toward War," 315–26; Richard N. Lebow, "Generational Learning and Conflict Management," 555–85; Ole R. Holsti and James N. Rosenau, "Does Where You Stand Depend on When You Were Born?" 1–22; and Michael Roskin, "From Pearl Harbor to Vietnam," 563–88.

7. Daniel Schorr, "The Dread of Appeasement."

8. David W. Levy, *The Debate over Vietnam*, 19.

Chapter 1. Munich and Vietnam: Lessons Drawn

1. For the definitive account of the Munich Conference, see Telford Taylor, *Munich: The Price of Peace*.

2. See Martin Thomas, "France and the Czechoslovak Crisis," 122–59; and Eric Goldstein, "Neville Chamberlain, the British Official Mind, and the Munich Crisis," 276–92.

3. Quoted in Taylor, *Munich*, 884.

4. Henry Kissinger, *Diplomacy*, 317; emphasis in original.

5. For a detailed assessment of the European military balance at the time of

Munich, see Williamson Murray, *The Change in the European Balance of Power, 1938–1939,* 217–63.

6. William L. Shirer, *The Rise and Fall of the Third Reich,* 426; emphasis in original.

7. Ibid., 423–24.

8. See Liddell Hart, *The German Generals Talk,* 31–34; Walter Goerlitz, *History of the German General Staff,* 304–39; Richard Overy, "Germany and the Munich Crisis," 191–215; Taylor, *Munich,* 681–731; and Shirer, *Rise and Fall of the Third Reich,* 404–14.

9. N. H. Gibbs, *History of the Second World War: Grand Strategy,* 1:642–48.

10. See Robert Allan Doughty, *The Seeds of Disaster,* 14–40.

11. Graham Stewart, *Burying Caesar: The Churchill-Chamberlain Rivalry,* 313.

12. Ibid., 297.

13. Doughty, *Seeds of Disaster,* 36, 38.

14. See Martin Gilbert and Richard Gott, *The Appeasers,* 248–352.

15. "The Munich Agreement," speech by Winston S. Churchill before the House of Commons, October 5, 1938; reprinted in Churchill, *Blood, Sweat, and Tears,* 61.

16. William L. Shirer, *Berlin Diary,* 145, 146.

17. B. H. Liddell Hart, *History of the Second World War,* 7, 22.

18. Churchill, *Blood, Sweat, and Tears,* 58.

19. See Robert J. Beck, "Munich's Lessons Reconsidered," 161–91.

20. See discussion in Stewart, *Burying Caesar,* 275–313.

21. Quoted in ibid., 300.

22. Quoted in Ronald Steel, *Walter Lippmann and the American Century,* 371, 374.

23. Hemmer, *Which Lessons Matter,* 4.

24. Lebow, "Generational Learning and Conflict Management," 562.

25. David Fromkin and James Chace, "What *Are* the Lessons of Vietnam?" 745, 746.

26. See, for example, W. W. Rostow, "The Case for the Vietnam War," 39–50.

27. Quoted in George McT. Kahin, *Intervention,* 249.

28. Quoted in Tom Wells, *The War Within,* 99.

29. Dean Rusk, with Richard Rusk and Daniel S. Papp, *As I Saw It,* 472.

30. Carl von Clausewitz, *On War,* 608.

31. For an exhaustive treatment of civil-military relations on Vietnam policy issues during the period 1961–65, see H. R. McMaster, *Dereliction of Duty.*

32. See Richard Nixon, *No More Vietnams,* 18; and W. Thomas Smith Jr., "An Old Warrior Sounds Off," 133.

33. Vo Nguyen Giap, *Big Victory, Great Task,* 74.

34. See Lewis Sorley, *A Better War.*

35. See Jeffrey Record, *The Wrong War,* 10.

36. Michael Lind, *Vietnam: The Necessary War.*

37. See, for example, George C. Herring, *America's Longest War;* and Gabriel Kolko, *Anatomy of a War.*

38. For the best representative expression of this school, see U. S. G. Sharp, *Strategy for Defeat: Vietnam in Retrospect.*

39. Nixon, *No More Vietnams,* 237; emphasis in original.

40. See McMaster, *Dereliction of Duty;* Andrew Krepinevich, *The Army and Vietnam;* Bruce Palmer Jr., *The Twenty-five Year War;* Dave Richard Palmer, *Summons of the Trumpet;* and Harry G. Summers Jr., *On Strategy.*

41. Kissinger, *Diplomacy,* 628.

42. Quoted in Stanley Weintraub, *MacArthur's War,* 5.

43. Summers, *On Strategy.*

44. Eric R. Alterman, "Thinking Twice," 94.

45. Caspar W. Weinberger, *Fighting for Peace,* 8.

46. See "Appendix B, The Weinberger Doctrine," in Michael I. Handel, *Masters of War,* 307–26.

47. Excerpts from the Weinberger speech appearing in the above and following paragraphs are drawn from "The Uses of Military Power," speech before the National Press Club, Washington, D.C., November 28, 1984, reprinted in Handel, *Masters of War,* 329–445; emphasis in original.

48. Maxwell D. Taylor, *Swords and Plowshares,* 403, 404, and 406.

49. Weinberger, "The Uses of Military Power," 159.

50. Ibid., 161.

51. See Lawrence Freedman, ed., *Strategic Coercion: Concepts and Cases;* and Alexander L. George and William E. Simons, eds., *The Limits of Coercive Diplomacy.*

52. Colin Powell, with Joseph E. Persico, *My American Journey,* 148.

53. Ibid., 149.

54. Colin L. Powell, "U.S. Forces: Challenges Ahead," 38, 39, 40.

55. *A National Security Strategy for a New Century,* 19, 20.

56. Ibid., 20.

57. Andrew J. Bacevich, "The Limits of Orthodoxy," 184.

58. Norman Podhoretz, *Why We Were in Vietnam,* 12.

Chapter 2. Truman in Korea

1. Bernard Brodie, *War and Politics,* 118.

2. Levy, *The Debate over Vietnam,* 14–15.

3. See John Lewis Gaddis, *Strategies of Containment.*

4. X [pseud.], "The Sources of Soviet Conduct," 566–83.

5. George F. Kennan, *Memoirs,* 497.

6. "The Statement and Testimony of the Honorable George F. Kennan" before the Senate Foreign Relations Committee, February 10, 1966; reprinted in *The Vietnam Hearings,* 108.

7. "Special Message to the Congress on Greece and Turkey: The Truman Doctrine," March 12, 1947, in Harry S. Truman, *Public Papers of the Presidents, January 1 to December 31, 1947*, 178–79.

8. Ibid., 178.

9. For a discussion of NSC-68, see Gaddis, *Strategies of Containment*, 89–126; and Marc Trachtenberg, "Making Grand Strategy," 33–40.

10. "NSC-68: a Report to the National Security Council by the Executive Secretary on United States Objectives and Programs for National Security, April 14, 1950," 61–62.

11. Ibid., 64–65.

12. Ibid., 53.

13. Ibid., 56.

14. Ibid., 59.

15. Ibid., 83.

16. Truman, *Memoirs*, 2:335.

17. Reprinted in *The Pentagon Papers*, 589.

18. Kissinger, *Diplomacy*, 479.

19. Richard E. Neustadt and Ernest R. May, *Thinking in Time*, 48.

20. Bruce Cumings, *Korea's Place in the Sun*, 263; and Don Oberdorfer, *The Two Koreas*, 9.

21. Sergei N. Goncharov, John W. Lewis, and Xue Litai, *Uncertain Partners*, 131.

22. William T. Lee, *The Korean War Was Stalin's Show*, 48–55.

23. Goncharov et al., *Uncertain Partners*, 141–42; and William Steuck, *The Korean War*, 32.

24. Steuck, *The Korean War*, 32–41.

25. Lee, *The Korean War Was Stalin's Show*, 31.

26. See Shen Zhihua, "Sino-Soviet Relations and the Origins of the Korean War."

27. Kissinger, *Diplomacy*, 290.

28. Robert Mann, *A Grand Delusion*, 36.

29. Dean Acheson, *The Korean War*, 32–33.

30. Quoted in Rosemary Foot, *The Wrong War*, 23.

Chapter 3. Eisenhower in Indochina

1. Quoted in Mann, *A Grand Delusion*, 97.

2. Dwight D. Eisenhower, *Mandate for Change*, 373.

3. Excerpted in Robert J. McMahon, ed., *Major Problems in the History of the Vietnam War*, 120.

4. Excerpted in ibid., 122.

5. Excerpted in ibid., 121–22.

6. "The Threat of a Red Asia," address by Secretary of State John Foster Dulles before the Overseas Press Club of America, March 29, 1954; reprinted in *Department of State Bulletin*, April 12, 1954, 539, 540.

7. Nixon, *No More Vietnams*, 31.

8. Herbert S. Parmet, *Eisenhower and the American Crusades,* 364.

9. Ibid., 357.

10. Nixon, *No More Vietnams,* 31.

11. *Pentagon Papers,* 1:94; and Matthew B. Ridgway, *Soldier,* 275–78.

12. Ridgway, *Soldier,* 277.

13. Ibid.

14. See Gaddis, *Strategies of Containment,* 127–97; and Eisenhower, *Mandate for Change,* 445–58.

15. Parmet, *Eisenhower and the American Crusades,* 361–63; and Jeffrey Record, *Revising U.S. Military Strategy: Tailoring Means to Ends,* 16.

16. Eisenhower, *Mandate for Change,* 454.

17. Record, *The Wrong War,* 13–35; Daniel S. Papp, *Vietnam: The View from Moscow, Peking, Washington,* 10; and William J. Duiker, *Sacred War,* 89–91.

18. Reprinted in *The China White Paper, August 1949,* xiv, xv–xvi, and xvi.

19. Tang Tsou, *America's Failure in China,* 398. Also see Richard C. Thornton, *China: A Political History,* 160–224.

Chapter 4. Kennedy and Johnson in Vietnam and the Caribbean

1. See Peter Collier and David Horowitz, *The Kennedys,* 104–7.

2. Quoted in Guenter Lewy, *America in Vietnam,* 12.

3. Quoted in Theodore C. Sorenson, *Kennedy,* 703.

4. Ernest R. May and Philip D. Zeilkow, eds., *The Kennedy Tapes,* 3.

5. Doris Kearns, *Lyndon Johnson and the American Dream,* 252.

6. Quoted in Michael Beschloss, ed., *Taking Charge,* 248.

7. Ibid., 250.

8. Johnson's reference was to the umbrella Chamberlain carried as he announced "peace in our time" after he stepped off the airplane in the rain on his return from the Munich Conference. Eric F. Goldman, *The Tragedy of Lyndon Johnson,* 330–31.

9. Rusk, *As I Saw It,* 404.

10. Quoted in John B. Henry II and William Espinosa, "The Tragedy of Dean Rusk," 185.

11. Kai Bird, *The Color of Truth,* 107, 317.

12. Yuen Foong Khong, *Analogies at War,* 58–62.

13. Ibid., 97.

14. Robert D. Schulzinger, *A Time for War,* 45.

15. Record, *The Wrong War,* 38–39.

16. Quoted in Richard Reeves, *President Kennedy: Profile in Power,* 444.

17. Quoted in Robert Buzzanco, *Masters of War,* 143.

18. Quoted in Kearns, *Lyndon Johnson and the American Dream,* 252.

19. Quoted in Brian VanDeMark, *Into the Quagmire,* 204.

20. Lyndon Baines Johnson, *The Vantage Point,* 151–52.

21. Gaddis, *Strategies of Containment,* 209.

22. The argument is most comprehensively presented in David Kaiser, *American Tragedy.*

23. Quoted in David Halberstam, *The Best and the Brightest,* 76.

24. Clausewitz, *On War,* 88.

25. See William J. Duiker, *The Rise of Nationalism in Vietnam;* John T. McAlister Jr., *Vietnam: The Origins of Revolution;* and David G. Marr, *Vietnamese Anticolonialism* and *Vietnamese Tradition on Trial.*

26. Quoted in Leslie H. Gelb and Richard K. Betts, *The Irony of Vietnam,* 42.

27. John Kenneth Galbraith, *How to Get out of Vietnam,* 19.

28. Quoted in E. J. Kahn, *The China Hands,* 23.

29. Quoted in Gibbons, *The U.S. Government and the Vietnam War,* 2:161.

30. Lind, *Vietnam: The Necessary War,* xi, 1.

31. Ibid., 48.

32. Ibid., 48.

33. Nixon, *No More Vietnams,* 13.

34. Herring, *America's Longest War,* 314.

35. Hans J. Morgenthau, "We Are Deluding Ourselves in Vietnam."

36. See Trumbull Higgins, *The Perfect Failure;* and Peter Wyden, *Bay of Pigs.*

37. Address before the American Society of Newspaper Editors, April 20, 1961, in John F. Kennedy, *Public Papers of the Presidents, January 20, 1961, to December 31, 1961,* 304.

38. Radio and television report to the American people on the Soviet arms buildup in Cuba, in Kennedy, *Public Papers of the Presidents, January 1 to December 31, 1962,* 809.

39. See Mark J. White, ed., *The Kennedys and Cuba.*

40. Aleksandr Fursenko and Timothy Naftali, *"One Hell of a Gamble,"* 188.

41. Ibid., 806.

42. Quoted in May and Zeilkow, *The Kennedy Tapes,* 235.

43. Quoted in ibid., 127.

44. Quoted in ibid., 115.

45. Quoted in ibid., 122.

46. Quoted in ibid., 207.

47. Quoted in Evan Thomas, *Robert Kennedy: His Life,* 215.

48. Quoted in May and Zeilkow, *The Kennedy Tapes,* 244.

49. See Theodore Draper, *The Dominican Revolt.* For more comprehensive accounts of the Dominican intervention, see Piero Gleijeses, *The Dominican Crisis;* and John Bartlow Martin, *Overtaken by Events.*

50. Lyndon B. Johnson, *The Vantage Point,* 188, 199.

51. Robert Dallek, *Flawed Giant,* 265.

52. George W. Ball, *The Past Has Another Pattern,* 330–31.

Chapter 5. Nixon and Kissinger in Vietnam

1. Arnold R. Isaacs, *Without Honor*, 496–97.

2. Henry Kissinger, *White House Years*, 292.

3. Nixon, *No More Vietnams*, 212.

4. Ibid., 12, 13.

5. Quoted in Stephen E. Ambrose, *Nixon*, 48.

6. Quoted in ibid., 78.

7. Quoted in Jeffrey Kimball, *Nixon's Vietnam War*, 38.

8. Richard Nixon, *The Memoirs of Richard Nixon*, 269–70.

9. Quoted in Kimball, *Nixon's Vietnam War*, 52.

10. Ibid., 161–62.

11. Kissinger, *White House Years*, 262; emphasis added.

12. Nixon, *No More Vietnams*, 80.

13. "A Conversation with the President about Foreign Policy, July 1, 1970"; reprinted in Richard Nixon, *Public Papers of the Presidents, 1970*, 551.

14. Stephen E. Ambrose, "The Christmas Bombing," 555, 557.

15. Earl H. Tilford Jr., *Setup*, 264; also see Kimball, *Nixon's Vietnam War*, 358–71.

16. Richard Nixon, *The Real War*, 105–6; also see Record, *The Wrong War*, 70–71.

17. Kimball, *Nixon's Vietnam War*, ix.

18. Informal remarks in Guam with newsmen, July 25, 1969, in Nixon, *Public Papers of the Presidents, 1970*, 554.

19. Ibid., 555.

20. Address to the nation on the war in Vietnam, November 3, 1969, in ibid., 906.

21. Ibid., 905, 906.

22. Second annual report to Congress on United States foreign policy, February 25, 1971, in Nixon, *Public Papers of the Presidents, 1971*, 225, 226.

Chapter 6. Reagan in Lebanon, Grenada, Central America, and Afghanistan

1. Address at commencement exercises at the University of Notre Dame, May 22, 1977, in Jimmy Carter, *Public Papers of the Presidents, 1977*, 1:955, 956, 957.

2. See Kenneth E. Morris, *Jimmy Carter, American Moralist*, 262–72; and Peter G. Bourne, *Jimmy Carter*, 380–92.

3. Address by Jimmy Carter to the American Chamber of Commerce in Tokyo, Japan, May 28, 1975; quoted in Robert Kagan, *A Twilight Struggle*, 51.

4. Address to the nation, January 4, 1980, in Carter, *Public Papers of the Presidents, 1980–1981*, 1:22, 24.

5. The State of the Union, January 23, 1980, in ibid., 195, 196, 197.

6. Interview with Lou Cannon, quoted in Lou Cannon, *President Reagan*, 406.

7. See Richard A. Gabriel, *Operation Peace for Galilee*, especially pp. 60–68; and Ze'ev Schiff and Ehud Ya'ari, *Israel's War in Lebanon*, especially pp. 41–44.

8. Richard N. Haass, *Intervention*, 105.

9. Ibid., 24.

10. Remarks in a question-and-answer session with regional editors and broadcaster on the situation in Lebanon, White House, October 24, 1983, in Ronald Reagan, *Public Papers of the Presidents, 1983*, 2:1500–1504.

11. Reagan, "Lebanon and Grenada," 67.

12. Weinberger, "The Uses of Military Power," 156, 160.

13. *Report of the Department of Defense Commission on Beirut International Airport Terrorist Act, October 23, 1983*, 24.

14. In a 1989 interview, Robert C. "Bud" McFarlane told Reagan biographer Lou Cannon: "Ronald Reagan called Lebanon vital to United States security interests, which in any context, it is not. If Lebanon disappeared, it wouldn't affect United States' security interests very much" (quoted in Cannon, *President Reagan*, 449).

15. *Report of the Department of Defense Commission*, 44.

16. *Adequacy of the U.S. Marine Corps Security in Beirut*, 33.

17. Ronald Reagan, *An American Life*, 442–46.

18. Richard A. Gabriel, *Military Incompetence*, 122.

19. George P. Shultz, *Turmoil and Triumph*, 233.

20. Ibid., 231.

21. See Norman Cigar, "Iraq's Strategic Mindset and the Gulf War," 29.

22. Reagan, *An American Life*, 466.

23. For an excellent and well-informed account of the U.S. invasion and the political events in Grenada that prompted it, see Mark Adkin, *Urgent Fury*.

24. Haass, *Intervention*, 25.

25. Shultz, *Turmoil and Triumph*, 340.

26. Reagan, *An American Life*, 456.

27. Remarks in Bridgetown, Barbados, following a luncheon meeting with leaders of eastern Caribbean countries, April 8, 1982, in Reagan, *Public Papers of the Presidents, 1982*, 1:448.

28. Reagan, *An American Life*, 451.

29. Quoted in Frances Fitzgerald, *Way out There in the Blue*, 109.

30. Cannon, *President Reagan*, 335–36.

31. Quoted in ibid., 348.

32. Excerpts from an interview with Walter Cronkite of CBS News, March 3, 1981, in Reagan, *Public Papers of the Presidents, 1981*, 1:195.

33. Remarks on presenting the Presidential Citizen's Medal to Raymond Weeks at a Veteran's Day ceremony, November 11, 1982, in Reagan, *Public Papers of the Presidents, 1982*, 2:1146.

34. Radio address to the nation on defense spending, February 19, 1983, in Reagan, *Public Papers of the Presidents, 1983*, 1:258.

35. Karen Elliot House, "Reagan's World: Republican Policies Stress Arms Buildup, a Firm Line to Soviet," *Wall Street Journal*, June 3, 1980.

36. Quoted in Charles W. Kegley Jr. and Eugene R. Wittkopf, *American Foreign Policy*, 426.

37. The president's news conference, March 6, 1981, in Reagan, *Public Papers of the Presidents, 1981*, 1:207.

38. Remarks on signing the Captive Nations Week Proclamation, July 19, 1982, in Reagan, *Public Papers of the Presidents, 1982*, 2:936.

39. Remarks on the Caribbean Basin Initiative to the Permanent Council of the Organization of American States, February 24, 1982, in ibid., 2:214.

40. Address before a joint session of the Congress on Central America, April 27, 1983, in Reagan, *Public Papers of the Presidents, 1983*, 1:607.

41. Kagan, *A Twilight Struggle*, 167.

42. Shultz, *Turmoil and Triumph*, 311.

43. Remarks at the National Leadership Forum of the Center for International and Strategic Studies of Georgetown University, April 6, 1984, in Reagan, *Public Papers of the Presidents, 1984*, 1:484.

44. Charles Krauthammer, "The Reagan Doctrine," 54–56.

45. James M. Scott, *Deciding to Intervene*, 16; emphasis in original. Also see Peter W. Rodman, *More Precious than Peace*, 259–88.

46. Alexander M. Haig Jr., *Caveat*, 122.

47. Quoted in Isaacs, *Without Honor*, 148.

Chapter 7. Bush in Panama, the Persian Gulf, and Somalia

1. Steve C. Ropp, "The Bush Administration and the Invasion of Panama," 81.

2. For the best account of the intervention, see Thomas Donnelly, Margaret Roth, and Caleb Baker, *Operation Just Cause*. Also see Richard H. Shultz Jr., *In the Aftermath of War;* and Martha L. Cottam, *Images and Intervention*, 141–62.

3. Address to the nation announcing United States military action in Panama, in George Bush, *Public Papers of the Presidents, 1989*, 1:1723.

4. Ibid., 1:1722.

5. See Powell, *My American Journey*, 418–20; and Susan G. Horowitz, "Indications and Warning Factors," 55.

6. Bush, *Public Papers of the Presidents, 1989*, 1393.

7. Ropp, "The Bush Administration and the Invasion of Panama," 85.

8. Powell, *My American Journey*, 428.

9. Ropp, "The Bush Administration and the Invasion of Panama," 101.

10. Figures taken from Karl W. Eikenberry, "Take No Casualties," 113.

11. Horowitz, "Indications and Warning Factors," 59.

12. James A. Baker III, with Thomas M. DeFrank, *The Politics of Diplomacy*, 194.

13. Powell, *My American Journey*, 434.

14. See Yuen Foong Khong, "Vietnam, the Gulf, and U.S. Choices," 74–95.

15. Herbert S. Parmet, *George Bush*, 464.

16. George Bush and Brent Scowcroft, *A World Transformed*, 303.

17. Ibid., 326.

18. Ibid., 340.

19. Quoted in George Bush, *All My Best,* 497.

20. Ibid., 375.

21. Ibid., 354.

22. Khong, "Vietnam, the Gulf, and U.S. Choices," 88.

23. Address to the nation announcing the deployment of United States armed forces to Saudi Arabia, August 8, 1990, in Bush, *Public Papers of the Presidents, 1990,* 2:1108.

24. Remarks at the annual conference of the Veterans of Foreign Wars in Baltimore, Maryland, August 20, 1990, in ibid., 1150.

25. Remarks to officers and troops at Hickam Air Force Base in Pearl Harbor, Hawaii, October 28, 1990, in ibid., 1483.

26. The president's news conference in Orlando, Florida, November 1, 1990, in ibid., 1514.

27. The president's news conference on the Persian Gulf crisis, January 9, 1991, in Bush, *Public Papers of the Presidents, 1991,* 1:20.

28. Address to the nation announcing allied military action in the Persian Gulf, January 16, 1991, in ibid., 44.

29. Remarks to the Reserve Officers Association, January 23, 1991, in ibid., 60.

30. Bush, *All My Best,* 511.

31. Bush and Scowcroft, *A World Transformed,* 354.

32. Quoted in Robert W. Tucker and David C. Hendrickson, *The Imperial Temptation,* 152.

33. Arnold Isaacs, *Vietnam Shadows,* 76.

34. See Donald Kagan, "Colin Powell's War," 41–45.

35. See Bob Woodward, *The Commanders,* 60–61; and Michael R. Gordon and Bernard E. Trainor, *The Generals' War,* 123–58.

36. Bush and Scowcroft, *A World Transformed,* 431.

37. John Mueller, "The Perfect Enemy," 77–117.

38. See Jeffrey Record, *Hollow Victory,* 57–69.

39. See Cigar, "Iraq's Strategic Mindset and the Gulf War," 1–29.

40. Donald Kagan and Frederick W. Kagan, *While America Sleeps,* 377.

41. Gordon and Trainor, *The Generals' War,* xv.

42. Haass, *Intervention,* 111–13; and John R. Bolton, "Wrong Turn in Somalia," 56–66.

43. Mark Bowden, *Black Hawk Down,* 354.

44. Powell, *My American Journey,* 564–65.

45. William J. Durch, "Introduction to Anarchy," 320–21.

46. James L. Woods, "U.S. Government Decisionmaking Processes during Humanitarian Operations in Somalia," 169.

47. William G. Hyland, *Clinton's World,* 54.

48. Elizabeth Drew, *On the Edge,* 319.

49. Quoted in Hyland, *Clinton's World,* 57.

50. Richard Holbrooke, *To End a War,* 217.

51. *New York Times,* August 8, 1992; quoted in Khong, "Vietnam, the Gulf, and U.S. Choices," 89.

52. Powell, "Why Generals Get Nervous."

53. Quoted in Tim Judah, *Kosovo: War and Revenge,* 73–74.

Chapter 8. Clinton in Haiti and the Balkans

1. Quoted in Ole R. Holsti and James N. Rosenau, "Does Where You Stand Depend on When You Were Born?" 2.

2. James MacGregor Burns and Georgia J. Sorenson, *Dead Center,* 302, 323.

3. Hyland, *Clinton's World,* 15–27.

4. Ibid., 200, 20l.

5. Quoted in Thomas L. Friedman, "Clinton's Foreign Policy Agenda Reaches across Broad Spectrum."

6. Interview with Tom Brokaw of NBC News, June 5, 1994, in William J. Clinton, *Public Papers of the Presidents, 1994,* 1:1038.

7. Remarks at the Joint Service Review at Wheeler Army Airfield in Honolulu, September 1, 1995, in Clinton, *Public Papers of the Presidents, 1995,* 2:1277.

8. Interview with Tom Brokaw, 1040.

9. Susan L. Woodward, "Upside-down Policy," 128.

10. Ivo H. Daalder and Michael E. O'Hanlon, *Winning Ugly,* 209.

11. See Wayne Bert, *The Reluctant Superpower,* 107–23.

12. Drew, *On the Edge,* 146, 148, 155–56.

13. Ivo H. Daalder, *Getting to Dayton,* 118.

14. Powell, "U.S. Forces: Challenges Ahead," 39–40.

15. James Gow, *Triumph of the Lack of Will,* 306.

16. Richard Holbrooke, *To End a War,* 92–93.

17. Quoted in Thomas W. Lippman, *Madeleine Albright and the New American Diplomacy,* 89.

18. Ibid., 90–91.

19. Quoted in ibid., 95.

20. Hyland, *Clinton's World,* 21. Also see Owen Harries, "Madeleine Albright's 'Munich Mindset.'"

21. Quoted in Walter Isaacson, "Madeleine's War," 29.

22. Quoted in "Lessons from the War in Kosovo," 5.

23. Quoted in Ethan Bronner, "Historians Note Flaws in President's Speech."

24. President's radio address, March 27, 1999, in Clinton, *Public Papers of the Presidents, 1999,* 1:461.

25. Secretary Albright, "The Importance of Kosovo," remarks at the U.S. Institute for Peace, Washington, D.C., May 4, 1999; reprinted in *U.S. Department of State Dispatch* (January/February 1999): 5.

26. Dusko Doder and Louise Branson, *Milosevic,* 210.

27. Quoted in Daalder and O'Hanlon, *Winning Ugly,* 101.

28. Michael Ignatieff, *Virtual War,* 203.

29. Quoted in Doder and Branson, *Milosevic,* 263.

30. Ignatieff, *Virtual War,* 41.

31. Eliot A. Cohen, "What's Wrong with the American Way of War."

32. See Jeffrey Record, *Serbia and Vietnam.*

33. Tim Judah, *Kosovo: War and Revenge,* 228–29.

34. *Kosovo/Operation Allied Force After-Action Report to the Congress* (Washington, D.C.: Department of Defense, January 31, 2000), 10–11.

35. Charles K. Hyde, "Casualty Aversion," 17–27.

36. Judah, *Kosovo: War and Revenge,* 311; and R. Jeffrey Smith, "A GI's Home Is His Fortress."

37. John Sweeney, "Stuck in Haiti," 150.

38. Hyland, *Clinton's World,* 64.

39. See Bob Shacochis, *The Immaculate Invasion,* 30–34.

40. The author served on the Senate Armed Services Committee staff during this period and was in charge of organizing an account of the Carter-Powell-Nunn meetings with Cedras and other Haitian officials based on Senator Nunn's handwritten notes and subsequent oral testimony. According to Nunn, Cedras initially refused to believe that the United States would use force against him. Powell assured him as a fellow professional military man that it would; Nunn assured Cedras that Congress, while hardly enthusiastic about military action, would not block it.

41. Drew, *On the Edge,* 333–35; and Burns and Sorenson, *Dead Center,* 181.

42. Shacochis, *The Immaculate Invasion,* 254.

Chapter 9. Legacies of Munich and Vietnam for the Post–Cold War World

1. Robert S. McNamara, "Misreading the Enemy."

2. Robert S. McNamara, with Brian VanDeMark, *In Retrospect;* and Robert S. McNamara, *Argument without End.*

3. NSC-68, 56.

4. Handel, *Masters of War,* 314.

5. Michael Kinsley, "Is There a Doctrine in the House?"

6. Colin S. Gray, *Modern Strategy,* 102.

7. George P. Shultz, "The Ethics of Power," speech given before the convocation of Yeshiva University, New York, December 9, 1984; reprinted in *Ethics and American Power,* 12, 13.

8. Caspar W. Weinberger, "The First Priority for Our New President."

9. Ibid., 13.

10. Nixon, *No More Vietnams,* 13.

11. Ibid., 220, 221.

12. Ibid., 221.

13. Ibid., 224.

14. Ibid., 226.

15. McNamara, *Argument without End*, 370.

16. Quoted in Isaacs, *Without Honor*, 72–73.

17. Shultz, *Turmoil and Triumph*, 646, 650.

18. Powell, *My American Journey*, 576.

19. Quoted in Haass, *Intervention*, 15.

20. Jane E. Holl, "We the People Don't Want No War: Executive Branch Perspectives on the Use of Force," in *The United States and the Use of Force in the Post–Cold War Era*, an Aspen Strategy Group Report (Queenstown, Md.: Aspen Institute, 1995), 124.

21. Holbrooke, *To End a War*, 27.

22. Bert, *The Reluctant Superpower*, 241.

23. Alterman, "Thinking Twice," 107.

24. Kagan and Kagan, *While America Sleeps*, 425.

25. Bert, *The Reluctant Superpower*, xxv.

26. Ibid., xxv.

27. See Record, "Weinberger-Powell Doctrine Doesn't Cut It Anymore," 35–36.

28. Leslie H. Gelb, "Quelling the Teacup Wars," 5.

29. Michael Ignatieff, *The Warrior's Honor*, 104–5.

30. Philippe Delmas, *The Rosy Future of War*, 7.

31. Record, "Force Protection Fetishism."

32. William S. Cohen and Gen. Henry Shelton, "Joint Statement on Kosovo: After-Action Review," 27.

33. Wesley K. Clark, "The United States and NATO," 8–9.

34. See Richard K. Betts, "What Will It Take to Deter the United States?"; Andrew P. N. Erdmann, "The Presumption of Quick, Costless Wars"; and John Mueller, "Public Support for Military Ventures Abroad."

35. See Hyde, "Casualty Aversion"; and the following studies performed by the Rand Corporation of Santa Monica, California: Mark Lorrell and Charles Kelley Jr., *Casualties, Public Opinion, and Presidential Policy during the Vietnam War*, 1985; Benjamin C. Schwarz, *Casualties, Public Opinion, and U.S. Military Intervention*, 1994; and Eric V. Larson, *Casualties and Consensus*, 1996.

36. See John Mueller, *Policy and Opinion in the Gulf War*, 45, 124, 306–7.

37. Erdmann, "The Presumption of Quick, Costless Wars," 375–76.

38. Digest of Findings and Studies Presented to the Conference on the Military and Society, Catigny Conference Center, 1st Division Museum, October 28–29, 1999, 5. http://www.unc.edu/depts/tiss/CIVMIL.htm.

39. Peter D. Feaver and Christopher Gelphi, "How Many Deaths Are Acceptable?"

40. Ibid.

41. Ibid.

42. Hyde, "Casualty Aversion," 25.

43. Quoted in Feaver and Gelphi, "How Many Deaths Are Acceptable?"

44. Quoted in Hyde, "Casualty Aversion."

45. Vincent J. Goulding Jr., "From Chancellorsville to Kosovo," 12.

46. Clausewitz, *On War*, 88.

47. Bert, *The Reluctant Superpower*, 247.

48. Ibid., 163.

49. See Michael Pillsbury, *China Debates the Future Security Environment*; Richard Bernstein and Ross H. Munro, *The Coming War with China*; and Robert Kagan, "What China Knows That We Don't," 22–27.

50. For a comprehensive analysis of China's security challenges, see Andrew J. Nathan and Robert S. Ross, *The Great Wall and the Empty Fortress*.

51. Ian Johnson, "China's Economic Health Raises Doubts."

52. Gerald Segal, "Does China Matter?" 28.

53. Ibid., 3.

54. Bill Owens with Ed Offley, *Lifting the Fog of War*, 14.

55. Joseph S. Nye Jr. and William A. Owens, "America's Information Edge," 25.

56. Burns and Sorenson, *Dead Center*, 306; and Dick Morris, *Behind the Oval Office*, 253–54.

57. Carl von Clausewitz's monumental *On War* treats war as an art, whereas Antoine Henri de Jomini's *The Art of War* approaches it as primarily a science. For the best recent discussion of what war is all about, see Gray, *Modern Strategy*; also see Stephen M. Walt, "The Search for a Science of Strategy."

58. See Barry D. Watts, *Clausewitzian Friction and Future War*.

59. Lawrence Freedman, *The Revolution in Strategic Affairs*, 41.

Chapter 10. Using Force, Thinking History

1. Bert, *The Reluctant Superpower*, 111.

2. Paul M. Kattenburg, *The Vietnam Trauma in American Foreign Policy*, 98.

3. Ernest R. May, *"Lessons" of the Past*, 121.

4. Chester L. Cooper, *The Lost Crusade*, 422.

5. Neustadt and May, *Thinking in Time*, 75–90.

6. George F. Kennan, "The Origins of Containment," 25, 26.

7. Kennan, *Memoirs*, 486.

8. Ibid., 487.

9. Quoted in Lawrence Freedman, *Kennedy's Wars*, 33.

10. Mann, *A Grand Delusion*, 68.

11. McNamara, *Argument without End*, 40.

12. William J. Duiker, *Ho Chi Minh*, 569–77.

13. Alexander M. Haig Jr., with Charles McCarry, *Inner Circles*, 127.

14. Ibid., 133–34.

15. See Daniel Yergin, *Shattered Peace*.

16. John Lewis Gaddis, *We Now Know: Rethinking Cold War History*, 284.

17. "Bush Outlines His Goals."

Bibliography

Acheson, Dean. *The Korean War.* New York: W. W. Norton, 1971.

Adequacy of the U.S. Marine Corps Security in Beirut. Report of the Investigations Subcommittee of the House Armed Services Committee. 98th Congress, 1st session, 28-6470. Washington, D.C.: U.S. Government Printing Office, December 19, 1983.

Adkin, Mark. *Urgent Fury: The Battle for Grenada.* Lexington, Mass.: D. C. Heath, 1989.

Alterman, Eric R. "Thinking Twice: The Weinberger Doctrine and the Lessons of Vietnam." *Fletcher Forum* 10 (winter 1986): 93–109.

Ambrose, Stephen E. "The Christmas Bombing." In *America at War: An Anthology of Articles from MHQ, the Quarterly Journal of Military History,* ed. Calvin L. Christman, 553–55. Annapolis: Naval Institute Press, 1991.

———. *Nixon: The Triumph of a Politician, 1962–1972.* New York: Simon and Schuster, 1989.

Bacevich, Andrew J. "The Limits of Orthodoxy: The Use of Force after the Cold War." In *The United States and the Use of Force in the Post–Cold War Era.* An Aspen Strategy Group Report. Queenstown, Md.: Aspen Institute, 1995.

Baker, James A. III, with Thomas M. DeFrank. *The Politics of Diplomacy: Revolution, War and Peace.* New York: Putnam, 1995.

Ball, George W. *The Past Has Another Pattern: Memoirs.* New York: W. W. Norton, 1982.

Beck, Robert J. "Munich's Lessons Reconsidered." *International Security* 14 (fall 1989): 161–91.

Bernstein, Richard, and Ross H. Munro. *The Coming War with China*. New York: Alfred A. Knopf, 1997.

Bert, Wayne. *The Reluctant Superpower: United States Policy in Bosnia, 1991–1995*. New York: St. Martin's Press, 1997.

Beschloss, Michael, ed. *Taking Charge: The Johnson White House Tapes, 1963–1964*. New York: Simon and Schuster, 1997.

Betts, Richard K. "What Will It Take to Deter the United States?" *Parameters* 25 (winter 1995–96): 70–79.

Bird, Kai. *The Color of Truth. McGeorge Bundy and William Bundy: Brothers in Arms*. New York: Simon and Schuster, 1998.

Bolton, John R. "Wrong Turn in Somalia." *Foreign Affairs* 73 (January/February 1994): 56–66.

Bourne, Peter G. *Jimmy Carter: A Comprehensive Biography from Plains to Post-presidency*. New York: Scribner, 1997.

Bowden, Mark. *Black Hawk Down: A Story of Modern War*. New York: Penguin Books, 1999.

Brodie, Bernard. *War and Politics*. New York: Macmillan, 1973.

Bronner, Ethan. "Historians Note Flaws in President's Speech." *New York Times*, March 26, 1999.

Burns, James MacGregor, and Georgia J. Sorenson. *Dead Center: Clinton-Gore Leadership and the Perils of Moderation*. New York: Scribner, 1999.

"Bush Outlines His Goals: 'I Want to Change the Tone of Washington.'" *New York Times*, August 4, 2000.

Bush, George. *All My Best: My Life in Letters and Other Writings*. New York: Scribner, 1999.

———. *Public Papers of the Presidents of the United States: George Bush 1989–1992*. 4 vols. Washington, D.C.: U.S. Government Printing Office, 1990–93.

Bush, George, and Brent Scowcroft. *A World Transformed*. New York: Alfred A. Knopf, 1998.

Buzzanco, Robert. *Masters of War: Military Dissent and Politics in the Vietnam Era*. New York: Cambridge University Press, 1996.

Cannon, Lou. *President Reagan: The Role of a Lifetime*. New York: Simon and Schuster, 1991.

Carter, Jimmy. *Public Papers of the Presidents of the United States: Jimmy Carter, 1977–1981*. Washington, D.C.: U.S. Government Printing Office, 1978–82.

The China White Paper, August 1949. Stanford: Stanford University Press, 1967.

Churchill, Winston S. *Blood, Sweat, and Tears*. New York: Putnam, 1941.

Cigar, Norman. "Iraq's Strategic Mindset and the Gulf War: Blueprint for Defeat." *Journal of Strategic Studies* 15 (March 1992): 1–29.

Clark, Wesley K. "The United States and NATO: The Way Ahead." *Parameters* 29 (winter 1999–2000): 2–14.

Clausewitz, Carl von. *On War*. Edited and translated by Michael Howard and Peter Paret. Princeton: Princeton University Press, 1976.

Clinton, William J. *Public Papers of the Presidents of the United States: William J. Clinton, 1994–1999.* Washington, D.C.: U.S. Government Printing Office, 1995–2000.

Cohen, Eliot A. "What's Wrong with the American Way of War." *Wall Street Journal,* March 30, 1999.

Cohen, Secretary of Defense William S., and Gen. Henry Shelton, Chairman of the Joint Chiefs of Staff. "Joint Statement on Kosovo: After-Action Review." Testimony before the Senate Armed Services Committee, October 14, 1999.

Collier, Peter, and David Horowitz. *The Kennedys: An American Drama.* New York: Summit Books, 1984.

Cooper, Chester L. *The Lost Crusade: America in Vietnam.* New York: Dodd, Mead, 1970.

Cottam, Martha L. *Images and Intervention: U.S. Policies in Latin America.* Pittsburg: University of Pittsburg Press, 1994.

Cumings, Bruce. *Korea's Place in the Sun: A Modern History.* New York: W. W. Norton, 1977.

Daalder, Ivo H. *Getting to Dayton: The Making of America's Bosnia Policy.* Washington, D.C.: Brookings Institution, 2000.

Daalder, Ivo H., and Michael E. O'Hanlon. *Winning Ugly, NATO's War to Save Kosovo.* Washington, D.C.: Brookings Institution, 2000.

Delmas, Philippe. *The Rosy Future of War.* New York: Free Press, 1995.

Digest of Findings and Studies Presented to the Conference on the Military and Society. Catigny Conference Center, 1st Division Museum, October 28–29, 1999. http://www.unc.edu/depts/tiss/CIVMIL.htm.

Doder, Dusko, and Louise Branson. *Milosevic: Portrait of a Tyrant.* New York: Free Press, 1999.

Donnelly, Thomas, Margaret Roth, and Caleb Baker. *Operation Just Cause: The Storming of Panama.* New York: Lexington Books, 1991.

Doughty, Robert Allan. *The Seeds of Disaster: The Development of French Army Doctrine 1919–1939.* Hamden, Conn.: Archon Books, 1985.

Draper, Theodore. *The Dominican Revolt: A Case Study in American Policy.* New York: A Commentary Report, 1968.

Drew, Elizabeth. *On the Edge: The Clinton Presidency.* New York: Simon and Schuster, 1994.

Duiker, William J. *Ho Chi Minh: A Life.* New York: Hyperion, 2000.

———. *The Rise of Nationalism in Vietnam.* Ithaca: Cornell University Press, 1976.

———. *Sacred War: Nationalism and Revolution in a Divided Vietnam.* New York: McGraw-Hill, 1995.

Durch, William J. "Introduction to Anarchy: Humanitarian Intervention and 'State Building' in Somalia." In *UN Peacekeeping, American Politics, and the Uncivil Wars of the 1990s,* ed. William J. Durch, 311–65. New York: St. Martin's Press, 1996.

Eikenberry, Karl W. "Take No Casualties." *Parameters* 25 (summer 1996): 109–18.

Eisenhower, Dwight D. *Mandate for Change, 1953–1956.* Garden City, N.Y.: Doubleday, 1963.

Erdmann, Andrew P. N. "The Presumption of Quick, Costless Wars." *Orbis* 43 (summer 1999): 363–81.

Feaver, Peter D., and Christopher Gelphi. "How Many Deaths Are Acceptable? A Surprising Answer." *Washington Post,* November 7, 1999.

Fitzgerald, Frances. *Way out There in the Blue: Reagan, Star Wars and the End of the Cold War.* New York: Simon and Schuster, 2000.

Foot, Rosemary. *The Wrong War: American Policy and the Dimensions of the Korean Conflict, 1950–1953.* Ithaca: Cornell University Press, 1985.

Freedman, Lawrence. *Kennedy's Wars: Berlin, Cuba, Laos, and Vietnam.* New York: Oxford University Press, 2000.

———. *The Revolution in Strategic Affairs.* Adelphi Paper 318. London: International Institute for Strategic Studies, April 1998.

———, ed. *Strategic Coercion: Concepts and Cases.* New York: Oxford University Press, 1998.

Friedman, Thomas L. "Clinton's Foreign Policy Agenda Reaches across Broad Spectrum." *New York Times,* October 4, 1992.

Fromkin, David, and James Chace. "What *Are* the Lessons of Vietnam?" *Foreign Affairs* 63 (spring 1985): 722–46.

Fursenko, Aleksandr, and Timothy Naftali. *"One Hell of a Gamble": Khrushchev, Castro, and Kennedy, 1958–1964.* New York: W. W. Norton, 1997.

Gabriel, Richard A. *Military Incompetence: Why the American Military Doesn't Win.* New York: Hill and Wang, 1985.

———. *Operation Peace for Galilee: The Israeli-PLO War in Lebanon.* New York: Hill and Wang, 1984.

Gaddis, John Lewis. *Strategies of Containment: A Critical Appraisal of Postwar American Security Policy.* New York: Oxford University Press, 1982.

———. *We Now Know: Rethinking Cold War History.* New York: Oxford University Press, 1997.

Galbraith, John Kenneth. *How to Get out of Vietnam.* New York: Signet Books, 1967.

Gelb, Leslie H. "Quelling the Teacup Wars: The New World's Constant Challenge." *Foreign Affairs* 73 (November/December 1994): 2–6.

Gelb, Leslie H., and Richard K. Betts. *The Irony of Vietnam: The System Worked.* Washington, D.C.: Brookings Institution, 1979.

George, Alexander L., and William E. Simons, eds. *The Limits of Coercive Diplomacy.* Boulder, Colo.: Westview Press, 1994.

Gibbons, William Conrad. *The U.S. Government and the Vietnam War: Executive and Legislative Roles and Relationships.* Part 2. Washington, D.C.: U.S. Government Printing Office, 1984.

Gibbs, N. H. *History of the Second World War: Grand Strategy.* Volume 1: *Rearmament Policy.* London: Her Majesty's Stationery Office, 1976.

Gilbert, Martin, and Richard Gott. *The Appeasers.* 1963. Reprint, London: Phoenix Press, 2000.

Gleijeses, Piero. *The Dominican Crisis: The 1965 Constitutionalist Revolt and American Intervention.* Translated by Lawrence Lipson. Baltimore: Johns Hopkins University Press, 1978.

Goerlitz, Walter. *History of the German General Staff.* Boulder, Colo.: Westview Press, 1985.

Goldman, Eric F. *The Tragedy of Lyndon Johnson.* New York: Alfred A. Knopf, 1969.

Goldstein, Eric. "Neville Chamberlain, the British Official Mind, and the Munich Crisis." *Diplomacy and Statecraft* 10 (July–November 1999): 276–92.

Goncharov, Sergei N., John W. Lewis, and Xue Litai. *Uncertain Partners: Stalin, Mao, and the Korean War.* Stanford: Stanford University Press, 1993.

Gordon, Michael R., and Bernard E. Trainor. *The Generals' War: The Inside Story of the Conflict in the Gulf.* New York: Little, Brown, 1995.

Goulding, Vincent J. Jr. "From Chancellorsville to Kosovo: Forgetting the Art of War." *Parameters* 30 (summer 2000): 4–18.

Gow, James. *Triumph of the Lack of Will: International Diplomacy in the Yugoslav War.* New York: Columbia University Press, 1997.

Gray, Colin S. *Modern Strategy.* Oxford: Oxford University Press, 1999.

Haass, Richard N. *Intervention: The Use of American Force in the Post–Cold War World.* Washington, D.C.: Carnegie Endowment for International Peace, 1994.

Haig, Alexander M. Jr. *Caveat: Realism, Reagan, and Foreign Policy.* New York: Macmillan, 1984.

Haig, Alexander M. Jr., with Charles McCarry. *Inner Circles: How America Changed the World. A Memoir.* New York: Warner Books, 1992.

Halberstam, David. *The Best and the Brightest.* New York: Random House, 1969.

Handel, Michael I. *Masters of War: Classical Strategic Thought.* Portland, Ore.: Frank Cass, 2000.

Harries, Owen. "Madeleine Albright's 'Munich Mindset.'" *New York Times,* December 19, 1996.

Hart, B. H. Liddell. *The German Generals Talk.* New York: Quill Press, 1979.

———. *History of the Second World War.* New York: Putnam, 1971.

Hemmer, Christopher. *Which Lessons Matter? American Foreign Policy Decision Making in the Middle East, 1979–1987.* Albany: State University of New York Press, 2000.

Henry, John B. II, and William Espinosa. "The Tragedy of Dean Rusk." *Foreign Policy* 18 (fall 1972): 166–92.

Herring, George C. *America's Longest War: The United States in Vietnam, 1950–1975.* Third edition. New York: McGraw-Hill, 1996.

Higgins, Trumbull. *The Perfect Failure: Kennedy, Eisenhower, and the C.I.A. at the Bay of Pigs.* New York: W. W. Norton, 1987.

Holbrooke, Richard. *To End a War.* New York: Random House, 1998.

Holsti, Ole R., and James N. Rosenau. "Does Where You Stand Depend on When You Were Born? The Impact of Generation on Post-Vietnam Foreign Policy Beliefs." *Public Opinion Quarterly* 10 (spring 1980): 1–22.

Horowitz, Susan G. "Indications and Warning Factors." In *Operation Just Cause: The U.S. Intervention in Panama,* ed. Bruce W. Watson and Peter G. Tsouras, Boulder. Colo.: Westview Press, 1990: 49–64.

Houghton, David Patrick. "The Role of Analogical Reasoning in Novel Foreign-Policy Situations." *British Journal of Political Science* 26 (1996): 523–52.

House, Karen Elliot. "Reagan's World: Republican Policies Stress Arms Buildup." *Wall Street Journal,* June 3, 1980.

Hyde, Charles K. "Casualty Aversion: Implications for Policy Makers and Senior Military Officers." *Aerospace Power Journal* 14 (summer 2000): 17–27.

Hyland, William G. *Clinton's World: Remaking American Foreign Policy.* Westport, Conn.: Westview Press, 1999.

Ignatieff, Michael. *Virtual War: Kosovo and Beyond.* New York: Henry Holt, 2000.

———. *The Warrior's Honor: Ethnic War and the Modern Conscience.* New York: Henry Holt, 1997.

Isaacs, Arnold R. *Vietnam Shadows: The War, Its Ghosts, and Its Legacy.* Baltimore: Johns Hopkins University Press, 1997.

———. *Without Honor: Defeat in Vietnam and Cambodia.* New York: Vintage Books, 1984.

Isaacson, Walter. "Madeleine's War." *Time,* May 17, 1999, 29.

Jervis, Robert. *Perception and Misperception in International Politics.* Princeton: Princeton University Press, 1976.

Johnson, Ian. "China's Economic Health Raises Doubts." *Wall Street Journal,* May 31, 2000.

Johnson, Lyndon Baines. *The Vantage Point: Perspectives of the Presidency 1963–1969.* New York: Holt, Rinehart and Winston, 1971.

Judah, Tim. *Kosovo: War and Revenge.* New Haven: Yale University Press, 2000.

Kagan, Donald. "Colin Powell's War." *Commentary* 99 (June 1995): 41–45.

Kagan, Donald, and Frederick W. Kagan. *While America Sleeps: Self-Delusion, Military Weakness, and the Threat to Peace Today.* New York: St. Martin's Press, 2000.

Kagan, Robert. *A Twilight Struggle: American Power and Nicaragua 1977–1990.* New York: Free Press, 1996.

———. "What China Knows That We Don't." *Weekly Standard,* January 2, 1997, 22–27.

Kahin, George McT. *Intervention: How America Became Involved in Vietnam.* New York: Alfred A. Knopf, 1986.

Kahn, E. J. *The China Hands: America's Foreign Service Officers and What Befell Them.* New York: Viking Press, 1972.

Kaiser, David. *American Tragedy: Kennedy, Johnson, and the Origins of the Vietnam War.* Cambridge: Belknap Press of the Harvard University Press, 2000.

Kattenburg, Paul M. *The Vietnam Trauma in American Foreign Policy.* New Brunswick, N.J.: Transaction Books, 1980.

Kearns, Doris. *Lyndon Johnson and the American Dream.* New York: Harper and Row, 1976.

Kegley, Charles W. Jr., and Eugene R. Wiffkopf. *American Foreign Policy, Pattern and Process.* Third edition. New York: St. Martin's Press, 1987.

Kennan, George F. *Memoirs 1925–1950.* New York: Pantheon Books, 1967.

———. "The Origins of Containment." In *Containment, Concept and Policy,* vol. 1, ed. Terry L. Deibel and John L. Gaddis, 24–31. Washington, D.C.: National Defense University Press, 1986.

Kennedy, John F. *Public Papers of the Presidents of the United States: John F. Kennedy, 1961–1962.* Washington, D.C.: U.S. Government Printing Office, 1962–63.

Khong, Yuen Foong. *Analogies at War: Korea, Munich, Dien Bien Phu, and the American Decisions of 1965.* New York: Simon and Schuster, 1992.

———. "Vietnam, the Gulf, and U.S. Choices: A Comparison." *Security Studies* 5 (autumn 1992): 74–95.

Kimball, Jeffrey. *Nixon's Vietnam War.* Lawrence: University of Kansas Press, 1998.

Kinsley, Michael. "Is There a Doctrine in the House?" *Washington Post,* August 9, 2000.

Kissinger, Henry. *Diplomacy.* New York: Simon and Schuster, 1994.

———. *White House Years.* Boston: Little, Brown, 1979.

Kolko, Gabriel. *Anatomy of a War: Vietnam, the United States, and the Modern Historical Experience.* New York: New Press, 1985.

Krauthammer, Charles. "The Reagan Doctrine." *Time,* April 1, 1985, 54–56.

Krepinevich, Andrew. *The Army and Vietnam.* Baltimore: Johns Hopkins University Press, 1986.

Larson, Eric V. *Casualties and Consensus: The Historical Role of Casualties in Domestic Support for U.S. Military Operations.* Santa Monica, Calif.: Rand Corporation, 1996.

Lebow, Richard Ned. "Generational Learning and Conflict Management." *International Journal* 40 (autumn 1985): 555–85.

Lee, William T. *The Korean War Was Stalin's Show.* Charlottesville: Center for National Security Law, University of Virginia Law School, 1999.

"Lessons from the War in Kosovo." Heritage Foundation *Backgrounder,* no. 1311, July 22 1999, 5.

Levy, David W. *The Debate over Vietnam.* Second edition. Baltimore: Johns Hopkins University Press, 1995.

Lewy, Guenter. *America in Vietnam.* New York: Oxford University Press, 1973.

Lind, Michael. *Vietnam: The Necessary War. A Reinterpretation of America's Most Disastrous Military Conflict.* New York: Free Press, 1999.

Lippman, Thomas W. *Madeleine Albright and the New American Diplomacy.* Boulder, Colo.: Westview Press, 2000.

Lorrell, Mark, and Charles Kelley Jr. *Casualties, Public Opinion, and Presidential Policy during the Vietnam War.* Santa Monica, Calif.: Rand Corporation, 1985.

McAlister, John T. *Vietnam: The Origins of Revolution.* Garden City, N.Y.: Doubleday, 1971.

McMahon, Robert J., ed. *Major Problems in the History of the Vietnam War.* Second edition. Lexington, Mass.: D. C. Heath, 1995.

McMaster, H. R. *Dereliction of Duty: Lyndon Johnson, Robert McNamara, the Joint Chiefs of Staff, and the Lies That Led to Vietnam.* New York: HarperCollins, 1997.

McNamara, Robert S. *Argument without End: In Search of Answers to the Vietnam Tragedy.* New York: Public Affairs, 1999.

———. "Misreading the Enemy." *New York Times,* April 21, 1999.

McNamara, Robert S., with Brian VanDeMark. *In Retrospect: The Tragedy and Lessons of Vietnam.* New York: Random House, 1995.

Mann, Robert. *A Grand Delusion: America's Descent into Vietnam.* New York: Basic Books, 2001.

Marr, David G. *Vietnamese Anticolonialism, 1885–1925.* Berkeley: University of California Press, 1971.

———. *Vietnamese Tradition on Trial.* Berkeley: University of California Press, 1985.

Martin, John Bartlow. *Overtaken by Events: The Dominican Crisis from the Fall of Trujillo to the Civil War.* Garden City, N.Y.: Doubleday, 1966.

May, Ernest R. *"Lessons" of the Past: The Use and Misuse of History in American Foreign Policy.* New York: Oxford University Press, 1973.

May, Ernest R., and Philip D. Zeilkow, eds. *The Kennedy Tapes: Inside the White House during the Cuban Missile Crisis.* Cambridge: Belknap Press of the Harvard University Press, 1997.

Morgenthau, Hans J. "We Are Deluding Ourselves in Vietnam." *New York Times Magazine,* April 18, 1965, 25, 85–87.

Morris, Dick. *Behind the Oval Office: Winning the Presidency in the Nineties.* New York: Random House, 1997.

Morris, Kenneth E. *Jimmy Carter, American Moralist.* Athens: University of Georgia Press, 1996.

Mueller, John. "The Perfect Enemy: Assessing the Gulf War." *Security Studies* 5 (autumn 1995): 77–117.

———. *Policy and Opinion in the Gulf War.* Chicago: University of Chicago Press, 1994.

———. "Public Support for Military Ventures Abroad: Evidence from the Polls." Paper presented at the Conference on the Real Lessons of the Vietnam War: Reflections Twenty-five Years after the Fall of Saigon. University of Virginia School of Law, Charlottesville, Virginia, April 28–29, 2000.

Murray, Williamson. *The Change in the European Balance of Power, 1938–1939: The Path to Ruin.* Princeton: Princeton University Press, 1984.

Nathan, Andrew J., and Robert S. Ross. *The Great Wall and the Empty Fortress: Chi-*

na's Search for Security. New York: W. W. Norton, 1997.

A National Security Strategy for a New Century. Washington, D.C.: The White House, December 1999.

Neustadt, Richard E., and Ernest R. May. *Thinking in Time: The Uses of History for Decision-Makers.* New York: Free Press, 1986.

Nixon, Richard. *The Memoirs of Richard Nixon.* New York: Grosset and Dunlap, 1978.

———. *No More Vietnams.* New York: Avon Books, 1985.

———. *Public Papers of the Presidents of the United States: Richard Nixon, 1969–1971.* Washington, D.C.: U.S. Government Printing Office, 1970–72.

———. *The Real War.* New York: Warner Books, 1980.

"NSC-68: A Report to the National Security Council by the Executive Secretary on United States Objectives and Programs for National Security, April 14, 1950." Reprinted in *Naval War College Review* 27 (May–June 1975): 51–108.

Nye, Joseph S. Jr., and William A. Owens. "America's Information Edge." *Foreign Affairs* 75 (March/April 1996): 20–36.

Oberdorfer, Don. *The Two Koreas: A Contemporary History.* Reading, Mass.: Addison-Wesley, 1997.

Overy, Richard. "Germany and the Munich Crisis: A Mutilated Victory?" *Diplomacy and Statecraft* 10 (July–November 1999): 191–215.

Owens, Bill, with Ed Offley. *Lifting the Fog of War.* New York, Farrar, Straus, and Giroux, 2000.

Palmer, Bruce Jr. *The Twenty-five Year War: America's Role in Vietnam.* Lexington: University of Kentucky Press, 1984.

Palmer, Dave Richard. *Summons of the Trumpet: A History of the Vietnam War from a Military Man's Viewpoint.* New York: Ballantine Books, 1978.

Papp, Daniel S. *Vietnam: The View from Moscow, Peking, Washington.* Jefferson, N.C.: MacFarland, 1981.

Parmet, Herbert S. *Eisenhower and the American Crusades.* New York: Macmillan, 1972.

———. *George Bush: The Life of a Lone Star Yankee.* New York: Scribner, 1997.

Pentagon Papers. The Defense Department's History of United States Decisionmaking on Vietnam. 4 vols. Senator Gravel Edition. Boston, Mass.: Beacon Press, 1971.

Pillsbury, Michael. *China Debates the Future Security Environment.* Washington, D.C.: National Defense University Press, 2000.

Podhoretz, Norman. *Why We Were in Vietnam.* New York: Simon and Schuster, 1982.

Powell, Colin L. "U.S. Forces: Challenges Ahead." *Foreign Affairs* 71 (1992): 32–45.

———. "Why Generals Get Nervous." *New York Times,* October 8, 1992.

Powell, Colin L., with Joseph E. Persico. *My American Journey.* New York: Random House, 1995.

Reagan, Ronald. *An American Life.* New York: Simon and Schuster, 1990.

———. "Lebanon and Grenada: The Use of U.S. Armed Forces." Address to the nation, October 27, 1983. Reprinted in *Vital Speeches of the Day.* Volume 50, November 15, 1983, 66–69.

———. *Public Papers of the Presidents of the United States: Ronald Reagan, 1981–1984.* Washington, D.C.: U.S. Government Printing Office, 1982–85.

Record, Jeffrey. "Force Protection Fetishism: Sources, Consequences, and (?) Solutions." *Aerospace Power Journal* 14 (summer 2000): 4–11.

———. *Hollow Victory: A Contrary View of the Gulf War.* New York: Brassey's, 1993.

———. *Revising U.S. Military Strategy: Tailoring Means to Ends.* Washington, D.C.: Pergamon-Brassey's, 1984.

———. *Serbia and Vietnam: A Preliminary Comparison of U.S. Decisions to Use Force.* Occasional Paper No. 8. Maxwell Air Force Base, Ala.: Center for Strategy and Technology, Air War College, May 1999.

———. "Weinberger-Powell Doctrine Doesn't Cut It Anymore." *Proceedings* 126 (October 2000): 35–36.

———. *The Wrong War: Why We Lost in Vietnam.* Annapolis: Naval Institute Press, 1998.

Reeves, Richard. *President Kennedy: Profile in Power.* New York: Simon and Schuster, 1993.

Report of the Department of Defense Commission on Beirut International Airport Terrorist Act, October 23, 1983. Washington, D.C.: Department of Defense, December 20, 1983.

Ridgway, Matthew B. *Soldier: The Memoirs of Matthew B. Ridgway.* New York: Harper Brothers, 1956.

Rodman, Peter W. *More Precious than Peace: The Cold War and the Struggle for the Third World.* New York: Scribner, 1994.

Ropp, Steve C. "The Bush Administration and the Invasion of Panama: Explaining the Choice and Timing of the Military Option." In *United States Policy in Latin America: A Decade of Crisis and Challenge,* ed. John D. Martz, 80–109. Lincoln: University of Nebraska Press, 1995.

Roskin, Michael. "From Pearl Harbor to Vietnam: Shifting Generational Paradigms and Foreign Policy." *Political Science Quarterly* 89 (fall 1974): 563–88.

Rostow, W. W, "The Case for the Vietnam War." *Parameters* 26 (winter 1996–1997): 39–50.

Rusk, Dean, with Richard Rusk and Daniel S. Papp. *As I Saw It.* New York: W. W. Norton, 1990.

Schiff, Ze'ev, and Ehud Ya'ari. *Israel's War in Lebanon.* Edited and translated by Ina Friedman. New York: Simon and Schuster, 1984.

Schorr, Daniel. "The Dread of Appeasement." *Christian Science Monitor,* June 6, 1999.

Schuman, Howard, and Cheryl Rieger. "Historical Analogies, Generational Effects, and Attitudes toward War." *American Sociological Review* 57 (June 1992): 315–26.

Schwarz, Benjamin C. *Casualties, Public Opinion and U.S. Military Intervention: Implications for U.S. Regional Deterrence Strategies.* Santa Monica, Calif.: Rand Corporation, 1994.

Scott, James M. *Deciding to Intervene: The Reagan Doctrine and American Foreign Policy.* Durham: Duke University Press, 1996.

Segal, Gerald. "Does China Matter?" *Foreign Affairs* 78 (September/October 1999): 24–36.

Shacochis, Bob. *The Immaculate Invasion.* New York: Penguin Books, 1999.

Shultz, George P. "The Ethics of Power." In *Ethics and American Power.* Washington, D.C.: Ethics and Policy Center, 1984.

———. *Turmoil and Triumph: My Years as Secretary of State.* New York: Charles Scribner, 1993.

Shultz, Richard H. *In the Aftermath of War: U.S. Support for Reconstruction and Nation-Building in Panama following Just Cause.* Maxwell Air Force Base, Ala.: Air University Press, 1993.

Schulzinger, Robert D. *A Time for War: The United States and Vietnam, 1941–1975.* New York: Oxford University Press, 1997.

Sharp, U. S. G. *Strategy for Defeat: Vietnam in Retrospect.* San Rafael, Calif.: Presidio Press, 1978.

Shirer, William L. *Berlin Diary.* New York: Alfred A. Knopf, 1941.

———. *The Rise and Fall of the Third Reich: A History of Nazi Germany.* New York: Simon and Schuster, 1960.

Smith, R. Jeffrey. "A GI's Home Is His Fortress: High Security, High Comfort U.S. Base in Kosovo Stirs Controversy." *Washington Post,* October 5, 1999.

Smith, W. Thomas. "An Old Warrior Sounds Off." *George* (November 1998): 91–92, 132–133.

Sorenson, Theodore C. *Kennedy.* New York: Harper and Row, 1965.

Sorley, Lewis. *A Better War: The Unexamined Victories and Final Tragedy of America's Last Years in Vietnam.* New York: Harcourt Brace, 1999.

Steel, Ronald. *Walter Lippmann and the American Century.* New York: Random House, 1980.

Steuck, William. *The Korean War: An International History.* Princeton: Princeton University Press, 1995.

Stewart, Graham. *Burying Caesar: The Churchill-Chamberlain Rivalry.* Woodstock, N.Y.: Overlook Press, 2001.

Summers, Harry G. Jr. *On Strategy: A Critical Analysis of the Vietnam War.* Novato, Calif.: Presidio Press, 1982.

Sweeney, John. "Stuck in Haiti." *Foreign Policy* 102 (spring 1996): 143–51.

Tang Tsou. *America's Failure in China, 1941–50.* Chicago: University of Chicago Press, 1963.

Taylor, Maxwell D. *Swords and Plowshares.* New York: W. W. Norton, 1972.

Taylor, Telford. *Munich: The Price of Peace.* Garden City, N.Y.: Doubleday, 1979.

Thomas, Evan. *Robert Kennedy: His Life.* New York: Simon and Schuster, 2000.

Thomas, Martin. "France and the Czechoslovak Crisis." *Diplomacy and Statecraft* 10 (July–November 1999): 122–59.

Thornton, Richard C. *China: A Political History, 1917–1980.* Boulder, Colo.: Westview Press, 1982.

Tilford, Earl H. *Setup: What the Air Force Did in Vietnam and Why.* Maxwell Air Force Base, Ala.: Air University Press, 1991.

Timberg, Robert. *The Nightingale's Song.* New York: Simon and Schuster, 1995.

Trachtenberg, Marc. "Making Grand Strategy: The Early Cold War Experience." *SAIS Review* 19 (winter–spring 1999): 33–40.

Truman, Harry S. *Memoirs.* Volume 1: *Years of Decisions;* volume 2: *Years of Trial and Hope, 1946–1952.* Garden City, N.Y.: Doubleday, 1956.

———. *Public Papers of the Presidents of the United States: Harry S. Truman, January 1 to December 31, 1947.* Washington, D.C.: U.S. Government Printing Office, 1963.

Tucker, Robert W., and David C. Hendrickson. *The Imperial Temptation: The New World Order and America's Purpose.* New York: Council on Foreign Relations Press, 1992.

VanDeMark, Brian. *Into the Quagmire: Lyndon Johnson and the Escalation of the Vietnam War.* New York: Oxford University Press, 1995.

The Vietnam Hearings. New York: Vintage Books, 1966.

Vo Nguyen Giap. *Big Victory, Great Task.* New York: Praeger, 1968.

Walt, Stephen M. "The Search for a Science of Strategy." *International Security* 12 (summer 1987): 140–60.

Watts, Barry D. *Clausewitzian Friction and Future War.* McNair Paper 52. Washington, D.C.: Institute for National Strategic Studies, National Defense University, October 1996.

Weinberger, Caspar W. *Fighting for Peace: Seven Critical Years in the Pentagon.* New York: Warner Books, 1990.

———. "The First Priority for Our New President." *Forbes,* January 22, 2001. http://ebird.dtic.mil/Jan2001/e20010105first.htm.

Weintraub, Stanley. *MacArthur's War: Korea and the Undoing of an American Hero.* New York: Free Press, 2000.

Wells, Tom. *The War Within: America's Battle over Vietnam.* New York: Henry Holt, 1994.

White, Mark J., ed. *The Kennedys and Cuba: The Declassified Documentary History.* Chicago: Ivan R. Dee, 1999.

Woods, James L. "U.S. Government Decisionmaking Processes during Humanitarian Operations in Somalia." In *Learning from Somalia: The Lessons of Armed Humanitarian Intervention,* ed. Walter Clarke and Jeffrey Herbst, 151–72. Boulder, Colo.: Westview Press, 1997.

Woodward, Bob. *The Commanders.* New York: Simon and Schuster, 1991.

Woodward, Susan L. "Upside-down Policy: The U.S. Debate on the Use of Force and the Case of Bosnia." In *The Use of Force after the Cold War*, ed. H. W. Brands, with Darren J. Pierson and Reynolds S. Kiefer. College Station: Texas A & M University Press, 2000.

Wyden, Peter. *Bay of Pigs: The Untold Story.* New York: Simon and Schuster, 1979.

X [pseudonym for George F. Kennan]. "The Sources of Soviet Conduct." *Foreign Affairs* 25 (July 1947): 566–83.

Yergin, Daniel. *Shattered Peace: The Origins of the Cold War and the National Security State.* Boston: Houghton Mifflin, 1977.

Zhihua, Shen. "Sino-Soviet Relations and the Origins of the Korean War: Stalin's Strategic Goals in the Far East." *Journal of Cold War Studies* 2 (spring 2000): 44–68.

Index

About the Author

Jeffrey Record is a professor in the Department of Strategy and International Security at the U.S. Air Force's Air War College in Montgomery, Alabama. He received his doctorate at the Johns Hopkins School of Advanced International Studies and is the author of four books and a dozen monographs, including *Revising U.S. Military Strategy: Tailoring Means to Ends; Beyond Military Reform: America's Defense Dilemmas;* and *The Wrong War: Why We Lost Vietnam.*

Dr. Record has served as the assistant province adviser in the Mekong Delta during the Vietnam War, the Rockefeller Younger Scholar on the Brookings Institution's Defense Analysis Staff, and senior fellow at the Institute for Foreign Policy Analysis, the Hudson Institute, and the BDM International Corporation. He also has extensive Capitol Hill experience, serving as legislative assistant for national security affairs to senators Sam Nunn and Lloyd Bentsen, and later as a professional staff member of the Senate Armed Services Committee.